Reality Check

Reality Check

The Business and Art of Producing Reality TV

Michael Essany

ELSEVIER

AMSTERDAM • BOSTON • HEIDELBERG • LONDON
NEW YORK • OXFORD • PARIS • SAN DIEGO
SAN FRANCISCO • SINGAPORE • SYDNEY • TOKYO
Focal Press is an imprint of Elsevier

Focal
Press

Focal Press is an imprint of Elsevier
30 Corporate Drive, Suite 400, Burlington, MA 01803, USA
Linacre House, Jordan Hill, Oxford OX2 8DP, UK

Library of Congress Cataloging-in-Publication Data
Application Submitted

British Library Cataloguing-in-Publication Data
A catalogue record for this book is available from the British Library.

ISBN: 978-0-240-81030-0

For information on all Focal Press publications
visit our website at www.elsevierdirect.com

08 09 10 11 12   5 4 3 2 1

Printed in the United States of America

For Christa.

Table of Contents

Author Bio

Michael Essany is a published author and columnist who has been featured on *Oprah* and *The Tonight Show* and in *Time, People, TV Guide,* and *Entertainment Weekly.* Michael has produced and written for local and national television since 1997. A graduate of Valparaiso University, he hosted *The Michael Essany Show* on E! Entertainment Television for two seasons prior to the program's syndication overseas. Michael is currently married and resides in Valparaiso, Indiana, where he is the Vice President of Marketing and Product Development for Indiana Grain Company, LLC. He can be reached at michaelessany@comcast.net.

Foreword

So you want to break into reality TV? You've picked up the right book, one that will tell you precisely what you need to know before you jump head-first into this medium that can be as rewarding as it is demanding and as brutal as it is enlightening.

Starting up any television show is a daunting prospect. You know that feeling when it's time to clean out the garage for the first time in a decade? There are so many chores and tasks before you, you don't know which one to do first. This book will serve as your compass, not only showing you where to start but advising you as to what tasks are worth pursuing at all and which are best left behind.

The problem with making your name known in this crowded field is that you'll be competing against thousands of other aspiring producers who have the same ambition. "I'll go to Hollywood," they're all saying right now. "I'll take my idea and turn it into gold, become famous and sit at the helm of my own hit network reality series."

Not so fast. The road to stardom is littered with the dead careers of those who dove into this hot pursuit with the best of intentions but no plan. They had no knowledge of major players in the biz, how to pitch ideas, how to formulate a proposal to produce and promote a series, or how to protect those ideas so others can't claim them as their own.

Before going any further, you might want to consider whether you're really cut out for this competitive industry. Are you thin-skinned, resistant to change, bruised by any criticism, a loner, shunning any teamwork and tending to fly solo? Then maybe you're considering the wrong line of work. This book will help you find out if reality TV is the genre for you.

Maybe you're a curious onlooker, wondering if all this overexposure, emotions-laid-bare entertainment is even ethical. Is it okay for us to be amused by the misfortunes of others, and by extension, to create and promote vehicles through which such humiliations can be carried out? When does entertainment turn into exploitation? Explore those moral questions between these covers as well.

A refreshing aspect of the book you're about to read is its frank discussions of the sinister underbelly of the reality TV business. For example, is it ethical for producers and camera people to allow (or encourage) a contestant to drive drunk? Certainly such a taped sequence could make for some great TV, but where do a reality TV producer's obligations to the interests of the program conflict with common decency and responsibility for our fellow human beings?

This book isn't just a stab in the dark by an armchair "expert," either. Author Michael Essany blends in his own experiences producing and starring in his own reality TV series, showing you how he got his show produced and how he was able to receive nationwide exposure on the E! Network and beyond. Find out if it was a pleasant experience, a nightmare, or a combination of the two.

You'll go far beyond one man's experiences, too; inside you'll find valuable listings of not only nearly every reality television series that's ever been produced, but names of and contact info for agents, networks, and production companies that are the most likely to be interested in your pitch for a new idea. Sure, your idea seems unique, but is it really? Here you can find out whether your concept has been done before in the largest, most convenient, and easy-to-browse listing of reality television programs ever assembled in one place.

What about the budget for a reality TV show? Michael is intimately familiar with the inside story of budgets for network-level productions; he shows you how to decide what to spend your production's money on as well as money pits that are best avoided.

Taking the how-to theme beyond that, Essany also offers his take on the whys and hows of reality shows: Why are some programs popular while others tank after a few episodes? Why are some cast members more entertaining than others, and how can you spot a winner? How can you protect yourself legally as a producer from disgruntled contestants? And how do you craft a contract that will protect your interests as well as those of people appearing on your production?

This business of creating an original TV series can be bewildering. Is it a good thing to go straight to a TV network with your idea? Or is it better to go to a production company known for its reality TV productions? How about getting an agent to help you promote your idea? What approach gives your idea the best odds of success? Michael has been there and sorts out this puzzling labyrinth for you.

We hear from other experts in the field of reality TV production as well. Mark Burnett, one of the most well-known reality TV creators, who made his name with *Survivor* and continues to score hit after hit, talks with the author and gives his advice for success. We get cautionary advice from others, too, as well as the author himself.

Perhaps the best advice is to keep an eye on the types of reality shows that are popular now and develop that uncanny knack of being able to predict the trends. Which shows will be popular next year? How about two or five years ahead? Learn what's being done now, and then you'll be able to refine your own prognostications about what's around the corner.

Are you cut out for this kind of work? You've found the right book, so let's follow Michael on his journey from unknown host of his own homegrown talk show to the national level at a major cable network, hobnobbing with the stars, appearing on *The Tonight Show with Jay Leno*, mingling with celebrities, and learning a lot of useful information about the television industry along the way. In this book, he shares it all with you.

—Charlie White

Charlie White is an Emmy Award-winning television producer, director, author, and consultant who has worked in television and radio broadcasting since 1974.

Acknowledgments

No book truly worth reading is ever produced by the author alone. Without the unfaltering support of countless individuals, *Reality Check* would likely have never become a reality itself.

Of the many publishers and editors with whom I have worked over the years, the people at Focal Press are sincerely among the finest professionals I have ever had the privilege of knowing.

A big Italian bear-hug of affection is particularly warranted for both Elinor Actipis and Michele Cronin. At the beginning of the project, Elinor was kind enough to endure my incessant emails and phone calls when others might have notified the authorities to report some form of editorial harassment. She has truly been as gracious as she is talented.

Equally deserving of my genuine gratitude is Michele Cronin. From holding my hand throughout the entire process to never making me feel that a big bad editor was waiting to tear my manuscript apart, Michele has been as big a blessing to me as she undoubtedly is to Focal Press.

Of course, I must also thank my beautiful and tremendously understanding wife, Christa. Not only has she patiently shared me with two other women for the last year, she also ungrudgingly tolerated my incurable author's insomnia as I worked on this manuscript many late evenings instead of going to sleep with her like a normal husband. Thank you for not leaving me for one of those types.

A sincere thank you is also in order for my mother and father. God bless them. They encouraged me to follow my dreams from the time I was old enough to possess any dream at all. Indeed, they gave me the love and support to reach all that was once far beyond my juvenile grasp.

Naturally, without the opportunities I have been given in the world of reality television, the inspiration for this book as well as the means to produce it would likely be nonexistent today. First and foremost I would like to extend a heartfelt thanks to Leeza Gibbons, one of the kindest, smartest, and most talented women I have ever known in the entertainment business. Without her vision and her investment of inspiration, *The Michael Essany Show* would have certainly never found its way into the homes of millions around the world on E! Entertainment Television. Along with Leeza, Rachel Karzen and Paul Hecht are equally deserving of my thanks for their friendship, their talents, and their commitment to the quality and integrity of their work on our show.

Perhaps most important, I should thank the countless producers interviewed in depth for this project but who then refused to be quoted when discussing their negative experiences in reality television. Their overpowering concern with possibly "offending certain networks and producers" only served to further illustrate the need for a brutally honest and contemporary exploration of the ugly underside of the unscripted television industry. To be sure, this is a magnificent business, but it comes with its caveats, and the aspiring producer deserves to know exactly what they are.

I would also be remiss if I did not express my appreciation to both Caroline Stack and Charlie White for their insightful input and careful assistance with many aspects of this project. They, along with several individuals I interviewed either specifically for this book or at some time in the past (including Mark Burnett, Nigel Lythgoe, Simon Cowell, Phil Potempa, and Dick Clark), deserve a heartfelt round of applause for contributing their knowledge, experiences, and wisdom.

To Mike Randazzo, my lifelong best friend and on-air sidekick for *The Michael Essany Show*, thank you for your constant support, your precious humor, and your trusted guidance. You are my brother not by blood, but by choice.

What's more, a very warm thank you is in order for Tom Grisafi: a boss, a mentor, and an enormously supportive friend. You and your family have been a blessing in my life and provided a reality check that continues to prove that good people with true talents and generous hearts still exist in this world.

I would also like to thank my hometown of Valparaiso, Indiana, for always supporting one of their own. Valparaiso has never failed to give me the hope, encouragement, and inspiration to shine a positive light through my work on our wonderful community. May God continue to bless our beloved hometown.

Finally, I want to thank those aspiring producers and entertainers who hold dreams worth pursuing. Indeed, your inspiration to succeed is my inspiration for this book.

If I am forgetting anyone else by name, I am certainly remembering you in my heart.

—Michael Essany

Introduction

For most of the afternoon, things were relatively quiet in the dimly lit hallway. Occasionally someone would walk past my door, but there wasn't sufficient clamor to warrant closing it.

For nearly an hour I had been sitting on the sofa intently reviewing my notes and perusing the day's agenda. My attention would have probably remained undisturbed if not for a mysterious phantom rushing past my door.

When I got up to investigate, I noticed others across the hall following suit.

As we collectively laid eyes on this charging presence in the distance, I knew exactly what I was looking at: Oprah Winfrey. And she was in a hurry.

I stepped back into my dressing room and quickly glanced up at the television monitor where Oprah was bolting through the studio doors to surprise her audience with an impromptu appearance.

Apparently, the studio audience warm-up guy was joking with the crowd about having never seen Oprah without makeup. Not missing a beat, Ms. Winfrey sprang from her office, jaunted down the hallway, and barged directly into the studio to display her natural beauty for all to see.

Looking back, I doubt this memory will ever leave me. It was a moment that more than simply represented Oprah's incomparable sense of humor and down-to-earth nature. It also illustrated her remarkable ability to create a magical opportunity for excitement and humility from practically nothing.

As a privileged guest on Oprah's couch that morning, I was afforded an occasion to publicly reflect on my own unlikely personal journey, one that was similarly born of creating opportunities where few initially seemed available.

For me, however, the medium that provided such empowerment and the opportunity to live an improbable dream is the same medium that has shattered others. It is a genre of television programming that commands global attention for all the right *and* wrong reasons. It is a business that produces new millionaires on a daily basis. It is an art that inspires the creative talents of millions. It is, for all its commendation and condemnation, the juggernaut format of reality television.

A wildly accepted genre of programming recognized and defined by its cast of nonprofessional participants, reality television isn't as new as its contemporary popularity might otherwise suggest. From the earliest black-and-white days of *Candid Camera* to more recent rodent-eating adventures on a deserted island, the birth of "unscripted programming," in all actuality, coincided with the birth of the television medium itself.

The modern resurgence of reality TV's global popularity, however, portrays a format dramatically dissimilar from its innocent origins. Yet today the genre can now be instructively analyzed, with perspective, to reveal how it has matured (or not), how it profoundly reflects and impacts society, and how it can be successfully tackled head-on by a new generation of producers who will inherit the industry and influence programming for decades to come.

To its proponents, of course, reality TV is quality and purposeful entertainment of the people, by the people, and for the people. To its critics, reality TV is a degenerate medium that exposes individual frailties and naïveté to a ravenous cultural appetite for human embarrassment and unparalleled degradation.

But no matter how you slice it, the booming business of unscripted programming isn't going anywhere. Although most who seek short-term fame and fortune from reality television do so in front of the cameras, the majority of aspiring professionals looking to cultivate meaningful, lasting careers within the genre are the hopeful producers trying to paint their creative portraits on reality television's enormous and surprisingly welcoming canvas.

As the creator, executive producer, and star of my own reality television program, I have both witnessed and lived the tumultuous ups and downs common to working in the genre. And, despite the way its harshest critics might testify, I have observed the ways in which reality television is a distinct art form. Unfortunately, I have also observed that those who typically fail to make a splash in the genre are also those who fail to understand the business behind this unique art.

Anchored in my extensive knowledge of reality television and inspired by my heartfelt enthusiasm for the television industry, *Reality Check* is a personal account and knowledgeable guide for those seeking to produce, promote, and profit in television's hottest industry.

In addition to providing a discerning look behind the scenes of reality television production and culling helpful insights from gurus of the industry, *Reality Check* offers compelling advice on how you can:

- Better understand the nature, complexities, and potential of the reality genre
- Physically produce original reality programming
- Deliver quality pitches to major networks and production companies
- Legally protect yourself, your work, and your intellectual property
- Learn from glories and gaffes of those who toiled before you
- Utilize the Internet and other multimedia outlets to create and generate revenue from reality programming
- Avoid the professional pitfalls of the reality TV industry
- Parlay reality television projects into a successful and enduring career

Perhaps most importantly, *Reality Check* comprehensively addresses ways to protect your credibility in a highly accessible genre that can seriously devastate unprepared players in the reality TV game.

As we will explore, reality television is an art *and* a business. *Reality Check* is an essential guide to both.

Chapter one

Welcome to Reality

On the first day of filming for the second season of *The Michael Essany Show*, I was introduced to the new slate of producers hired by E! Entertainment Television. Incredibly, among the talented newcomers on our team was Colleen Haskell, the "girl next door" castaway from the first season of *Survivor*.

Genuinely dismayed by her overexposed reality TV debut, Colleen was hoping to maintain a formidable presence in the entertainment industry but in a less conspicuous role, behind the camera. Fortunately for me, this bright and wily veteran of unscripted programming landed first on my show.

Working with Colleen Haskell subsequently introduced me to an interesting paradox unique to the television medium. It's a trend that sees former reality TV stars routinely wanting to become reality TV producers. Conversely, reality TV producers typically avoid at all costs any opportunity to become a reality TV star.

For Colleen Haskell and scores of other producers who once dabbled in front of the lens, reality television can be a perilous means of employment. Nonetheless, some were still astonished by Haskell's decision not to return to *Survivor* during the 2004 all-star edition produced by Mark Burnett. But, as Burnett later publicly explained, Colleen had chosen to move on with her life and "just genuinely didn't want to go through that again."

Television audiences, though, have not proven as easily disenchanted. Reality TV, in fact, has emerged as the veritable junk-food equivalent of our daily entertainment consumption. Simply put, it's addictive, easy to digest, and usually devoid of any significant nourishment. Yet just like the drive-through that beckons our appetite on a steadily recurring basis, reality TV has more than enough fanatics to perpetuate its existence, conceivably, for generations to come.

The popularity of reality television signifies a workable marriage of convenience and contentment between networks and viewers. For the vast television audience desirous of brainless, flashy entertainment, reality TV is the answer. Equally, for programming executives habitually grappling with slumping ratings and rising expenses, reality TV presents a cost-effective remedy for programming ailments facing the networks.

Unscripted programming, for example, obviously doesn't require a team of highly compensated writers. So, in this regard, the 2007–2008 season might have actually resulted in a counterproductive consequence. During this period networks realized that unscripted programming was enormously popular with contemporary audiences. Not helping the writers was the stark realization that it frequently costs upward of $3 million to produce a single episode of scripted drama or comedy. On the other hand, reality programming can easily be produced in most cases for well under $1 million per episode.

At the beginning of the Fall 2007 writer's strike, some observers cynically speculated that networks might actually be pleased with the strike. Union writers' pickets provided a compelling excuse for launching more reality programs while simultaneously canning a bouquet of scripted programs that are more expensive to produce and largely less profitable than most reality programs. Ironically, it had been the previous writers' strike of 1988 that introduced viewing audiences to a wide array of new reality television shows, including *Cops*, a forerunner of many contemporary unscripted series.

Of course, reality television also has writers, or "story producers," a fact that has finally been introduced as a point of both contention and negotiation for the Writers Guild of America. Unfortunately, a survey conducted by the WGA revealed that only 10 percent of 1500 reality TV writers and producers have healthcare or a retirement plan. As a result, the WGA worked diligently to secure a deal that would aid reality TV producers and writers to a greater extent. The networks, however, continue exhibiting indications that they are more than willing to replace many of their scripted programs and high-salaried writers with new reality series and their corresponding inexpensive "story producers."

> "The secret about reality TV isn't that it's scripted, which it is; the secret is that reality TV is a 21st-century telecommunications industry sweatshop."
> **—Daniel Petrie, Jr., former president WGA West**

Ultimately, the 2007–2008 writers guild strike can be said to have helped further illustrate how the prevalence of reality TV has just as much to do with its mainstream popularity as its ease of inexpensive production. What's more, as a result of its ubiquitous presence in modern pop culture, television viewers have been dubbed "consumers" for their ravenous consumption of whatever flash-in-the-pan reality programming reaches their living rooms on a given weeknight.

A fair analysis of the symbiotic relationship between networks and viewers, however, would also reveal that the very industry pumping out hundreds of hours of reality programming every week also fits the description of an insatiable consumer. It's no exaggeration in the least to assert that the reality television business regularly consumes the lives of its most innocent and unsuspecting participants—both those in front of and behind the lens.

Certainly, there are some things in life that just never sound like a good idea. Skydiving without a parachute, for instance, readily comes to mind. Having a root canal without anesthetic is another. And perhaps equally harrowing, yet rarely acknowledged as such, is pursuing a career in the alluring realm of reality television.

Though the rigors of reality TV stardom are obvious even to those outside the entertainment industry, people looking to find success behind the cameras as producers of unscripted programming aren't off the hook by any stretch of the imagination. They, too, regularly face similar professional challenges, ethical dilemmas, and an unending series of threats to their credibility, reputations, and job security.

Few new entrants, if any, truly understand what they're getting into with reality TV. Of course, this juggernaut genre of programming can be vastly rewarding, both creatively and financially, for those who capably harness its colossal power. And all criticisms aside, reality TV genuinely provides a matchless artistic workshop for talented producers as well as a powerful vehicle for equally powerful ideas. But for those who imprudently proceed without complete and utter caution, reality television can permanently damage one's professional—and personal—future.

My ominous perception of this "dark side" of the genre often conveys the incorrect suggestion that I'm not among its legions of fans. In reality—pun intended—I was once an ambitious aspirant to reality TV stardom, a dream that eventually afforded me numerous opportunities to learn precisely what I now wish I had known before pursuing that lofty dream.

Despite seeming astonishingly transparent, reality television has latent complexities that are nearly as widespread as the format's global popularity. From breaking into this highly accessible industry and producing quality programming to surviving the common pratfalls of the business and using the genre as a launching pad for higher achievement, reality television could easily encompass a serious four-year program of study at any accredited college in the United States.

But due in large part to continually evolving programming trends in response to viewer whims and market preferences, it is practically impossible for anyone to become a veritable Ph.D. of unscripted television. Thankfully, at least, the core elements of reality TV have remained unchanged since the genre's advent. And it is from this remarkably unaffected foundation that all reality TV careers, successful or shameful, are launched.

According to some players currently earning a substantial living from this occasionally serious, often silly programming format, it is absolutely imperative for anyone training their professional sights on reality television to have more than just a tenuous grasp on all that encompasses the genre. It's a process that begins with asking a simple question to which we mistakenly expect to already have a sufficient answer: What exactly *is* reality TV?

> "Reality is merely an illusion, albeit a very persistent one."
>
> **—Albert Einstein**

In a later era Einstein could have been accurately referring to the present-day world of network and cable reality television. The majority of unscripted programming, after all, is far less "authentic" than even some professionals in the entertainment industry realize.

Although unscripted television is commonly thought a type of programming that ostensibly presents unrehearsed, unscripted, and largely unplanned documentary-style coverage of people, places, and events, the reality of reality television is something of an acceptably duplicitous misnomer. In most cases, programming developed under the rubric of reality is less a product of authentic circumstance and more the result of off-screen manipulation by producers, executives, and, naturally, post-production "tweaking."

Say to anybody in the business that you want to produce reality TV and they will look at you the perplexed way a restaurant server would if you simply perused a menu and ordered nothing more specific than "food." When it comes to unscripted television, nuance is what separates the men and women from the boys and girls.

Whether to make the most of the primordial soup that may currently be your idea for a reality series or to simply delve deeper into your preferential wing of the reality industry, the journey to becoming a savvy warrior of reality TV begins with understanding the assorted subcategories within this thriving genre.

- Documentary Reality
- Competition Reality
- Celebrity Reality
- Personal Improvement and Makeover Reality
- Renovation and Design Reality
- Professional Reality
- Forced Environment Reality
- Romance Reality
- Aspiration Reality
- Fear-Based Reality
- Sports Reality
- Undercover Reality

DOCUMENTARY REALITY

The truest form of reality television programming is that which almost entirely eliminates a conscious entertainment perspective from the production process. Regrettably, because such dedication to authenticity effectively removes producers' ability to affect ratings-friendly twists and turns in the developing story line, few programs committed to the documentary reality format are produced for mainstream commercial network or cable television. The 1973 PBS series *An American Family*, for example, which chronicled an "ordinary" American family's struggle to cope with divorce, masterfully captured this fly-on-the-wall method of documentary reality programming.

Similar endeavors to capture genuine situations still exist, but they typically fall victim to post-production interventions before reaching viewers. More commonly, though, producers now confer prior to physical production, to efficiently storyboard a series of events they would like to see transpire on screen.

Before being shuffled over to my series, one of the producers of *The Anna Nicole Show* revealed that he had concocted the idea to have Anna, who purportedly couldn't drive, take driving lessons on her show. Although Anna might have eventually signed up for driver's education even without the hovering of an omnipresent camera crew, arranging an instructor who couldn't speak English was a definite "plant." Beyond Anna not having a license, every other component of this particular episode was preconceived long before the cameras had speed.

COMPETITION REALITY

The 1983 debut of Ed McMahon's *Star Search* ushered in an era of talent-driven reality programming that eventually paved the way for such contemporary incarnations as *American Idol*, *America's Got Talent*, and *So You Think You Can Dance*, to name only a select few.

Though the embellished elements of these talent-based competition reality series usually center on the cast of charismatic hosts and cantankerous judges who spice things up with witty banter and biting commentary, this format—arguably the most popular of all reality formats—characteristically enables talented young performers from all facets of entertainment to compete with their peers in a chiefly unaffected setting.

Many shows within this category have given legs to upstart careers, but none has launched superstars to the extent or degree that *American Idol* has since the summer of 2002. Kelly Clarkson's first-season victory, in fact, illustrates reality television's ability to produce what is now regarded as an "overnight celebrity."

In addition to the talent-driven variety of competition-based reality programming, reality game shows can also be lumped into this broad category. *Survivor* and *Big Brother* are internationally recognized as two of the most successful nontalent-based competition series of the post-2000 reality boom. These series often showcase ordinary people—who just happen, in some cases, to resemble European models—competing for a cash prize while living together, normally in a remote or confined environment. One by one, participants are booted off the show, either by a collective decision from the competitors themselves or via an interactive vote from the engrossed, or grossed-out, viewing audience.

Unlike talent-based programming, which mainly omits relationship dynamics from the dramatic lure of the series, competitive shows like *Survivor* heighten the audience's awareness of the lives and relationships of their participants. Frequently, challenges and contests within these series are manufactured by clever producers to build upon a particular rivalry or romance that may have already emerged between competitors or partners during filming. Inducing lovers or enemies to share the same tent, for example, radically amplifies viewer interest by cultivating the chemistry or combativeness between the show's spotlight characters until a desired climax or eventuality is produced.

Such techniques consequently result in more than spiked ratings and an augmented fan base. The Television Academy frequently recognizes the intense drama and pageantry of competitive reality programming with Emmy nominations and awards for Outstanding Reality Competition Program.

CELEBRITY REALITY

The Osbournes, Nick and Jessica Simpson's *Newlyweds*, and, of course, *The Anna Nicole Show* have all contributed heavily to the emergent and seemingly unbridled popularity of celebrity reality TV. Although these programs, along with *Hogan Knows Best*, *Dice: Undisputed*, and *Gene Simmons Family Jewels*, are at least somewhat rooted in reality (i.e., the celebrities play themselves, they reside in their own homes, and they largely conduct ordinary day-to-day activities), the category of celebrity reality programming is by no means restricted to stars willing to subject their real lives to 24/7 fishbowl surveillance.

The Surreal Life, for instance, represents a brand of celebrity reality programming that doesn't even begin to pretend to be real—at least not beyond having past-their-prime celebrities portray themselves. In other words, unless you genuinely believe that Florence Henderson would otherwise be living with Gary Coleman and Vanilla Ice in a cartoon-colorful townhouse in Southern California if cameras were not present, everything about programs like *The Surreal Life* is completely unnatural and altogether contrived.

The ridiculous number of celebrity reality series that have either already been cancelled, are currently airing, or are preparing for broadcast next season represents the public's continued wholesale interest in the lives (genuine or fabricated) of celebrities and their families. As a result, production companies and television networks are experiencing an enormous surge in show pitches from aspiring producers with the "next big idea" for a celebrity reality series. And because the reality genre has helped a number of former child stars and out-of-work actors find renewed fame and some degree of fortune, scores of aspiring producers have experienced relative ease in getting celebrities on board their projects even before a network picks up the series.

PERSONAL IMPROVEMENT AND MAKEOVER REALITY

From *The Biggest Loser* and *Queer Eye for the Straight Guy* to *Extreme Makeover* and *Miami Slice,* personal improvement and makeover reality programming is among the least expensive and most popular forms of reality programming being produced.

Programs within this category differ in terms of content and the areas of personal improvement they target, but the structure of this format usually remains unchanged. Normally, a worthy makeover candidate is introduced. Then a skilled authority or a rabid team of experts is unleashed to assess the challenge. Finally, we bear witness to the impressive start-to-finish transformation of the episode's formerly downtrodden subject.

Appealing to the average viewer's own desire for self-improvement, this reality format often packs as much of an emotional punch for viewers as it does the participants experiencing the all-expense-paid metamorphosis.

Interestingly, the widespread popularity of personal improvement and makeover reality programming has been used to argue against the absorbed theory that reality TV is only in vogue because it exploits unsuspecting participants and enables a "mean-spirited audience" to mock and ridicule. If anything, the majority of makeover programming leaves viewers feeling almost as uplifted and inspired as those who underwent a positive life-changing transformation on television.

The only perceived downside of the budding popularity of makeover and self-improvement reality programming is the growing number of patients visiting plastic surgeons and requesting the same often risky procedures they learned from shows like E!'s *Dr. 90210* and MTV's *I Want a Famous Face*.

According to a study reported in a July 2007 issue of *Newsweek*, seventy-nine percent of the patients surveyed by the academic journal *Plastic and Reconstructive Surgery* said that television influenced their decision to have a cosmetic surgery procedure. Only 12 percent of the patients wanting plastic surgery said that reality television played no part in their decision to go under the knife.

RENOVATION AND DESIGN REALITY

Personal improvement and makeover reality programming focuses on an individual; similarly, renovation and design reality series commonly tackle one's home. HGTV, for example, has quickly become an entire cable network devoted almost exclusively to renovation and design reality programming. *Design on a Dime*, one of the channel's most popular series, follows a small team of design experts into a ho-hum bedroom or living space. With a scant budget and boundless creativity, these wizards of design perform an impressive renovation (or miracle) that easily resembles something entirely less affordable.

HGTV, TLC, and, more recently, DIY (the Do It Yourself network) closely follow and emulate an established paradigm for producing quality renovation and design reality programming. It's a three-step approach that centers on a tangible result, an emotional response, and an enjoyable experience. In other words, the metamorphosis of the living space must be obvious and impressive. A challenging life story of the homeowner must be illuminated and must consequently tug at the viewer's emotional heartstrings. And, last but not least, the technical and poignant aspects of the program require fusion through the charming presence and thoughtful labor of a likeable host or design expert.

Though design and renovation reality programming accounts for an enormous chunk of all reality TV produced, this variety primarily appeals to a niche market and rarely comes to the forefront of mainstream network reality television. However, with more cable networks than ever allocating airtime for design and renovation series, numerous opportunities exist for producers eager and capable of tapping into this niche market with their own distinctive ideas for this remarkably straightforward format.

PROFESSIONAL REALITY

The category of professional reality television features only two varieties of programming. The first concentrates on the daily performance of a particular occupation, such as *The First 48, Cops, Miami Ink*, and their ilk. *American Chopper*, as a key example, follows Paul Teutul, Sr., and his son, Paul Teutul, Jr., as they quarrel, goof, and banter for the cameras while meeting accelerated deadlines for building custom-designed choppers. A father-and-son team with undeniable chemistry as they toil in their chosen craft essentially embodies the nature of programming in this specialized category.

Given the number of lively characters and interesting professions across the American landscape, it's no wonder that the genre of professional reality programming has received considerable attention from aspiring producers looking for the next big show.

Programs like *Making the Band* and *The Apprentice*, though incorporating some elements of competitive reality programming, primarily focus on individuals pursuing a career in a particular area of expertise. HGTV's *Design Star* is another professional reality series that showcases a small number of talented designers competing for the ultimate dream job: hosting their own design series.

Apart from the stark realization that reality shows are now being produced about people who want their own reality shows, there are, of course, more absurd variations of the professional reality series. The Sci-Fi network's *Who Wants to Be a Superhero?* is a perfect illustration of such programming trends. Individuals who have always dreamed of being crime-fighting caped crusaders like those from Marvel comic strips now have an opportunity to transform their childhood passion into a professional reality.

FORCED ENVIRONMENT REALITY

Similar, at least in appearance, to the documentary reality format, forced environment reality series like *The Real World, Big Brother*, and *Road Rules* confine previously (supposedly) unintroduced participants to a feigned living environment suited to the production and content needs of the shows' producers.

Watching ill-advised social pairings cohabitate is, without a doubt, a major component of this popular format's proven success and track record with reality TV fans. Forced environment reality programming, though, is often criticized for pushing ethical boundaries by overtly invoking racial, gender, and socioeconomic conflicts purely to heighten dramatic effect.

In this realm, Fox's now defunct *Temptation Island* was quickly chastised for its platform of "stranding" a handful of purportedly happy couples on an island surrounded by sexy, promiscuous single young men and women. The obvious plot driver of the series—pushing the limits of couples' fidelity—was morally condemned on numerous fronts. But because it was a novel idea that promised to draw huge numbers in the midst of such controversial hype, Fox pushed ahead with its overexposed *Temptation Island* until audiences, consequently, were no longer tempted to watch.

As of late 2007, forced environment reality series seemed to have reached the downswing of their popularity. Largely responsible, according to many, is the pervasiveness of celebrity reality programming, which, incidentally, recurrently includes forced environment scenarios.

Of course, the reality television fan base represents a market that habitually fluctuates between which lives, celebrity or civilian, prove more interesting to voyeuristically monitor. Some believe other factors are at work in determining which is more popular at any given time, but I personally maintain that the charisma of the celebrities and ordinary folks selected for such programming is the primary determining factor.

ROMANCE REALITY

A cursory glance at the contemporary landscape of romance reality TV illustrates just how much times have changed since *The Dating Game* was television's preeminent dating series.

In 2001, beginning with *The Bachelor*, continuing with *The Bachelorette*, and culminating with *Who Wants to Marry a Multi-Millionaire?* the romance reality series dominated, in number and popularity, every other reality series broadcast during that period.

So profound was the romance reality impact of 2001 that several years now removed from its white-hot popularity, we still see former stars like Trista Rehn gracing the occasional magazine cover or appearing on one of the many daytime talk shows and newsmagazines seemingly riveted by the lives of current or former reality show stars that won our hearts or repulsed our senses.

A mind-boggling number of variations on the classic dating show (which features an attractive "catch" selecting a potential mate from a group of equally attractive suitors) have been produced over the last half century, but producers are still finding innovate new ways to package their romance reality programming. As a result, television audiences have remained incredibly welcoming of dating-based competition shows long after their predicted and anticipated demise.

Today, the popularity of programs like *Cheaters, Blind Date,* and *Elimidate,* not to mention *Flavor of Love* and its two spin-offs, *I Love New York* and *Rock of Love,* prove that romance reality programming will remain a major force in unscripted programming, at least for the foreseeable future.

ASPIRATION REALITY

The aspiration reality format is an interesting category of reality programming because it frequently encompasses a variety of components from other reality TV subcategories, specifically competitive and professional reality programming. Aspiration reality differs, however, in that it doesn't necessarily result in a designated winner or loser. In effect, aspiration reality is about a process. *Project Greenlight,* for example, chronicles an aspiring filmmaker struggling to produce his or her film with limited resources but boundless passion.

Aspiration programming focuses on real people who were specifically cherry-picked for the series by producers who prescreened their skills prior to filming. But because of the transparent vulnerability of aspiring entertainers, chefs, models, and the like, aspiration reality TV, perhaps above all other varieties of reality TV programming, can be incredibly risky for potential participants. Often, some aspiring subjects are selected only because they are so unknowingly untalented or unlikely to succeed that it's "a mesmerizing train wreck" to watch them fall short of their dreams on national television.

Indeed, reality television has been just as vicious toward as it has been supportive of would-be performers and professionals. Nonetheless, aspiration reality programming remains a juggernaut brand that continues to draw fire, praise, and every emotion in between from fans, critics, and former contestants alike.

FEAR-BASED REALITY

MTV launched the first fear-based reality series of the modern unscripted programming boom—conveniently titled *Fear*—in 2000. This commercially and critically successful show featured a group of five or more contestants spending the weekend in an allegedly "haunted" locality while enduring a succession of fear-related challenges.

Although *Fear* lasted only two seasons, it was not cancelled in response to dwindling viewership. Rather, the exorbitant cost of producing each episode was ultimately responsible for *Fear's* untimely demise.

Similarly, the 2003 original Sci-Fi series *Scare Tactics* also sought to jolt the daylights out of its jumpy participants. But unlike *Fear*, which politely showcased a weekly cast of characters who knowingly signed up for the program, *Scare Tactics* was mostly a hidden-camera show made possible by the thoughtful coordination of "friends" of an unsuspecting victim. Regarded for its outlandish stunts punctuated by cinema-quality special effects and monster-movie makeup, *Scare Tactics* also lasted only a few short seasons.

Luckily for the growing fan base longing for fear-centric programming, network and cable television networks soon launched a horde of new series that followed the accepted pattern of placing everyday people in frightening situations. NBC's *Fear Factor*, while less scary in a horror-movie sense, rose to immediate popularity by parading its weekly cast of intrepid contestants through a barrage of always hair-raising, usually grotesque stunts in hopes of winning a cash prize.

Though certainly not poised to altogether disappear or, conversely, rise to the forefront of all reality programming, the future of fear-based reality television is somewhat uncertain. Although still popular with large segments of the reality TV viewership, the inclusion of fear-centric stunts on other popular reality series like *Survivor* has at least partially removed the unique lure of stand-alone fear-based reality programs. The October 2006 launch of the *Celebrity Paranormal Project*, however, further proved that producers will continue pushing fear-based reality programming in intermittent segments until the next *Fear* is found.

SPORTS REALITY

Clearly a less prevalent form of reality programming than the others described, sports-based reality programming is relatively new to the contemporary market. As its category heading otherwise suggests, sports reality programming largely incorporates elements of both competitive and aspiration reality into a season-long contest where athletes jockey for the top spot within their chosen sport.

Derived from the inspirational legacy of the *Rocky* films, for example, host Sylvester Stallone teamed with producer Mark Burnett to create *The Contender*, a sports reality series pitting amateur boxers against one another until only a single contender remains at the end of the season.

Following the time-honored reality TV trend of illuminating characters and relationships, *The Contender* also chronicled the lives and families of the featured pugilists. Regrettably, though, it is believed that *The Contender* is the first American reality series to have prompted a former contestant to commit suicide after failing to win the grand prize.

WWE's *Tough Enough* and UFC's *Ultimate Fighter* have also emerged as somewhat well-liked sports reality installments, but this genre has primarily served as a promising workshop for producers looking to fuse the popularity of sports with the lure of reality programming. To date, a powerhouse sports reality series is yet to take the airwaves by storm in the same way that other reality series have in their respective subcategories.

UNDERCOVER REALITY

Long before Ashton Kutcher lurked in the bushes on MTV's *Punk'd*, 1948's *Candid Camera* introduced the world to what is probably best described today as undercover reality TV.

A format primarily recognized for hilariously and harmlessly (in most cases, anyway) capturing random unsuspecting individuals in outrageous stunts and practical jokes, undercover reality programming has assumed a diminished role in recent years.

Though viewers still appreciate a well-executed prank, reality television has strayed from the simple hidden-camera show in favor of more elaborate programming that closely resembles that found within the previously acknowledged subcategories of reality TV.

Strangely enough, as stale as undercover reality programming has grown on network and cable television, the Internet has seen a considerable explosion of entertaining hidden-camera pranks on popular video-sharing websites like YouTube. Today, a number of web-based video programs regularly feature many of the same gags and stunts once in vogue on mainstream commercial television.

Accordingly, many industry watchers have speculated that the Internet is steadily becoming an outstanding barometer for predicting which recycled programming trends will soon resurface with a bang into the mainstream.

IN CONCLUSION

Speaking with friends in the entertainment business about the categories described here, I was inundated with additional suggestions for reality television subcategories.

Some proposed the inclusion of nature reality, which, in all actuality, has given rise to cable networks solely dedicated to outdoor or animal-oriented reality programming.

I was also lobbied for a subcategory in honor of spiritual reality programming, such as Oprah's *Big Give* and Amy Grant's *Three Wishes*. But before I could even finish noting all the shows that would appropriately belong among this uplifting group, I was chastised for having also failed to include the subcategory of medical reality and its swath of real-life hospital dramas that are best remembered for their moving but graphic presence on Discovery.

Of course, I was additionally reminded of what some have called significant life event reality TV—one of the few subcategories of reality programming that even my anti-reality TV wife regularly enjoys. From *A Wedding Story* and *For Better Or for Worse* to *Whose Wedding Is It Anyway?* and *Perfect Proposal*, cable networks are hastily devoting significant blocks of airtime to reality programming that revolves around the major life events to which we can all relate—particularly weddings.

Although it's not often lumped into the generic genre of reality programming, I was strongly encouraged to throw the oldest programming format of all into the reality TV fray: the obligatory television talk show.

In keeping with the basic criteria of what constitutes a reality program, the standard interview-based talk show certainly fits the bill. But once you begin differentiating between the nature of daytime and late-night talk shows (mindful of the nuances, for example, separating Dr. Phil from David Letterman), you have yet another laundry list of subcategories within the talk show category of reality television programming.

Needless to say, the more I reflected on these and other appropriate suggestions, the more I realized that they were all relevant and worthy of discussion. Unfortunately, a likely consequence of including them in this book would be that a third of it would consist of nothing but descriptions of reality television subcategories.

Ultimately, given that the reality TV programming subcategories are always growing and changing in response to industry trends, production innovations, and audience preferences, there can truly be no definitive catalogue of all things reality television.

And, incredibly, therein lies perhaps the greatest attribute of the genre: it's as malleable as your own imagination.

As we've seen, there are myriad varieties of reality programming. Most represent the art of reality TV production. All represent the business. Whether it's talk-based, competitive, fear-centric, or a yet to be discovered or defined subcategory of this popular and lucrative genre, reality television is a legitimate friend to any producer eager to create his or her own show or contribute to an already established series.

Unlike the highly inaccessible world of scripted television, the reality TV industry is an ever-inviting pillar of opportunity. Still extremely competitive and as cutthroat as any other wing of the business, reality television is exceedingly accessible to the average person because, to no small degree, the average person is at the core of reality television.

Consequently, in exploring the heights possible for their reality TV ambitions, aspiring producers are limited only by their own creativity. To think that the industry is too crowded, too complicated, or too uncompromising for you and your talents is an altogether unrealistic outlook on the world of reality TV.

Chapter | two

Reality's Long Reel

Depending on who you ask, reality television is either the newest trend in contemporary programming or the oldest format of the entire broadcast medium. To a degree, however, both perspectives are accurate. Reality television has existed since the advent of television itself, yet only recently has the genre emerged as the preeminent programming format of the modern era.

The 1948 debut of *Candid Camera* is often hailed as the epic birth of reality television. True to its format, *Candid Camera's* pioneering host, Allen Funt, cleverly placed real people in contrived situations to elicit humorous but otherwise harmless reactions. Two years later, *Truth or Consequences* borrowed the emergent hidden-camera technique and achieved similar ratings success during television's famed golden era.

But for the next quarter century, the bulk of reality programs were predominately of the game show variety, continuing the emphasis on nonprofessional actors in the cast. Although programs like *What's My Line? To Tell the Truth*, and *I've Got a Secret* are relatively innocuous by present standards, at the time these innovative programs were equally trendy—albeit less controversial—as contemporary unscripted programming. Needless to say, the sensationalized era of reality television was still unborn in the late 1940s and early 1950s. But despite common misperceptions, it was ultimately not the viewing audience's reaction to innovative programming that changed the scope and landscape of modern reality television. In fact, it was the medium itself that reacted to growing changes within the American population, particularly among the youth of a new generation.

The Ebb and Flow of Reality TV: A Timeline of Genre Benchmarks

1947: *Candid Microphone*, the wildly popular precursor to *Candid Camera*, debuts on radio, June 28, 1947

1948: *Candid Camera*, the television spin-off of *Candid Microphone*, debuts as the first reality TV show

1973: The first modern reality series, *An American Family*, premieres on PBS

1989: In the wake of a Writers Guild strike, Fox launches *Cops*, the inspiration for the cinéma vérité appearance of subsequent reality programming

1992: MTV introduces *The Real World* and the production idea of forcing complete strangers into a single living environment while documenting the resulting drama

2000: The contemporary reality boom is born with the 1999 launch of ABC's *Who Wants to Be a Millionaire?* Followed by *Survivor*, *Temptation Island*, and *The Mole*, reality television largely replaced scripted television on the top perch of network and cable ratings glory

During the relatively conservative decade of the 1950s, American culture was dominated by an almost spiritual commitment to patriotism at home and the fight for democracy abroad. At the beginning of the 1960s, though, the nation endured an enormous period of radical change, marked by the civil rights movement, the "sexual revolution," growing antiwar sentiment, and the emergence of "flower children" and the Woodstock generation. But it was the no-nonsense, free-spirited mentality of coming-of-age Baby Boomers that did more than anything else to usher in a new generation of mainstream entertainment conducive to its newly liberated audience. As a result, television programming became relatively "obscene" in comparison to TV of only a decade earlier. By the close of the 1960s, unabashed candor and unbridled self-autonomy were the preferable alternatives to previously shared conservative values and established modesty.

Often regarded as the principal forerunner of modernized documentary-style reality programming, PBS's *An American Family* was shot in 1971 and later broadcast in installments in 1973 to an average audience of more than 10 million.

An American Family, which consisted of 12 episodes culled from 300 hours of footage, showcased a "typical" nuclear family in southern California. Cameras chronicled the Loud family during a particularly difficult period when the parents, Bill and Pat Loud, separated and later divorced.

Of the five children on the program, Lance Loud, a 20-year-old gay man, became somewhat of an icon for gays and lesbians by being the first openly gay figure on national television. As such, the common dysfunction captured by PBS not only forever altered perspectives on the "normal American family," it also permanently influenced the style and scope of documentary-style reality programming in the United States.

The incredible popularity of *An American Family* illustrated to subsequent generations of producers that audiences were compelled *en masse* toward real drama rooted in highly relatable personal and family-related struggles.

THE ORDINARY STAR IS BORN

In the aftermath of *An American Family*, audiences had not only grown comfortable with such unconventional and brutally honest programming, they had also come to eagerly anticipate it. Although these and other emerging styles of reality television largely offered unaffected portrayals of real people in real situations, the alluring drama of scripted television was still present. Surprisingly, reality television had proven itself also capable of telling a compelling story.

Pioneering Audience Participation

America's Most Wanted, the longest-running series in the history of the Fox network, is regularly credited with inspiring the phenomenon of audience participation in reality television programs. With its established function of publicly profiling fugitives in hopes of assisting law enforcement in bringing them to justice, *America's Most Wanted* has aired consistently for more than 20 years. Hosted by John Walsh, *America's Most Wanted* is responsible for an estimated 1000 captures of lawbreakers, the majority of which were brought about through direct audience involvement.

Real People and *That's Incredible* in the early 1980s further contributed to the growth of reality programming by actively removing cameras from the studio and taking them directly to places where good stories were waiting to be told—even someone's living room. Simplifying the production process was the development and relative affordability of RCA's TK-76 camera (not to mention the Ikegami HL-77 and HL-79), which made remotes, or portable video shoots, easier than ever. Those behind Westinghouse Broadcasting's syndicated newsmagazine, *PM Magazine,* were among the first to capitalize on this new technology and paved the way for others to do the same. Within only a few years, Sony's revolutionary Betacam further elevated the ease and quality of on-location production, as evidenced by the subsequent groundswell of reality-based programs that followed: *Unsolved Mysteries* (1987), *America's Most Wanted* (1988), *Cops* (1989), *Rescue 911* (1989), and more. In 1990, following the debut of *America's Funniest Home Videos*, audiences became a part of the reality TV genre itself, a development rooted in the advent of the home video camera (the VHS camcorder).

The bulk of reality programming in the early 1990s, however, concentrated on scenarios in which "reality" could transpire within forced living environments. The leading example of such programming was MTV's *The Real World*, which debuted in 1992.

The Real World fused the emotional powder-keg elements of *An American Family* with the voyeuristic style of *Candid Camera* and presented a culturally and socially relevant program that wasn't afraid to explore an assortment of issues facing American youth. For some cast members, *The Real World* provided an opportunity for first encounters with people of different races or sexual orientations. Over the course of 18 subsequent seasons, many episodes of *The Real World* have documented arguments and discussions over these and other sensitive issues.

The fusion of production and storytelling techniques utilized by the producers of *The Real World* engendered a reality TV format that was considered more "structured" than its predecessors. This structure resulted from the ways in which producers purposefully selected the city of production location, the cherry-picking of a cast of desirable characters, eliciting emotions and candid revelations in video testimonials, and shooting unprecedented amounts of tape to deliver more options for editing and creating storylines. These thoughtful, comprehensive, and occasionally duplicitous techniques paved the way for producers of reality shows like *Big Brother* and *Survivor* to achieve similar structure.

REGURGITATED REALITY

Since 2000, many critics of reality television have condemned the genre for regurgitating and borrowing many previously used— and often abused—programming concepts. More recent trends, however, strongly suggest that though reality television remains globally popular, audiences are quickly tiring of rehashed ideas and are hungry for new shows that still fall under the rubric of reality programming.

Are You Smarter Than a 5th Grader?, which showcases scholarly and articulate fifth-grade students, often at the humorous expense of adults who occasionally prove to know less than the kids, reinvigorated audience interest in prime-time game shows. For several years, ratings had been dwindling in response to the incessant rehashing of old game show programs. But by continuing a proven, quiz-based competition with an entirely new generation of contestants, viewers initially rallied behind *Are You Smarter Than a 5th Grader?* to the tune of nearly 12.8 million viewers per episode.

According to *The New York Times*, in 2007 four of the top 10 TV searches on AOL.com were for reality television shows: *American Idol, Dancing with the Stars, Deal or No Deal,* and *Big Brother.* To be fair, however, most industry observers concur that the major networks have not cultivated a new juggernaut reality series since *Dancing with the Stars* debuted in the summer of 2005. In 2006, *Dancing* became one of the world's most popular series, reaching top 10 ratings status in 17 countries.

Early Predictors of Reality TV in Pop Culture

1949: George Orwell's *Nineteen Eighty-Four* portrays a world in which two-way television screens monitored ordinary people's activities 24/7

1958: Robert Sheckley's sci-fi novel *The Prize of Peril* presents a chilling tale of a game show where the contestant is hunted by killers for an entire week

1965: Before there was Mark Burnett, there was Walter F. Moudy, who foretells in *The Survivor* a tale of the 2050 "Olympic War Games;" waged between the US and the USSR, the "games" are played by soldiers on each side, with the goal of eliminating the opposing force while audiences look on

1968: *The Year of the Sex Olympics*, a controversial television play on the BBC, portrays a rebellious dissenter within a dictatorship who is dispatched to an island with the single responsibility of entertaining his countrymen on what is tantamount to a reality TV show

1974: Robert J. Stove's *The Unsleeping Eye* is a published novel about a woman with terminal cancer whose final days are uninterruptedly chronicled for a television show without her consent—or knowledge

1976: A story by science fiction writer Kate Wilhelm called *Ladies and Gentlemen, This Is Your Crisis* depicts a TV show in which contestants— among them an out-of-work actress looking for renewed fame—have to find their way out of the deserted wilderness into which they've been placed

1982: A work by Stephen King later produced as a film starring Arnold Schwarzenegger, *The Running Man* portrays a game show in which contestants must survive the hunters trying to kill them

THE REALITY ARCHIVE: REALITY TV THEN AND NOW

Abbey and Janice, 2007–
The Academy, 2007–
Ace of Cakes, 2006–
Adam and Joe Go Tokyo, 2003–2003
The Adam Carolla Project, 2005–
Adventure Camp, 2003–2007
Adventures in Hollyhood, 2007–
After Hours with Daniel Boulud, 2006–
After the Catch, 2007–
Against All Odds, 1992–1992
The Agency, 2007–
Airline, 2004–2005
All Out Christmas, 2005–
All-Star Holiday Cookies, 2007–
The Amazing Dunninger, 1955–1956
The Amazing Race, 2001–
The Amazing Race Asia, 2006–
Amazing Vacation Homes, 2004–2006
Ambush Makeover, 2004–2005
AMC Backstory, 2000–2004
AMC Naked Hollywood, 1991–1991
America or Busted, 2004–2005
America's Ballroom Challenge, 2006–
America's Funniest Home Videos, 1990–
America's Got Talent, 2006–
America's Greatest Pets, 1998–1999
America's Most Wanted, 1988–
America's Next Top Model, 2003–

America's Psychic Challenge, 2007–
America's Most Smartest Model, 2007–
American Candidate, 2004–2004
American Casino, 2004–
American Chopper, 2003–
American Chronicles, 1990–1991
American Dream Derby, 2005–2005
An American Family, 1973–1973
American Fighter Pilot, 2002–2002
American Gladiators, 1989–1997
American Gladiators, 2008–
American High, 2000–2000
American Hot Rod, 2004–
American Idol, 2002–
American Idol Extra, 2006–
American Inventor, 2006–
American Juniors, 2003–2003
American Justice, 1992–
American Princess, 2005–
American Start-Up, 2005–
Amish in the City, 2004–2004
Anatomy of a Scene, 2001–2001
Anatomy of Crime, 2000–2002
Anchorwoman, 2007–2007
The Andy Milonakis Show, 2005–
Animal Airport, 2007–
Animal Cops: Detroit, 2001–2005
Animal Face-Off, 2004–2004
Animal Hospital, 1994–2004
Animal Jam, 2003–2004
Animal Kidding, 2003–2004
Animal Miracles, 2001–

Continued...

Animal Precinct, 2001–

Animal Tails, 2003–2008

Animals Do the Funniest Things, 1999–

Animals, Animals, Animals, 1976–1981

Anna in Wonderland, 2002–

The Anna Nicole Show, 2002–2003

Anthony Bourdain: No Reservations, 2005–

Antiques Roadshow, 1997–

Any Dream Will Do, 2007–

Anything for Love, 2003–2003

The Apprentice, 2004–

The Apprentice: Martha Stewart, 2005–2007

Are You Hot?, 2003–2003

Armed & Famous, 2007–2007

Arrest & Trial, 2000–2002

The Ashlee Simpson Show, 2004–2005

Ask Rita, 2003–2004

Ask This Old House, 2002–

The Assistant, 2004–2004

At Home with the Eubanks, 2003–2004

Austin Stevens: Snakemaster, 2003–

Automaniac, 2005–

Autopsy, 1994–

AV Squad, 2003–2007

Average Jane, 2005–2006

Average Joe, 2003–2005

B. Smith Style, 1997–2005

The Baby Borrowers, 2008–

A Baby Story, 1998–

The Bachelor, 2002–

Bachelor Pad, 2004–2004

The Bachelorette, 2003–2005

Back to Reality, 2004–2004

Back to the Floor, 1997–2002

Back to the Grind, 2007–

Backyard Blitz, 2000–

The Bad Girls Club, 2006–

Baldwin Hills, 2007–

Ball Breakers, 2005–

Ballroom Bootcamp, 2005–2008

Bam's Unholy Union, 2007–2008

Band in a Bubble, 2007–2007

Bands on the Run, 2001–2001

Bands Reunited, 2004–2006

Barefoot Contessa, 2002–

Barely Famous, 2004–2005

Bargain Hunt, 2000–

Barking Mad, 1999–2000

Bash, 2006–

Bathroom Divas, 2006–

Battle Dome, 1999–2000

Battle for Ozzfest, 2004–2005

Battle of the Gridiron Stars, 2005–2006

Battle of the Network Reality Stars, 2005–

Battle of the Network Stars, 1976–2003

BattleBots, 2000–2002

Be Real, 2006–2006

Beach Patrol: Honolulu, 2007–

Beach Patrol: Miami Beach, 2006–2008

Beach Patrol: San Diego, 2006–

Beauty and the Geek, 2005–

Becoming, 2001–2002
Beef: The Series, 2006–
Before They Were Stars,
   1996–1996
Beg, Borrow & Deal, 2002–2003
Behind the Music, 1997–2006
Being Bobby Brown, 2005–2005
The Best of, 2000–
The Best of the Post, 1960–1961
BET Style, 2004–2006
Better Half, 2007–
Better Homes And Gardens, 1996–
Beyond Boiling Point, 2000–2008
Beyond Chance, 1999–2002
Beyond River Cottage, 2004–
Beyond the Bull, 2006–
The Big 4-0, 2008–
The Big Blue Marble, 1974–1983
Big Brother, 2000–
Big Man on Campus, 2004–2005
Big Medicine, 2007–
The Big Spender, 2006–
Big Strong Girls, 1999–2001
The Big Time, 1976–1980
Big Urban Myth Show,
   2003–2003
BIG! 2004–2004
The Biggest Loser, 2004–
Black. White., 2006–2006
Blind Date, 1999–2006
The Block, 2003–
Blow Out, 2004–2005
Blowin' Up: Fatty Koo, 2005–2005
Blueprint, 2001–
Bo! in the USA, 2006–2006
Boarding House: North Shore,
   2003–2003
The Bob Smith Gulf Show,
   1948–1949

Bob Vila, 2005–
Boiling Points, 2004–2005
Bondi Rescue, 2006–
Boneyard, 2005–
The Book of Lists, 1982–1982
Boot Camp, 2001–2001
Born American, 2003–2004
Bounty Girls, 2007–
Boy Meets Boy, 2003–2003
Boy Meets Grill, 2003–
Brat Camp, 2005–2005
Breaking Bonaduce, 2005–
Breaking the Band, 2006–
Breaking Up with Shannen Doherty,
   2006–2006
Bridezillas, 2004–
Bringing Home Baby, 2005–
Britain's Brainiest, 2001–2002
Britain's Got Talent, 2007–
Britain's Next Top Model, 2005–
Britney and Kevin: Chaotic,
   2005–2005
Brunch, 1997–1998
BSTV, 2005–2007
Bug Juice, 1998–1998
Bullrun, 2007–2007
But Can They Sing?, 2005–
Buy Me, 2006–2008
Buzz, 2000–
Buzzkill, 1996–1996

Caesars 24/7, 2005–2005
California's Gold, 1991–
The Call, 2007–
Call to Greatness, 2006–
Camp Jim, 2003–2003
Can We Help?, 2006–
Can't Get a Date, 2006–2006
Canada's Next Top Model, 2006–

Continued...

THE REALITY ARCHIVE: REALITY TV THEN AND NOW—CONTINUED

Canada's Worst Driver, 2005–
Canadian Idol, 2003–
Candid Camera, 1948–
Cannonball Run 2001, 2001–2001
Caprial and John's Kitchen: Cooking for Family and Friends, 2006–
Carol Vorderman's Better Gardens, 2000–
Carol Vorderman's Better Homes, 1999–2002
Carpocalypse, 2005–2006
Cash Cab, 2005–
Cash in the Attic, 2004–
The Casino, 2004–2004
Castaway 2000, 2000–2001
Cathouse: The Series, 2005–
Caught in the Moment, 2006–2006
CBBC at the Fame Academy, 2002–2005
Celebrities Uncensored, 2003–2004
Celebrities Under Pressure, 2003–2004
Celebrity Big Brother, 2001–
Celebrity Bootcamp, 2002–2002
Celebrity Challenge of the Sexes, 1978–1978
Celebrity Charades, 2005–
Celebrity Circus, 2005–
Celebrity Cooking Showdown, 2006–2006
Celebrity Dish, 2000–2001
Celebrity Dog School, 2003–2003
Celebrity Driving School, 2003–2003
Celebrity Duets, 2006–2006
Celebrity Expose, 2007–

Celebrity Extra, 2000–2001
Celebrity Eye Candy, 2005 –
Celebrity Fit Club, 2005–
Celebrity Justice, 2002–2005
Celebrity Love Island, 2005–
Celebrity Overhaul, 2005–2007
Celebrity Paranormal Project, 2006–2006
Celebrity Poker Showdown, 2003–
Celebrity Rap Superstar, 2007–2008
Celebrity Ready, Steady, Cook, 1997–2000
Celebrity Rehab with Dr. Drew, 2008–
Celebrity Undercover, 2001–2001
Celebrity Wrestling, 2005–
Chains of Love, 2001–2001
Change of Heart, 1998–2003
Change That, 1997–1998
Charm School, 2007–
Chasing Farrah, 2005–2005
Cheaters, 1999–
Cheerleader Nation, 2006–2006
Chevy Top 20, 1995–
Cheyenne, 2006–2006
The Chicas Project, 2007–
Chop Cut Rebuild, 2004–
The Christies: Committed, 2006–2008
Chuck Woolery: Naturally Stoned, 2003–2003
Ciao America with Mario Batali, 2003–2004
Citizen Reno, 2001–2001
Clash of the Choirs, 2007–

Classic Wide World of Sports, 1999–2000

Clean House, 2003–

Clean Sweep, 2003–2005

Click, 2007–

Club Reps, 2004–2004

Coach Trip, 2005–

Code Blue, 2002–2002

Cold Case Files, 1999–

Cold Turkey, 2004–2005

College Hill, 2004–

Colonial House, 2004–2004

Color Splash, 2007–

Combat Missions, 2002–2002

Combat Zone, 2007–2008

The Comeback, 2005–2005

Comic Relief Does Fame Academy, 2003–

Coming Out Stories, 2006–

The Complex: Malibu, 2004–2004

Con, 2005–2005

Confessions of Crime, 1991–1993

Conquest, 2002–2003

Conspiracies, 2001–2001

The Contender, 2005–

A Cook's Tour, 2002–2003

Cook-Off America, 1999–2003

Cooking It, 2007–

Cooking with Caprial & John! 2001–2001

COPS, 1989–

Corkscrewed: The Wrath of Grapes, 2006–

Corwin's Quest, 2005–

Country Fried Home Videos, 2006–

Country Style, 1950–1950

Courage, 2000–2001

Court TV, 2004–2004

Cover to Cover, 1991–1991

Cowboy U, 2003–

Crash Test Mommy, 2004–

Creative Juice for the Holidays, 2005–

Crime 360, 2008–

Crime Stories, 1999–1999

Crime Strike, 1998–1999

Crimes of the Century, 1988–1989

Crimewatch Solved, 1989–1990

Criss Angel Mindfreak, 2005–

The Croc Files, 1999–2001

The Crocodile Hunter, 1997–

The Crocodile Hunter Diaries, 2002–2004

Crossing over with John Edward, 2000–2004

Crowned, 2007–

Cupid, 2003–2003

Curb Appeal, 1999–

Curl Girls, 2007–

The Cut, 1998–1999

The D.A., 2004–2004

D.G.I.A.E., 2002–2002

Daisy Does America, 2005–2006

Dallas Cowboys Cheerleaders, 2006–

Dallas SWAT, 2006–

Damage Control, 2005–2005

The Dan Ho Show, 2007–

Dance 360, 2004–2005

Dance Party USA, 1986–1992

Dance Revolution, 2006–2007

Dance War: Bruno vs. Carrie Ann, 2008–

Dancelife, 2007–

Dancing on Ice, 2006–

Dancing on Ice: Defrosted, 2006–

Dancing with the Stars, 2005–

Continued...

THE REALITY ARCHIVE: REALITY TV THEN AND NOW—CONTINUED

Dane Cook's Tourgasm, 2006–2006

Date My Mom, 2004–2004

Dateline NBC, 1992–

The Dating Experiment, 2003–2003

Dating Games People Play, 2007–

David Blaine: Drowned Alive, 2006–

Day in Court, 1963–1965

Dead Tenants, 2005–

Deadliest Catch, 2005–

Deal or No Deal, 2005–

Dear Santa, 2005–

Debbie Does Dallas Again, 2007–2007

Debbie Travis' Facelift, 2003–2005

Debbie Travis' Painted House, 2004–

Decision House, 2007–

Decisiones, 2006–

Decorating Cents, 2006–

Degrassi Talks, 1992–1992

Degrassi Unscripted, 2004–

Derren Brown: Trick or Treat, 2007–2008

Deserving Design, 2007–

Design on a Dime, 2003–2006

Designed to Sell, 2006–

Designer Guys, 2002–

Designers' Challenge, 2000–

Designing for the Sexes, 1998–

Destination Truth, 2007–

Diary, 1999–

Diary of an Affair, 2004–

Dice Undisputed, 2007–2008

Dinner: Impossible, 2007–

Dirty Dancing: Living the Dream, 2006–

Dirty Jobs, 2003–

Dirty Sanchez, 2003–

Dirty Tricks, 2007–

Dismissed, 2001–

Divine Design, 2006–

Divorce Court, 1999–

DMX: Soul of a Man, 2006–

Dog Days, 2002–2003

Dog Eat Dog, 2002–2003

The Dog Whisperer, 2004–

Don't Forget the Lyrics, 2007–

Don't Forget Your Toothbrush, 2000–2001

Don't Sweat It, 2006–

The Dooley and Pals Show, 2000–2000

Double J News, 2006–

Downtown, 1999–1999

Dr. 90210, 2004–2007

Dr. Danger, 2007–

Dr. G: Medical Examiner, 2004–

Dr. Steve-O, 2007–

Dragon's Den, 2005–

Dream Girl of '67, 1966–1967

Dream Girl, U.S.A., 1986–1987

Dream House, 2000–

Dream Job, 2004–2006

Dream Maker, 1999–2000

Dress My Nest, 2007–

Driven, 2002–

The Dudesons, 2006–2006

Duel, 2007–

The Dunninger Show, 1955–1955

E! Behind the Scenes, 1991–
E! Celebrity Homes, 1999–2002
E!'s 101, 2003–
Eco-Challenge, 1995–2003
Ed vs. Spencer, 2007–
Ego Trip's Race-O-Rama, 2005–2008
Ego Trip's White Rapper Show, 2007–
elimiDATE, 2001–2006
Elimidate Deluxe, 2001–2001
eLove, 2007–
Embellish This!, 2003–
Emergency Vets, 1998–2001
Emeril Live, 1997–
Encounters with the Unexplained, 2000–2002
Endurance, 2002–
Engaged & Underage, 2007–
The Entertainer, 2005–2005
Epic Conditions, 2007–
Escape from Experiment Island, 2003–2003
Essence of Emeril, 1994–
European Poker Tour, 2005–
Everest: Beyond the Limit, 2006–2006
The Ex-Wives Club, 2007–2007
Expedition, 1960–1961
Extreme Contact, 2000–2000
EXTreme Dating, 2002–2004
Extreme Engineering, 2003–
Extreme Homes, 1997–1998
Extreme Makeover, 2002–
Extreme Makeover: Home Edition, 2003–
Extreme Truth, 2008–

The F Word, 2005–
The Fabulous Life of, 2003–
Faking It, 2000–
Faking the Video, 2004–2004
Fame Academy, 2002–2003
Fame, Fortune and Romance, 1986–1986
Family Bonds, 2004–
Family Business, 2003–2008
Family Face-Off: Hollywood, 2004–2004
Family Foreman, 2007–
Family Plots, 2004–
Famous Jury Trials, 1949–1952
FANatic, 1998–2000
The Farm, 2004–2005
Fashion Police, 2003–
The Fashion Story, 1948–1949
The Fashionista Diaries, 2007–
Fast Cars & Superstars, 2007–2007
Fast Inc., 2006–2006
Fat March, 2007–2008
FBI: The Untold Stories, 1991–1993
Fear, 2000–2002
Fear Factor, 2001–2006
Fight Back with David Horowitz, 1976–1992
Fight for Fame, 2005–
Fight Quest, 2008–
Fight School, 2005–
Film School, 2004–2004
Filthy Rich Cattle Drive, 2005–2005
Final Appeal, 1992–1992
Final Fu, 2006–2006

Continued...

Final Justice with Erin Brockovich, 2003–2003

Find & Design, 2006–

Fire Me, Please, 2005–2005

The Firm, 2007–

The First 48, 2004–

First Comes Love, 2007–

First Look, 1990–1991

First Person, 2000–2001

Fishing with John, 1991–1992

The Fix, 1998–1999

Flip This House, 2005–

Flipping Out, 2007–2008

Flog It!, 2002–

Food 911, 2000–

The Food Factory, 1999–1999

Food Jammers, 2006–

The Food Network Awards, 2007–

Food Network Challenge, 2006–

FoodNation with Bobby Flay, 2003–

For Love or Money, 2003–2004

For Better or for Worse, 2003–2005

Ford Bold Moves Documentary, 2006–

Forever Eden, 2004–2004

Forever Summer with Nigella, 2002–2002

Foul-Ups, Bleeps & Blunders, 1984–1984

Fraternity Life, 2003–2005

The French Chef, 1962–1973

Freshman Diaries, 2003–2003

From Flab to Fab, 2004–2004

From Here to Maternity, 2006–

From the Ground Up, 2006–

Frontier House, 2002–2002

Fugitive Strike Force, 2006–

Full Frontal Fashion, 2003–

Full Metal Challenge, 2002–2003

G-String Divas, 2000–

The Galloping Gourmet, 1969–1971

The Games, 2003–

Games People Play, 1980–1981

The Games: Live, 2005–

The Games: Live at Trackside, 2005–

GameSpot on the Spot, 2004–

Garage Takeover, 2005–

Gardener's World, 1969–

Gardens of the World, 1993–1993

Gastineau Girls, 2005–2006

Gay, Straight, or Taken?, 2007–

Gene Simmons Family Jewels, 2006–

Gene Simmons' Rock School, 2005–

Generation Renovation, 2005–

Get Out There!, 2006–

Get This Party Started, 2006–2006

Getaway, 1992–

Ghost Hunters, 2004–

Ghost Hunters International, 2008–

Ghost Stories, 1997–1998

Ghost Trackers, 2005–

Giant Step, 1956–1957

The Gift, 2006–

Gift Show, 2005–

Gifted, 2006–

Girls Behaving Badly, 2002–2006

The Girls Next Door, 2005–

Girls v. Boys, 2003–

Girlz TV, 2002–2005

The Glass House, 2001–2006

God or the Girl, 2006–

Going for a Song, 1997–

Going Tribal, 2005–

Good Deal with Dave Lieberman, 2005–

Good in the Hood, 2008–

Gordon Ramsay's Boiling Point, 2000–2008

The Graham Norton Variety Pack, 2007–2007

Grease Is the Word, 2007–

Grease: You're the One that I Want, 2007–2007

The Great Adventure, 1963–1964

The Great American Dream Vote, 2007–2007

Great Biker Build-Off, 2002–

Great Britons, 2002–2002

The Great Outdoors, 1994–

Great Pretenders, 1998–2002

Greece Uncovered, 1998–2000

Greek to Chic, 2006–

Ground Force, 1998–2005

Growing Up Gotti, 2004–2005

Guess Who's Coming to Dinner?, 1998–2004

Guinness World Records: Primetime, 1998–2001

Ham on the Street, 2006–2007

Hammered with John & Jimmy DiResta, 2006–

Hampton Court Palace, 1999–2000

Hard Copy, 1989–1999

Hard Knocks, 2001–2008

Hard Shine, 2007–2008

Harry's Practice, 1997–2003

Haunted Hotels, 2000–2005

A Haunting, 2005–

Haunting Evidence, 2005–

Have Fork, Will Travel, 2007–

He's a Lady, 2004–2004

Head 2 Toe, 2003–2005

Hear'Say It's Saturday, 2001–2001

Hell's Kitchen, 2005–

A Hero's Welcome, 2006–

Hey Paula, 2007–

Hey! Spring of Trivia, 2004–2005

Hi-Tech Vets, 2008–2008

Hidden Howie: The Private Life of a Public Nuisance, 2005–

Hider in the House, 2007–

High-Maintenance 90210, 2007–

High School Project U.S.A., 2004–2004

High School Stories, 2004–

Hilary Duff: This Is Now, 2007–2008

The Hills, 2006–

I Want to Be a Hilton, 2005–2005

History Alive, 2006–

Hit Me Baby One More Time, 2005–2005

Hogan Knows Best, 2005–2007

Hollywood and Crime, 2000–2001

Hollywood Hold 'Em, 2005–2005

Holmes on Homes, 2004–

Continued...

THE REALITY ARCHIVE: REALITY TV THEN AND NOW—CONTINUED

Home Again with Bob Vila, 1990–2005

Home Cooking with Amy Coleman, 2008–

Home Delivery, 2004–2005

Home Run Derby, 1960–1960

Home to Go, 2006–

Homewrecker, 2005–2005

Homicide Squad, 2001–

Honey, We're Killing the Kids!, 2006–

Hooking Up, 2005–

Hospital!, 2000–2000

We Got to Do Better, 2007–2008

Hot Pursuit, 2006–

Hot Ticket, 2001–2004

Hot Wax, 2001–2001

House Doctor, 1999–

House Hunters, 1999–

House of Boateng, 2006–

House of Carters, 2006–2006

House of Dreams, 2004–2004

The House of Tiny Tearaways, 2005–

The House of Tiny Terrors, 2006–2006

House Rules, 2003–2003

House Wars, 2003–2003

How Clean Is Your House?, 2002–

How Do I Look?, 2004–

How Do You Solve a Problem Like Maria?, 2006–

How I'm Livin', 2001–2003

How It's Made, 2001 –

How Low Can You Go?, 2005–

How to Be a Gardener, 2002–2002

How to Boil Water, 2000–

How to Get the Guy, 2006–2006

How to Look Good Naked, 2008–

How William Shatner Changed the World, 2005–

How'd They Do That?, 1993–1994

Human Weapon, 2007–2008

The Hypnotic World of Paul McKenna, 1993–1993

I Bet You, 2007–

I Bet You Will, 2002–2002

I Can't Believe You Said That!, 1998–1998

I Dare You, 2000–2000

I Do . . . Let's Eat, 2005–

I Know My Kid's A Star, 2008–

I Love the 1980s, 2001–2001

I Love the 1990s, 2001–2001

I Love the '70s, 2003–2003

I Love the '80s, 2002–2002

I Love the '80s Strikes Back, 2003–2003

I Love the '90s, 2004–2004

I Love the '90s, Part Deux, 2005–2005

I Married a Princess, 2005–2005

I Married . . ., 2003–2005

I Pity the Fool, 2006–2006

I Propose, 2007–

I Wanna Be a Soap Star, 2004–

I Want a Famous Face, 2004–2005

I Want That!, 2006–

I Witness Video, 1992–1994

I'm a Celebrity: Get Me Out of Here! 2002–

I'm Famous and Frightened, 2004–2005

I'm from Rolling Stone, 2007–

I'm Still Alive, 2004–2004

I'm With Busey, 2003–2003

I, Detective, 2001–

Ibiza Uncovered, 1997–1999

Ice-T's Rap School, 2006–2006

Identity, 2006–2006

Impact: Stories of Survival, 2002–2005

In Search of the Partridge Family, 2004–2004

In the Moment, 2004–

Incredible Sunday, 1988–1989

The Incurable Collector, 2001–2004

Indievelopment, 2007–

Infamous, 2003–2004

Inked, 2005–2006

The Inn Crowd, 2006–

Inside Fame, 2001–

Inside This Old House, 2003–

International King of Sports, 2002–2002

Intervention, 2005–

Intimate Portrait, 1995–2004

Inturn, 2006–

Invasion Iowa, 2005–2005

Invasion of the Hidden Cameras, 2002–2002

Investigative Reports, 1991–

Iron Chef, 1993–2006

Iron Chef America, 2004–

The It Factor, 2002–2003

It Takes Two, 2006–2007

It's a Miracle, 1998–2004

It's Christopher Lowell, 1999–

It's Good to Be . . ., 2003–2004

It's Your Show, 2007–

An Italian Christmas With Mario & Giada, 2004–

Ivana Young Man, 2006–

Jackass, 2000–2002

Jacob and Joshua: Nemesis Rising, 2006–

Jail, 2007–

The Jamie Kennedy Experiment, 2002–2004

Jamie Kennedy's Blowin' Up, 2006–

Jamie's Kitchen, 2004–

Jamie's School Dinners, 2005–2005

The Janice Dickinson Modeling Agency, 2006–

Jobs for the Boys, 1997–1999

Joe Millionaire, 2003–2003

John Edward Cross Country, 2006–2008

The John Henson Project, 2004–2004

John Ratzenberger's Made in America, 2003–

Jon and Kate Plus 8, 2007–

The Joy of Painting, 1983–1993

The JR Digs Show, 2001–

The Judge, 1986–1989

Judge Alex, 2005–

Judge for Yourself, 1994–1995

Judge Hatchett, 2000–

Judge Joe Brown, 1998–

Judge Judy, 1996–

Judge Maria Lopez, 2006–

Judge Mathis, 1999–

Judge Mills Lane, 1998–2001

Judge Wapner's Animal Court, 1998–2000

Junior Eurovision Contest, 2003–

Continued...

THE REALITY ARCHIVE: REALITY TV THEN AND NOW—CONTINUED

Junk Brothers, 2006–

Junkyard Wars, 1998–2004

Just for Laughs, 2007–

Just the Two of Us, 2006–2007

Juvies, 2007–

Kathy Griffin: My Life on the D-List, 2005–

Kathy's So-Called Reality, 2001–2001

Keeping Up with the Kardashians, 2007–

Kenny Chesney: Somewhere in the Sun, 2005–

Kenny vs. Spenny, 2003–

Kept, 2005–

Keys to the VIP, 2007–

Kicked Out, 2005–

Kid Nation, 2007–

Kids Say the Darnedest Things, 1998–2000

Kids Say the Funniest Things, 2000–2000

Kids' Choice Awards, 1987–

Kill Reality, 2005–

Kimora: Life in the Fab Lane, 2007–

King of Cars, 2006–

King of the Jungle, 2003–2004

Kitchen Accomplished, 2004–

Kitchen Nightmares, 2007–

Kitty Bartholomew: You're Home, 1994–1994

Knight School with Coach Bobby Knight, 2006–

Knock First, 2003–2004

Koffee with Karan, 2004–

Kyle's Academy, 2007–

LA Forensics, 2006–

LA Ink, 2007–

Ladette to Lady, 2006–

Lady or a Tramp, 2008–

Newport Harbor: The Real Orange County, 2004–

Landscapers' Challenge, 2006–

LAPD, 1995–1999

LAPD: Life on the Beat, 1995–1999

Las Vegas Garden of Love, 2005–2005

Last Chance Learners, 2007–

Last Comic Standing, 2003–

Last One Standing, 2007–

The Last Resort, 2002–2003

The Law Firm, 2005–

Leave Us Kids Alone, 2007–

Let's Just Play: Go Healthy Challenge, 2006–

Lie Detector, 2005–2005

Life Is Great With Brooke Burke, 2004–2005

Life Is Not a Fairy Tale: The Fantasia Barrino Story, 2006–

Life Moments, 2002–2003

A Life of Grime, 2006–2006

Life of Ryan, 2007–

Lifestories: Families in Crisis, 1992–1996

Lifestyle Magazine, 2001–2001

Lifestyles of the Rich and Famous, 1984–1995

Lil' Kim: Countdown to Lockdown, 2006–2006

The Linkletter Show, 1963–1963

Lisa Williams: Life among the Dead, 2006–
The List, 2006–2006
Little Angels, 2004–
Little People, Big World, 2006–
The Littlest Groom, 2004–2004
Livin' Large, 2002–2003
Living in TV Land, 2004–
Living It Up With Patti LaBelle, 2004–
Living Lahaina, 2007–2007
Living on the Edge, 2007–
Living the Dream, 2004–2004
Living With Ed, 2007–
Liza and David, 2002–2002
Lobster Wars, 2007–
London Ink, 2007–
Long Way Round, 2004–2004
The Look for Less, 2002–
Looking for Love: Bachelorettes in Alaska, 2002–2002
The Lost Book of Nostradamus, 2007–
The Lost Tomb of Jesus, 2007–
The Lost Tribes, 2007–2007
Love at Third Site, 2006–
Love Connection, 1983–1994
Love on a Saturday Night, 2004–2004
Love Stories, 1991–1992

Mad, Mad House, 2004–2004
Mad Mike and Mark, 2004–
Mad Money, 2006–
Madden Nation, 2005–
Made, 2002–
Made in the U.S.A., 2005–
Make Me a Supermodel, 2008–
Makeover Mamas, 2003–2004

A Makeover Story, 2000–
Making Menudo, 2007–
Making the Band, 2000–2002
Making the Band 2, 2002–2004
Making the Cut, 2004–
Making the Video, 1999–
Making the Video, 2002–
Man vs. Wild, 2006–
Manhunt, 2001–2001
Manor House, 2003–2003
The Mansion, 2004–2004
Marmalade Boy, 1994–1995
Married by America, 2003–2003
Martha, 2005–
Martha Stewart Living, 1997–2004
Master Blasters, 2005–2006
Master of Champions, 2006–2006
Masters of Illusion, 2000–2001
Matched in Manhattan, 2008–
Maternity Ward, 2000–2001
Maui Fever, 2007–2007
Maury, 1998–2007
Maxim's Girl Next Door, 2004–
Maximum Disclosure, 2005–
Maximum Exposure, 2000–2002
Me, My House, and I, 2003–
Meerkat Manor, 2006–
Meet Mister Mom, 2005–
Meet My Folks, 2002–
Meet or Delete, 2007–
Meet the Barkers, 2005–2006
Meet the Family, 2005–
Meet the Royals, 2003–2004
Meet Your Match, 2007–
Mental Block, 2003–
The Meow Mix House, 2006–
Merge, 2003–2005
The Messengers, 2006–
Miami Animal Police, 2004–

Continued...

THE REALITY ARCHIVE: REALITY TV THEN AND NOW—CONTINUED

Miami Ink, 2005–

The Michael Essany Show, 1998–2005

Million Dollar Idea, 2006–

Million Dollar Listing, 2006–

Minding the Store, 2005–2006

Miracle Workers, 2006–

Miss America: Reality Check, 2008–

Miss Seventeen, 2005–

Miss Universe Pageant, 1955–

Mix It Up, 2003–2004

Model Citizens, 2004–2004

A Model Life With Petra Nemcova, 2007–

The Mole, 2001–2004

Moment of Truth, 2008–

The Monastery, 2006–

The Money Program, 1966–

Monster Garage, 2002–2006

Monster House, 2003–2006

Moolah Beach, 2001–2001

Most Daring, 2007–

Most Extreme Elimination Challenge, 2003–

Most Haunted, 2002–

A Most Mysterious Murder, 2004–

Most Outrageous Moments, 2005–2008

Most Shocking, 2006–

Motormouth, 2004–

Mr. Chi Chi's Guide to the Universe, 2000–2001

Mr. Personality, 2003–2003

Mr. Romance, 2005–2005

MTV Cribs, 2000–

MTV Exposed, 2006–

MTV Movie Awards, 1992–

MTV Sports, 1992–1993

MTV's the '70s House, 2005–2005

Murder, 2007–

Murder by the Book, 2006–

Murder in Small Town X, 2001–2001

Murder Squad, 2006–

MuzikMafia TV, 2005–2005

My Bare Lady, 2006–2006

My Big Fat Obnoxious Boss, 2004–2004

My Big Fat Obnoxious Fiancé, 2004–2004

My Brand New Life, 2004–2006

My Fair Brady, 2005–

My First Place, 2006–

My House Is Worth What?, 2006–

My Life Is a Sitcom, 2003–2003

My New Best Friend, 2003–2008

My Own, 2005–

My Restaurant Rules, 2004–2005

My Super Sweet 16, 2005–

My Unique Family, 2007–

MythBusters, 2003–

Myths & Legends, 2007–

Naked Camera, 2005–

Name Your Adventure, 1992–1995

Nanny 911, 2004–

NASCAR Drivers: 360, 2004–2005

NASCAR in Primetime, 2007–2008

Nashville, 2007–2007

Nashville Star, 2003–

National Bingo Night, 2007–2007

The National Dog Show Presented by Purina, 1999–

The Natural World, 2005–

NBA Inside Stuff, 1990–
NBA Rookies, 2005–
Neat, 2004–
Nerd Nation, 2004–2004
New Attitudes, 1998–2000
The Newcomers, 1977–1980
Newlyweds: Nick and Jessica, 2003–2005
Next, 2005–
Next Action Star, 2004–2004
The Next Big Thing, 2007–
The Next Food Network Star, 2005–
The Next Great Champ, 2004–2004
The Next Iron Chef, 2007–
The Nick Cannon Show, 2002–2003
Nick Cannon Presents Wild 'N Out, 2005–
Nigel's Wild, Wild World, 2001–2001
Nitro Circus, 2006–
Nobody's Watching, 2007–
North Mission Road, 2003–
Now It Can Be Told, 1991–1992
NZ Idol, 2004–

Off the Leash, 2006–2006
Offbeat America, 2005–
On the Lot, 2007–
On the Verge, 2000–2002
One-Hit Wonders, 2002–2002
One Ocean View, 2006–2006
One Punk under God, 2006–
One Step Beyond, 2005–
The One: Making a Music Star, 2006–2006
Only in America, 2005–
Open Bar, 2005–2008

Oprah's Big Give, 2008–
The Osbournes, 2002–2005
Our Place, 2005–2005
Outback Jack, 2004–2004
Outtake TV, 2002–2006
Over Your Head, 2006–
Overhaulin', 2004–

The Pacific Life Holiday Bowl Parade, 2007–
Pageant Place, 2007–
The Papdits, 2006–2006
Paradise City, 2007–
Paradise Hotel, 2003–
Paramedics, 2006–
The Paranormal Borderline, 1996–1996
Paranormal State, 2007–
Parental Control, 2006–
Parenteen, 2006–
Party at the Palms, 2005–
Party/Party, 2005–
Pat Croce: Moving In, 2004–2005
Paula's Home Cooking, 2002–
Paula's Party, 2006–
The Pendletons, 2008–
People Are Funny, 1954–1961
People Are Funny, 1984–1984
People Do the Craziest Things, 1984–1985
The People's Court, 1981–
Pepsi Smash, 2003–2004
Perfect Match, 2003–2003
Performing As, 2003–2003
Pet Psychic, 2002–2003
Pet Star, 2002–
Phenomenon, 2007–2007
The Pick-Up Artist, 2007–
Pimp My Ride, 2004–
Pinks: All Out, 2007–

Continued...

THE REALITY ARCHIVE: REALITY TV THEN AND NOW—CONTINUED

Planet Earth, 2007–

The Planet's Funniest Animals, 1999–

The Player, 2004–2004

Playing It Straight, 2004–2006

Pole to Pole, 1992–1992

Police Camera Action, 1994–2002

Pop Idol, 2001–2003

Popstars, 2001–2002

Porno Valley, 2004–2004

Prank Patrol, 2006–

Prankville, 2007–

Pressure Cook, 2007–

Prime Time Pets, 1990–1990

Primetime Live, 1989–

The Princes of Malibu, 2005–2005

Princess Nikki, 2006–

The Priory, 1999–2001

Private Property, 1999–1999

Profiles in Courage, 1964–1965

Project Catwalk, 2006–

Project Greenlight, 2001–2005

Project Runway, 2004–

Project Runway Canada, 2007–

Proof Positive, 2004–2004

Property Ladder, 2005–

Pros vs. Joes, 2006–

Psychic Witness, 2005–

Punk'd, 2003–

Pussycat Dolls: The Search for the Next Doll, 2007–

Puttin' on the Hits, 1984–1988

Queer Eye for the Straight Girl, 2005–2005

Queer Eye for the Straight Guy, 2003–

R U the Girl with T-Boz & Chilli, 2005–2005

The Race, 2006–2006

Race to the Altar, 2003–2003

Race Around the World, 1997–1998

Rachael Ray's Tasty Travels, 2005–

Radio Music Awards, 2005–

Rally Round the House, 2003–2005

Random 1, 2005–2005

Ready, Steady, Cook, 2001–

The Real Estate Pros, 2007–

The Real Gilligan's Island, 2004–2005

The Real Housewives of Orange County, 2006–

The Real Hustle, 2007–

The Real Roseanne Show, 2003–2003

Real Time with Andy Kindler, 1998–1999

Real TV, 1996–2001

The Real Wedding Crashers, 2007–

The Real World, 1992–

The Real World/Road Rules Challenge, 1997–

The Reality Show, 2005–2005

Really Rich Real Estate, 2006–2006

The Rebel Billionaire, 2004–2005

Recipe for Success, 2004–

Red Handed, 1999–1999

Reel Wild Cinema, 1996–1997

Regency House Party, 2004–2004

Relationship Rehab, 2006–

Remaking, 2005–2005

Rendez-View, 2001–2002
Renovate My Family,
   2004–2004
Rent Free, 2002–2002
Rescue 911, 1989–1996
The Restaurant, 2003–2004
Restaurant Makeover, 2005–
Rich Girls, 2003–2003
The Rich List, 2006–2006
Ripley's Believe It or Not!,
   2000–2003
Rising Stars, 2001–2001
Road Hockey Rumble, 2007–
Road Rules, 1995–2007
Road Rules All Stars,
   1998–1998
Road to Menudo, 2007–
Rob & Amber: Against the Odds,
   2007–2007
Rob & Big, 2006–
Robot Wars, 2004–2006
Robot Wars: Extreme, 2001–2003
Robot Wars: Extreme Warriors,
   2001–2003
Robot Wars: Grand Champions,
   2002–2003
Rock Camp, 2004–2004
The Rock Life, 2007–2008
Rock of Ages, 1998–1998
Rock of Love with Bret Michaels,
   2007–
Rock Star, 2005–
Rocked with Gina Gershon, 2004–
Roker on the Road, 2006–
Rollergirls, 2006–
Rollerjam, 1999–2001
The Rookies, 2008–
Room by Room, 1994–
Room Raiders, 2003–

Rotten TV, 2000–2000
Rough Science, 2000–2005
Roush Racing: Driver X,
   2005–2006
Ruby Takes a Trip, 1991–1991
Ruby's Health Quest, 1995–1995
Run's House, 2005–

S.O.B., 2007–
The Salon, 2003–2004
The Salt 'N' Pepa Show, 2007–
Saturday Kitchen, 2006–
Saving Babies, 2007–
Say Yes to the Dress, 2007–
Scare Tactics, 2003–2006
The Scariest Places on Earth, 2000–
The Scholar, 2005–2005
Sci-Fi Investigates, 2006–
Score, 2007–2007
Scott Baio is 45 … and Single,
   2007–
Scream Play, 2004–2004
Scream Test, 2001–2001
Sea Rescue, 2007–
The Search, 2007–
The Search for the Next Elvira,
   2007–2007
The Next Great American Band,
   2007–
Second Verdict, 2004–2004
Secret Lives, 2003–2003
Secret Lives of Women,
   2007–2008
Secret Service, 1992–1992
Secret Service, 2002–2002
Secret, Strange & True,
   2002–2003
Secrets of Superstar Fitness,
   2002–

Continued...

THE REALITY ARCHIVE: REALITY TV THEN AND NOW—CONTINUED

Secrets of the Unknown, 1988–1989

Sell This House, 2003–

Sensing Murder, 2006–

Sexual Healing, 2006–

Sexy Urban Legends, 2001–

Shalom in the Home, 2006–

Shaq's Big Challenge, 2007–

Shear Genius, 2007–

Sheer Dallas, 2005–2006

Shipmates, 2001–2003

Shipwrecked, 2007–

Shock Treatment, 2006–2006

Shockwave, 2007–

Shooting Sizemore, 2007–2007

The Shot, 2007–

A Shot at Love with Tila Tequila, 2007–2007

Show Me the Funny, 1998–1999

Show Me the Money, 2006–2006

Showbiz Moms & Dads, 2004–2004

Showcase '68, 1968–1968

Side Effects, 1994–1996

Sidewalks: Video Nite, 1991–

The Simple Life, 2003–2007

Simply Delicioso, 2007–2008

Simply Quilts, 2003–

Situation: Comedy, 2005–2005

Six Experiments, 1999–1999

Skating with Celebrities, 2006–2008

Small Shots, 2001–2003

The Smoking Gun TV, 2003–2008

Snoop Dogg's Father Hood, 2007–

So You Think You Can Dance, 2005–

So You Think You Can Dance (Aus), 2008–

Soap Stars, 2001–2001

Soap World, 1982–1984

Songs of Praise, 1963–

Sonic Cinema, 2002–2002

Sons of Hollywood, 2007–

Sorority Life, 2002–2003

SOS: Coast Guard Rescue, 2005–

Spike TV's The Playbook, 2005–2006

Spike's Most Amazing Videos, 2006–

Split Ends, 2006–

Sports Illustrated: Model Search, 2005–2005

Sports Kids Moms & Dads, 2005–2006

The Springer Hustle, 2007–2007

Spy TV, 2001–2002

Stacked Poker, 2006–

Star Dates, 2002–2003

Star Racer, 2006–

Star Search, 1983–1995

Star Search, 2003–

Star Tomorrow, 2006–

The Starlet, 2005–2005

Stars in Their Eyes Kids, 2001–

Starting Over, 2003–2006

Stella Street, 1997–2001

Step It Up, 2008–

The Steph Show, 2006–2006

Steve-O, 2003–2003

Sticky Moments with Julian Clary, 1989–1990

Storm Chasers, 2007–

The Story of . . ., 2007–

Straight Plan for the Gay Man, 2004–2004
Stranded with Cash Peters, 2005–
Strange but True, 1994–1997
Strange Love, 2005–2005
Strange Universe, 1996–1997
Streetmate, 1998–2001
Streetwatch TV, 2007–
Strictly Dance Fever, 2005–
Strip Search, 2005–2005
Stuntdawgs, 2006–
Style Court, 2003–
Style Her Famous, 2006–
Style Me, 2006–2008
Style Star, 2002–
Successful Home Video, 1992–1992
Sugar Rush, 2006–2008
Summer Share, 2006–
Summer Storm, 2003–
Summer's Best, 2003–
Sunset Tan, 2007–
Super Agent, 2005–2005
SuperGroup, 2006–
Superior Court, 1986–1990
Supernanny, 2005–
Superstar, USA 2004–2004
Surf Girls, 2003–2003
Surfer Girls, 2005–
Surprise by Design, 2002–
The Surreal Gourmet, 2005–2008
The Surreal Life, 2003–
The Surreal Life: Fame Games, 2007–
Survival of the Richest, 2006–2006
Survive This, 2007–
Surviving Nugent, 2003–2004
Survivor, 2000–
Survivorman, 2005–

Swag, 2003–2008
The Swan, 2004–2004
Switched Up!, 2004–2004
Switched!, 2003–2004

Tabloid Tales, 2003–2004
TailDaters, 2002–2003
Take Hart, 1977–1983
Take-Home Chef, 2006–
Take-Home Handyman, 2007–
The Takedown, 2005–2005
Taking It Off, 2002–
Tales from River Cottage, 2006–
Tall Ships Chronicles, 2001–2002
TapouT, 2007–
Taradise, 2005 –
Tarrant on TV, 1992–
Taxicab Confessions, 1995–
Team Sanchez, 2005–
Teammates, 2005–
Tease, 2007–
Teen Big Brother, 2003–2003
The Teen Files, 2006–2006
Temptation Island, 2001–2003
The Test, 2001–2001
Tested to Destruction, 1999–1999
Texas Hardtails, 2005–
Texas Ranch House, 2006–
Texas S.W.A.T., 2006–
That Yin Yang Thing, 2005–
That's Funny, 2004–
That's Incredible, 1980–1984
That's My Baby, 2001–2003
There and Back: Ashley Parker Angel, 2006–
There's Something About Miriam, 2004–
Things to Try Before You Die, 2007–2007

Continued...

THE REALITY ARCHIVE: REALITY TV THEN AND NOW—CONTINUED

This Is David Gest, 2007–2008

This Is Your Life, 2006–

This Old House, 1980–

Those Amazing Animals, 1980–1981

Three Sheets, 2006–

Three Wishes, 2005–2007

Through the Keyhole, 1983–

Throwdown with Bobby Flay, 2006–

Tiara Girls, 2006–

Til Death Do Us Part, 2004–

Tim Gunn's Guide to Style, 2007–

The Time the Place, 1989–1990

Timeblazers, 2003–2005

TMZ on TV, 2007–

To Serve and Protect, 1993–

Todd TV, 2004–2004

Tommy Lee Goes to College, 2005–2005

Tomorrow's World, 1965–2002

Too Many Cooks, 2004–

Top 5, 2006–2006

Top Chef, 2006–

Top Cops, 1990–1993

Top Design, 2007–2007

Tori & Dean: Inn Love, 2007–

Total Drama Island, 2007–

Totally Circus, 2000–2000

Totally Hidden Video, 1989–1992

Totally Hoops, 2001–2001

Totally Obsessed, 2004–2004

Totally Outrageous Behavior, 2004–

Town Haul, 2005–2006

Tracey Takes On . . ., 1996–1999

Trading Spaces, 2000–

Trading Spaces: Boys vs. Girls, 2003–

Trading Spaces: Family, 2003–

Trading Spouses, 2004–2007

Traffic Cops, 2002–

Trailer Fabulous, 2005–

TransGeneration, 2005–2005

Trash or Treasure? 1952–1953

Trauma: Life in the E.R., 1997–2004

Treasure Hunters, 2006–2006

Trial by Jury, 1989–1990

Trick It Out, 2005–2008

Trick My Truck, 2006–

Trick My Trucker, 2007–

Trick of the Mind, 2004–2006

Trippin', 2005–2005

True Caribbean Pirates, 2006–2008

True Confessions, 1985–1986

True Detectives, 1990–1991

True Life, 1998–

Trust Me—I'm a Holiday Rep, 2005–2006

Truth or Scare, 2001–2003

Truth Quest: California, 2002–2002

Tuckerville, 2005–

Tuesday Night Book Club, 2006–2007

TV Bloopers and Practical Jokes, 1984–1986

TV Nation, 1994–1995

TV Reader's Digest, 1955–1956

Twentyfourseven, 2006–

The Two Coreys, 2007–

Two Dudes Catering, 2007–

Two Fat Ladies, 1996–

Two-a-Days, 2006–2007

Ty Murray's Celebrity Bull Riding Challenge, 2007–

Tycoon, 2007–
Tylers Ultimate, 2004–2005

The Ultimate Coyote Ugly Search,
  2006–2007
Ultimate Gamer, 2004–2006
Ultimate Home, 2004–2004
Ultimate Hustler, 2005–2006
The Ultimate Love Test,
  2004–2004
The Ultimate Revenge,
  2001–2003
Ultimate Transformations Live,
  2004–2004
Unan1mous, 2006–2006
UnCorked, 2007–
Under One Roof, 2002–2002
The Underdog Show, 2007–2008
Undersea World of Jacques
  Cousteau, 1966–1976
Unexplained Mysteries, 2003–2004
Unique Whips, 2005–
University Challenge, 1962–
Unsolved Mysteries, 1988–2002
Untitled Boy Band Project,
  2007–2008
Untitled Dave Ramsey Project,
  2006–

Venom ER, 2004–2004
Venus & Serena: For Real,
  2005–2005
Verdict, 1998–1998
The Verdict, 2007–
Vets in the Wild West, 2001–
VH1 Goes Inside, 2003–
VH1's (Inside) Out, 2003–
Victorian Scandals, 1976–1976
The Villa, 2007–

Viva la Bam, 2003–2005
VJ Search: The Series, 2006–2007

The Wade Robson Project,
  2003–2003
War of the Wives, 2006–
Warm Weather, White Christmas,
  2005–
The Way It Was, 1974–1978
Way of the Master, 2003–
Wayne Anderson: Singer of Songs,
  2006–2007
We the Jury, 2002–2003
The Weakest Link, 2002–2003
Weapon Masters, 2007–
Webdreams, 2005–
Wedding Day, 1981–1981
A Wedding Story, 1996–
The Week the Women Went,
  2008–
Weekend Makeover, 2006–
Weekend Warriors, 2000–2006
Weird U.S., 2005–
Wendy Williams Is on Fire,
  2003–2005
What Happened?, 1992–1992
What Not to Wear, 2003–
What's It Worth?, 1948–1953
When Jordan Met Peter,
  2004–2005
When Women Rule the World,
  2008–
Where Are They Now?, 1998–2003
While You Were Out, 2002–
Who Do You Think You Are?, 2004–
Who Wants to Be a Superhero?,
  2006–
Who Wants to Marry My Dad?,
  2003–2004

Continued...

THE REALITY ARCHIVE: REALITY TV THEN AND NOW—CONTINUED

Who's Your Daddy?, 2005–2005

Whose House Is It Anyway?, 2000–2001

Whose Wedding Is It Anyway?, 2006–

Wickedly Perfect, 2005–2005

Wide World of Sports, 1961–1997

Wife Mom Bounty Hunter, 2007–

Wife Swap, 2004–

Wild On!, 1999–2003

Wild Things, 1997–1998

Wild World of Spike, 2007–

Wildboyz, 2003–

The Will, 2005–2005

With a Little Help from My Friends, 2004–2005

Wolfgang Puck, 2001–

Work Out, 2006–

World Idol, 2003–2004

World in Action, 1963–1999

The World's Funniest!, 1997–2002

World's Most Amazing Video, 1999–

World's Wildest Police Videos, 1998–2005

Worst-Case Scenario, 2002–2002

WWE Tough Enough, 2001–2006

The X Effect, 2007–

The X Factor, 2004–

The Xtra Factor, 2004–

Yearbook, 1991–1991

Yo Momma, 2006–

You Are What You Eat, 2007–

You Asked for It, 1950–1959

You Lie Like a Dog, 2000–2000

You Spoof Discovery, 2007–

You Write the Songs, 1986–1987

You're Invited, 2002–

Your Kids Are in Charge, 2000–2000

Zoboomafoo, 1999–2001

Zoo Diaries, 2000–2004

Chapter three

From Fantasy to Reality

Standing next to Susan Sarandon in an elevator at the Hollywood Renaissance Theatre, I nervously bungle an attempt to break the ice with one of my favorite Academy Award-winning actresses.

"So, what brings you here, Ms. Sarandon?" I finally inquired.

"I'm presenting for the Television Critics Association," she responded, visibly aware of my childlike admiration and anxiety. "How about you?"

"I'm here for the convention, as well," I replied.

"Are you an actor?" she asked.

"No," I said. "I'm the star of a new reality TV series."

With that revelation, my conversation with Susan Sarandon ground to a halt. Her telling countenance in response to my announced status as a reality TV star communicated her genuine concern for my professional well-being.

Though extremely polite and gracious enough to even have her photo taken, Sarandon clearly saw me as an ambitious but innocent kid potentially in over his head.

To a considerable degree, Sarandon was correct. Although I had grown acclimated to spotting sharks, dodging shoddy deals, and sidestepping charlatans during the previous five years, my worst miscalculation in preparing for the big leagues of nationally televised reality programming was assuming that reality TV was unfailingly rooted at all times in actual reality.

FIGURE 3.1   Susan Sarandon and Michael Essany.

WAKING UP TO REALITY

Despite the style of a reality series—documentary, game show, fear-centric, and so on—its overarching aim never changes: to solicit a visceral response from the viewing audience. It doesn't matter if the response is laughter, sadness, joy, or even discomfort. Reality TV is in the business of selling relatable and emotive content. Whether we lambaste the performance of an unpopular contestant on *American Idol* or cringe at Donald Trump's scathing termination of our favorite would-be apprentice, the genre indisputably thrives on making us react in *some* visceral way.

As an unfortunate consequence of stage-managing reality programming to extract a desired emotional response from viewers, the subjects of these series are frequently rendered expendable components of the process. This is precisely what makes reality TV so highly exploitive. Its participants are always the means to an end: positive, negative, or somewhere in between.

I was only 19 years old when my life became the subject of a reality television series. Inspired by my unusual childhood ambition to one day host a late-night talk show, *The Michael Essany Show* was packaged as a reality program about the production of an

Indiana-based public access talk show and the interesting life and lofty goals of its "unorthodox teenage host."

When E! Entertainment Television purchased my series in late 2002, I was told that my work and life story would continue being represented according to the brand I had already created. Several years before *The Michael Essany Show* debuted nationally, I had already begun landing guest appearances on *Today, Oprah, Inside Edition, The Tonight Show,* and the like. Without fail, my story was always portrayed in a relatively accurate light. As a result, I effectively sold my show to an engrossed viewership long before E! entered the picture, presumably to perpetuate an already proven formula.

Looking back, this "formula" was the product of an unlikely dream that began during childhood. As I grew up in the small town of Hobart, Indiana, during the early 1980s, few joys in life rivaled staying up past my bedtime on an endless summer evening to watch *The Tonight Show* with my grandparents. Over time, my admiration for Johnny Carson and the nightly routine he made look so easy left me completely out of touch with reality in evaluating my own chances for a career in network television. Hosting a late-night

FIGURE 3.2 Behind the scenes with recording star Kelly Rowland for the premiere episode of *The Michael Essany Show* on E!

talk show, I thought, was a career option just as commonplace as any other trade.

Like a million hopeful entertainers before me, watching the King of Late Night gave rise to my own show business dream. The only real difference between me and the others is that I was much too impatient to comfortably put off the pursuit of my dream until I was older.

> **FACT**
>
> According to the Learning and Skills Council, one in seven British teenagers hopes to become rich and famous as a result of appearing on some form of reality television.

As I recall, the summer before my 12th birthday began my foray into the television industry in earnest. Oddly enough, it started with a weekend of simple research at the Valparaiso, Indiana, public library. For two straight afternoons I scoured tattered titles that boasted helpful how-to advice for individuals wanting to break into show business. Unfortunately, the advice I found (like the need to circulate glamorous headshots and colorful résumés to practically every legal resident of Southern California) consisted primarily of cookie-cutter tips with little relevance to me.

Given that I had no résumé or even a professional photo—excluding, of course, the Christmas portrait with Santa that adorned our living room mantle—I was desperate for sound advice that suited my uncommon situation.

Luckily, during my research I unearthed a fairly comprehensive guide to celebrity mailing addresses, which was designed for fan mail submissions, autograph requests, and, presumably, your run-of-the-mill psychotic celebrity stalkers. For me, though, the utility of this guide was its ability to connect me to those who had already traversed that perilous terrain between civilian and celebrity.

Subsequently, I began a letter-writing campaign to solicit advice from every famous person I thought would potentially respond. And, amazingly, the effort paid off. Whether endeared to a fellow soul enchanted with performing or simply riveted by a kid aiming too high for his own good, these celebrities sent me scores of cards and letters with thoughtful inscriptions.

> "Get in front of people," wrote Merv Griffin, one of television's most recognizable personalities and formidable innovators. "Don't waste your time trying to be discovered. Let others discover *you*!"

Griffin, along with Betty White, Joey Bishop, and Milton Berle, were among those who replied with unbelievably thoughtful counsel. Curiously, all had one overriding message in common: Start doing the work you want to do. The rest will follow.

DOWN THE BEATEN PATH

In the decades that preceded YouTube, MySpace, and the advent of mainstream Internet media, the only way for an ambitious, albeit untested and unprofessional, young performer like myself to reach the general public was to garner airtime on regional public access television. To be sure, this was a well-traveled road by others once in my shoes. Over the last quarter century, in fact, many show business professionals first cut their teeth in the creative workshop of public access.

As a result of the 1984 Cable Franchise Policy and Communications Act, all cable TV companies in the United States are now obligated, at their own expense, to provide free and accessible broadcast airtime to local residents. To this day, every cable provider designates one channel solely to "local origination programming," commonly referred to as public access TV. Typically, a semiprofessional television studio where programs can be produced is also found at the local cable provider's main office. The facilities, like airtime, are available at no cost and on a first-come, first-served basis.

The veritable rock-bottom of all broadcasting media, public access television always struck me as an unendingly fascinating entity. From mind-numbingly unoriginal banter on local interview programs to off-the-wall characters pretending to clash with plastic swords outside the neighborhood grocery store, there was no telling what practically unwatchable programming would air at any given moment. I've often remarked that the only thing more baffling than the existence of some of these programs was that people like me actually squandered brain cells watching them.

Nonetheless, during the summer of 1997, I signed up for my own weekly 60-minute show on the local station. Compelled by the unrealistic vision of a local talk show that could potentially rival those of late-night network television, my infinitely overconfident young brain began compiling a mental check list of all that I would need to attract A-list celebrities to my fledgling program.

First and foremost, I needed a clever twist to my relatively prosaic concept for a standard late-night talk show. Although I didn't want to stray considerably from my ideal format, I knew the program required a hook for it to be successful. To attract the audience I wanted, the show needed a shrewd gimmick capable of provoking an emotional reaction in viewers.

Borrowing a page from my mother's incessant promotion of honesty as the best policy, I decided to incorporate into my show an honest depiction of my life at that time. In other words, I intended to let the audience in on what was taking place both in front of and behind the cameras. Perhaps my experience as a young host struggling to book celebrity guests on an Indiana-based cable show would be both intriguing and hilarious to some. What's more, chronicling my efforts to disprove the scores of local critics doubting my success would also add a dramatic, inspirational hook to the show's comedic fodder.

Further punctuating this unusual concept was my hope to film the show outside the nondescript cable access studio in nearby Hammond, Indiana. In the spring of 1998, I presented my mom and dad with a quirky idea to host *The Michael Essany Show* from our house. One immediate advantage I would have over Leno and Letterman, I explained, is that my celebrity guests would feel much more *at home* on my show than they felt on any other. After the taping, for instance, we could invite guests to stay for dinner, enjoy a board game, and then kick back and relax with the hospitable Italian family of late night's youngest new host!

Although uncertain that my grandiose scheme would actually transpire as I had flamboyantly envisioned, my parents were willing to temporarily sacrifice their living room for my dream. Of course, Mom and Dad weren't wealthy, and together we had limited resources. But the family effort behind the growing momentum of this project would ultimately become a critical component of the show's popularity.

Luckily for the financing of the project, by the time I was 14 I had been limitedly self-employed for almost two years. Ever since I learned to use my dad's home video recorder when I was 12 I had offered my services as a "professional" videographer to friends and sometimes even complete strangers who wanted to capture a wedding, birthday, or similar family event for posterity. I was sort of like the A-Team: If you could find me, you could hire me.

Best of all, the 20 or so gigs I worked over this two-year period provided more than enough funding to augment our home entertainment equipment with the integral components needed to establish a functional production facility: two Hi8 camcorders, an SVHS editing deck, a four-channel sound mixer, and a set of two wireless handheld and lapel microphones.

IF YOU BUILD IT, THEY WILL COME

By the beginning of summer 1998, my old man and I had managed to construct a small backdrop for the living room set. With only a pile of discarded door hinges and threadbare plywood, my dad produced a three-paneled backdrop that was 14 feet wide and nearly 10 feet tall. Combined with the big city mural we unearthed from a Valparaiso wallpaper store and a freshly varnished desk that cost less than a latte from Starbucks, our living room soon breathed life into my original vision for this long-shot project.

Returning to the same handy celebrity reference guide from two years earlier, I soon blanketed the entertainment industry with interview requests for *The Michael Essany Show*. Although I received close to 1000 rejections during the first full year of trying to book guests, the local media eventually caught wind of my unorthodox dream and began publicizing the talk show even before it had a time slot or a single celebrity guest.

For the next five years, through all of high school and even the start of college, I pressed ahead with my original vision. Despite a bumpy start and a subsequent obligation that largely prevented me from enjoying my teenage years to the extent that I should have, at the end of four seasons on public access, my guest list rivaled that of any major network talk show. From Kevin Bacon and Jewel to Ray

FIGURE 3.3 With Jay Leno backstage at *The Tonight Show*, April 10, 2002.

Romano and Jeff Foxworthy, more than 100 celebrities granted interviews to *The Michael Essany Show*.

Since I didn't have an operating budget and couldn't compensate guests or even provide transportation, a significant number of celebrities traveled to Valparaiso, Indiana, which is about an hour east of Chicago, at their own expense.

At first, my notable guests received in return only the gratitude of a happy young man with an implausible dream. But with time my fan base grew. As a result, so did the national media's interest. Before long, celebrities arrived in Indiana to find more than home video cameras directed at them. From *Entertainment Weekly* to *TV Guide*, the nation was slowly introduced to *The Michael Essany Show*—a talk show available only to Hoosiers in the small northwestern corner of our humble state.

After only the first three seasons—or 72 episodes of weekly production—I received my inaugural entreaty from Hollywood. As it turned out, Columbia Tristar Television had taken notice of my show's "media darling" status and was interested in purchasing the rights to my story for a potential sitcom. However, because I wasn't an actor and refused to abandon my dream of hosting a national talk show in return for a quick lump sum of cash, at the age of 17 I politely informed Columbia Tristar that I would have to decline their offer.

Of course, I would be blatantly untruthful if I said I didn't heavily question my judgment while lying awake in bed for many weeks and months after that decision, which was considerably more difficult to make than I'm letting on. Perhaps I would have continued doubting myself indefinitely if not for an unexpected phone call I received in early 2001.

Having first appeared on my show during the second week of production, accomplished television producer and personality Leeza

Gibbons and I had not communicated in almost three years. Nonetheless, Leeza's former assistant, Rachel Karzen, who originally helped schedule my interview with Leeza, had since risen above the ranks of executive assistant to become vice president of creative development at Leeza's production company, Leeza Gibbons Enterprises (LGE). As it turned out, Rachel had stumbled across an article in *Details* magazine about comedian Jeff Foxworthy's recent visit to Valparaiso as a guest on my show. She and Leeza then decided to reach out to me with a development deal in hopes of taking my show to the next level.

Thankfully, Leeza and Rachel understood that the reason my show worked so well was because there was absolutely nothing contrived about my genuine desire to become a late-night talk show host or the massive support I received from family, friends, and some of the biggest names in show business. As a result, they were committed to maintaining the integrity of the series and the true story behind it.

After shopping the project for close to six months, LGE reached an exciting agreement with E! Entertainment Television. In late 2002, E! was euphoric in response to the much-hyped debut of

FIGURE 3.4 With Leeza Gibbons, executive producer of *The Michael Essany Show*, in January 2003.

The Anna Nicole Show. Trying to capitalize on the influx of viewers new to their network, the programming development team had grown fully vested in finding a series to immediately follow Anna's time slot. Incredibly, this is where my show landed.

> **FACT**
>
> An estimated 20 million people around the world have appeared on some variety or form of reality television programming.

Though somewhat taken aback by the prospect of being wedged between Anna Nicole Smith and Howard Stern, I was at least pleased to learn the particulars of the production responsibilities outlined by the executives. As part of their commitment to keep things real, I would not only remain host of *The Michael Essany Show*, I would also continue to write, produce, and direct all elements of the original talk show. Producers from E! would then be in charge of all production relating to the shooting of my life and day-to-day happenings.

With no additional concerns or tangible obstacles in my wake, I signed the proposed contract just days before my 20th birthday. Amazingly, two weeks later, producers from E! Entertainment Television arrived in Valparaiso to begin filming the first six episodes.

Reality Series Spin-Off . . . or Rip-Off?

The Ortegas, produced by Fox in late 2003, was described as an "inventive new series that blends comedy, reality, and improvisation into one wild, unique mix." The show follows a "likeable young host" of his very own late-night talk show. The aspiring host's generous parents, played by Cheech Marin and Terri Hoyos, built a fully functional television studio in the family's backyard. Each week, the family welcomes celebrity guests into their home, to share a meal and a talk show experience "truly like no other."

Invariably, reality programming centered on an individual subject is produced in one of only two possible ways. The first allows the star of the program to laugh *with* the audience in response to the peculiar and humorous happenings of his or her glorified daily existence. *Hogan Knows Best* is a great example of this approach.

The show, which chronicled (before the divorce, that is) the life of famed wrestler Hulk Hogan as he grappled with family, work, and managing the musical career of his daughter Brooke, is arguably about as "real" as any celebrity reality show is likely to be. In most cases, the Hogans are depicted as a relatively *normal* family—sans, of course, their obvious wealth and notoriety. Most people, including even Hulk and his charismatic kin, agree that the Hogan family is never misrepresented in a willfully negative light. Nothing to date, in fact, has been done to the Hogans through the manipulation of the reality TV lens that could somehow result in the degradation of their character or dignity. It should be noted, however, that Hulk Hogan later speculated that the strain of subjecting his family to a reality series may have played a factor in his eventual divorce from wife Linda.

Nonetheless, this ideal method of reality TV production differs considerably from its popular yet regrettable counterpart—a production approach that both allows and encourages the audience to laugh *at* the star, not *with* him.

Having spent the bulk of my adolescence cultivating *The Michael Essany Show* and its foundational story, I experienced a self-imposed apprenticeship on the inner workings of reality-based programming. I gained firsthand knowledge of the art behind relating a true story to viewers—a highly nuanced practice that requires both a commitment to the integrity of the story and an ability to interestingly translate that reality onto the screen.

Unfortunately, my working relationship with E! almost immediately illustrated another side of the reality TV experience. I'm referring to the business behind this art, a component that can stealthily subjugate any prior commitment to the art. It's an approach that naturally begs an obvious question: Why would any network essentially want to belittle or humiliate the subject of its own series? An honest response to this question centers squarely on the responsibility of reality TV producers to do whatever necessary to generate the highest ratings possible. Astonishingly, many reality programs are created to have a minimal shelf life. Thanks in part to their relative ease of inexpensive production, reality series can be used for a quick source of revenue, a platform for promoting other projects, or even a means for engendering short-term attention or controversy for a broader purpose.

AN UNWANTED REALITY

Reflecting today on my working relationship with E! Entertainment Television, I'm still not exactly sure what their true intentions were for *The Michael Essany Show*.

What is certain, though, was their eventual desire to change course and present my life and work in a radically different way from the successful approach taken by virtually every other national media outlet.

For the previous five years my program was commercially successful as both a provider of entertainment and as a human interest story. On account of my unusual ambitions, I was clearly a young man who didn't fit the mold of the typical college student. Admittedly, I was not your suave leading man type. Through a consistent use of self-deprecating humor on my show, I let audiences know that I didn't take myself very seriously. In short, I was comfortable being a dork. But instead of continuing to emphasize this Conan O'Brien-style of self-deprecation, some at E! clearly wanted to reverse this established brand. As far as I could tell, the goal of *The Michael Essany Show* was now to make people laugh *at* me instead of *with* me. It was a method also employed on *The Anna Nicole Show* and a sprinkling of other ephemeral series that ultimately brought as much shame on the network as it did the individuals who were embarrassed on national television.

To some producers within the reality genre, belittling the star of a series is a considerably easier goal to attain and certainly more instantly marketable than patiently crafting a meaningful body of work into a viable and lasting series. Because my reality show was one of the first individual-centered reality series of the contemporary reality boom, I was not initially as cautious as I should have been in adequately guarding against any and all threats to my on-camera dignity. From the get-go, I was naively preoccupied with all that reality TV could do *for* me, not *to* me.

Given how favorably the production team at E! reacted to my earlier appearance on *Oprah*, I was convinced that the queen of daytime had also convinced those at the network to follow her lead and continue presenting my work and life story exactly as they were.

Featured on an episode titled "People Who Love Their Jobs," I spent the seven most valuable minutes of my career sharing the stage with Oprah Winfrey. As many have astutely observed, Oprah and her extraordinary staff are capable of making anyone look good. This TV magic they masterfully work on featured guests unquestionably worked on me as well. In fact, immediately after appearing on *Oprah*—before my E! debut—not only did my street recognition skyrocket, I also began receiving thousands of fan letters from people curious about what would ultimately become of my talk show aspirations. Understandably, at the time I believed my subsequent series on E! would chronicle the journey that so many people around the country were interested to follow and eager to watch.

Instead, some of the producers assigned to my program quickly decided *The Michael Essany Show* would work best if it simply presented me as an awkward Indiana hick whose ambitions were worthy of mockery.

We had not yet completed a full week of production, in fact, before I was confronted with a producer's need to stage a few events for "expositional purposes." His idea was to present another dimension of my on-screen persona by placing me in an everyday situation removed from a talk show environment. Because I was keenly aware of the need to present my life in an interesting and marketable package, I was willing to go along with the idea. On the surface, anyway, it seemed relatively harmless.

As it turned out, one of my producers had already asked a student from Valparaiso University, whom I barely knew, to throw a party at his apartment in my "honor." It was explained to me that the purpose of this segment was to help endear me to a wider base of viewers. In other words, until now, viewers had only known me as a hard-working young television talk show host. I was told that shooting this party segment, which would essentially feature me hanging out with a bunch of fraternity brothers, would help me appear "cooler" and more like an average guy my age.

When the footage was finally broadcast, a number of television critics publicly referred to this segment as "unfortunate" and "uncomfortable to watch." They were reacting, without question, to the testimonial comments recorded by producers, unbeknownst to me, both before and after my visit to the party. Methodically, each partially wasted college guy was given an opportunity to insult anything and everything about me. As I recall, the harshest mockery was reserved for the fact that I didn't drink at the party.

Although I was presented as a mama's boy who presumably "couldn't handle beer," the truth of the matter was that I opted to not drink on national television because, at my age, I would have been breaking the law. Knowing what I now understand about the highly exploitive nature of reality television, it might have been an entirely premeditated ratings ploy to put me into a situation where I could have been busted for underage drinking. Of course, this is entirely speculation on my part. But what is incontrovertible is how I was routinely lured into situations like that of the frat party for no other reason than to make me a laughable human oddity.

What ultimately hurt most, however, were the times in which my family and friends were insulted on the show. Countless times my own mother and father were presented as cornfield simpletons. My longtime best friend and on-air sidekick, Mike Randazzo, was frequently portrayed in an equally unfavorable light. Even worse, so were some of our guests.

One of my favorite regulars over the years was Don Tersigni, a Valparaiso resident and an enormously talented, nationally recognized comedian. But when Don appeared on my E! series for the first time the footage was edited by producers to create the appearance that Don had utterly bombed. By removing the laughs he received and inserting inconsistent footage of blank-faced spectators, the editing magic made a cruel mockery of a good entertainer and a great man. Of course, it didn't matter to some at E! that this gifted comedian was needlessly and undeservingly embarrassed. To them, it looked funny to have a local stand-up comedian bomb on public access. It was wrong.

By the end of the first season it was perfectly clear to me and my family that we were being thoughtlessly mocked on many of the episodes. But since we all proceeded with greater caution to not leave ourselves vulnerable to further mockery in the second season, some of our producers caught on. As a result, they abandoned the ridicule and instead employed a new weapon to potentially boost ratings: sleaze, an altogether incongruous and inappropriate element given the established family-friendly nature of my show.

From trying to convince me to book porn stars to taping wild segments at local nightclubs, more than one executive sought to bring the *one* family-oriented show they had into the mature fold of their other signature programs.

Needless to say, I resisted with full force and never backed down. Yet despite my best efforts, and as I frequently wished for contract termination, some tried vigorously to work around me in achieving their objectives for our show. They even tried to sucker other on-air regulars to do the very things that I had refused to do myself.

Three episodes into our second season, Mike Randazzo was the newest target of these shifty maneuverings. Mike was told that they were filming a sketch with him where the audience would learn what nightlife is like for a sidekick in Valparaiso. By the time filming had begun Mike was under the impression that I had signed off on this sketch. In reality, producers reached Mike before I did. As a result, they simply informed him of what they wanted him to believe. Fortunately, Mike is a smart chap with an upstanding character. And once the producers told him what was about to happen—his limo would be filled with scantily clad women en route to a bar where he would be asked to autograph private parts—Mike adamantly refused. From that day forward Mike and I realized that we had to watch our backs at all times. We certainly weren't prudes, but we had to maintain the integrity of a program that families had been comfortably watching for more than five years.

Nonetheless, I honored my contract and continued hosting *The Michael Essany Show*, albeit with a more watchful, protective eye, for two seasons on E!. In 2004, the program's domestic distribution concluded and the program was sold overseas—remarkably, to a more popular tenure in Great Britain than in the United States.

The first graduation season after production wrapped, I began receiving invitations to lecture students of film and television at college campuses across the country. Although I never delivered a homogeneous, one-size-fits-all presentation about the nuts and bolts of reality television, a number of themes repeatedly surfaced in my candid talks—specifically, the need to protect oneself from the commonly overlooked dangers posed by the industry.

As a result of my outspoken rants, I often left the classroom feeling I had inadvertently discouraged the very core of aspiring young professionals that I had so passionately hoped to inspire. Today, however, with more time, perspective, and professional experience after the conclusion of my first reality TV series, I can confidently reflect on my journey from fantasy to reality and celebrate a number of invaluable lessons learned the hard way.

Chief among such insights was the heightened understanding that reality television simply cannot do anything to a person who doesn't knowingly want it done to them. For as much as I've tried to blame the producers and executives I initially held responsible for distorting the reality of my reality series beyond an acceptable range, ultimately, by not taking a more proactive stance in guarding myself from such distortion, I truly had no one but myself to blame for the outcome of my show and the telling of my story. To be sure, I'm not removing the need for accountability on the part of producers who willfully and inexcusably exploit talent. In my view, limiting the number of people burned by reality television is ultimately a two-way street. Yes, stars need to protect themselves. But producers should never be something that stars have to protect themselves from.

Auspiciously, the dangers of reality television are more widely understood today than at any other time in the history of the medium. Nevertheless, it remains remarkably easy for performers or producers to grow so comfortable with their positions that they still fall victim to the most common of pratfalls. After all, not everyone is injured by reality television right out of the gate. With this particular genre, the dangers are unpredictable and never out of range. That's exactly why I tell every young aspirant to reality programming that remaining invisibly cynical is the most important safeguard anyone can employ while working in front of or behind the cameras.

Naturally, the conclusion of my run on E! also brought with it a feeling of embarrassment for having my immediate body of work wholly represented by a reality television show that didn't wholly represent me. At that time, however, I was possessed of the incorrect notion that the perceived stigma associated with a reality TV failure is somehow indelible. In truth, the mainstream market for commercial network and cable programming is so saturated with reality programming that almost anyone can be redeemed (barring extreme circumstances) from their first negative experience with a future opportunity in the same genre—that is, of course, if the opportunity and the courage to endure another reality TV whirlwind exists.

Although we will explore in subsequent chapters the more concrete elements of reality TV (the physical production process, breaking into the genre, managing a career, and so on), perhaps the most helpful abstract lesson culled from my hands-on experience is that producers and performers alike often fail to recognize the vast creative license afforded them by this celebrated format.

Whether you're the lowliest of producers overshadowed by the bigwigs of your production or a star of a new series backed into a corner by network executives convinced of their creative genius, there is absolutely never an excuse for you to not exert creative influence on your project. This was a mistake I made and failed to recognize until it was too late.

I'm sorry to say that reality television has slowly begun sacrificing its most desirable production component—creative leniency—to the pervasive trend of repeating gimmicks used on other reality programs. As many viewers are increasingly witnessing, a lot of reality television has become repetitive. In this regard, the genre has come to resemble the established production paradigms of scripted dramatic and comedic programming.

My experience in the industry, however, has clearly illustrated that the best ideas are never used because few have the audacity or the know-how to break conventional molds, communicate the strength of their vision, or even let someone else take credit for their idea if it means saving a project or another person's dignity.

At all times, reality television should be thought of as big-budget public access programming. Just like the humble medium it mirrors, practically anything goes on reality television. At times it even appears that the casts of such programming are also selected on a first-come, first-served basis. Nonetheless, the regrettable trend of failing to use the very creative license that attracted many to the industry in the first place must be replaced with a broad understanding that the best ideas for reality programming have yet to be produced. The reality television industry is an evolutionary market, and never in the history of the genre has this market been more ready for or in need of change. Consequently, those looking to break into the business with their own creative vision should be encouraged to the hilt because, as we're poised to explore, the future of this highly accessible industry is fully dependent on what newcomers like yourself have to offer.

Chapter | four

Facing Reality

If you approach any person on the streets of Los Angeles and ask, "How's your screenplay coming along?" there's an excellent possibility that he or she will give you an elaborate spiel on their "exciting" project.

In recent years, reality television producers have grown just as omnipresent as the aspiring screenwriters often lampooned for their ubiquity. Nonetheless, whether you've written a project for film or developed a concept for reality TV, the industry is always looking for the next big thing—film, series, or whatever promises to generate the most revenue at the time.

Unfortunately, though, for the scores of talented producers who believe they have come up with "the next big reality show," there is little advice readily available for taking a project to that critical next level.

The shelves of major bookstores are continually replete with "how-to" titles boasting helpful guidance for would-be television producers, yet most works of this nature concentrate exclusively on how to sell your show with a winning pitch and then produce the project. Sadly, the majority of these titles fail to provide insight into what could very well amount to be the most laborious aspect of the entire selling process: getting an opportunity to pitch in the first place!

You could have the greatest idea for a series and a dynamite pitch prepared, yet neither will amount to anything without the initial opportunity to show your goods to the right people. And as almost anyone in the business will tell you, getting the opportunity to pitch is not an easy appointment to obtain—that is, of course, if you don't know what you're doing.

TAKING A SWING AT THE PITCH

So, then, how exactly does one go about landing the do-or-die pitch meeting with a prospective network? According to some, if you're new to the business and without a stellar résumé or vast reserves of professional experience, one way to get a network's attention is to first solicit the services of a renowned agent who can, in turn, reassure his or her network contacts that they aren't wasting their valuable time entertaining your underdeveloped pitch. Regrettably, though, finding an agent can frequently prove an even more daunting task than arranging a network pitch meeting all by your lonesome.

Ultimately, to sell a show to a network, it's imperative that you get in front of someone with the authorization to cut a check. Even if you manage to wrangle an agent to facilitate a pitch meeting, there's still another major hurdle to jump: Who is going to physically produce the project if it's green-lit?

In my experience, I have found it considerably easier to get a network's interest and money when you partner with a production company before you set foot in the pitch meeting. Similar to an agent who wields the power and credibility a newcomer may lack, many production companies carry enormous reputations that can elevate your own status merely by association. In other words, even if the television executive has never heard of you, if they know of the production company you're working with, they will be infinitely more inclined to take a meeting and give serious consideration to your project than if you just walked into the meeting as a lone entity. The old saying "Time is money" particularly holds true for network executives. If they think for an instant that you might be wasting their time, you'll never get a meeting. Like clockwork, they will only entertain pitches from those known to have the capability to formulate a workable concept and then produce it from beginning to end.

With very few exceptions, television networks view production companies more favorably than they do most agents and agencies. Conversely, networks are highly regarded "clients" of production companies in the television business model. By squeezing your way into the good graces of a reputable production company, your odds of getting an opportunity to successfully pitch your show to a network increase exponentially.

Needless to say, when a network green-lights a project or even simply orders a pilot, it is investing and entrusting enormous gobs of money in the hands of a select few. To get your hands on the gobs, you first need to earn the trust of those with the authority to spend a network's precious money. Understandably, this is a monumental challenge. But no matter how inexperienced you are as a producer, if your pitch is promising and you've secured the backing of a credible production company, this could very well be your entrée to a network with the interest and wherewithal to pick up your series.

For some reason or another, many producers new to the industry are convinced of an agent's integral role in the selling process. Since the major agencies all have departments devoted to reality television development, it's easy to follow the same beaten path that many others have already unsuccessfully traveled. Of course, there's certainly no harm in landing an agent to represent your project and open a few crucial doors. But no matter how many opportunities your agent delivers, a network still won't touch your project without being fully convinced of your ability to physically produce the series. In other words, a production company is bound to enter the picture sooner or later.

Your best bet is to cut out the middle man (the agent) and before pitching your show to a network, first pitch it to a production company with a track record of producing programs similar to yours. If they carry weight, your production company will serve the same function as an agent in using its esteem to get you into the networks and pitch directly to executives with the authority to write checks.

Fortunately—at least in my estimation—it's easier to find a production company with whom to pair than an agent. Production companies are always looking for quality programming concepts that they can readily produce with a network's money. To find one that might be interested in presenting your project to a network, simply watch the closing credits of any show that even moderately falls into the same genre as the type of show you're looking to produce. The production companies behind these similar series will be listed at the conclusion of the broadcast.

Afterward, a few minutes of online research will likely turn up current contact information for each production company you've discovered. Your next step then is to pitch your project directly to the production company, which will be much more inclined to take a face-to-face meeting with you than any major Hollywood talent agency or television network. There are literally hundreds of production companies in Southern California alone. Some, of course, are larger than others, yet they all serve the same function and any can be the conduit to a network launching your project.

As we've already discussed, networks are reluctant to waste time on an undeveloped pitch from a producer lacking the means to execute his or her vision. Networks, however, appreciate seeing a production company behind a project, even in the concept stage. Unlike a newcomer to the business, a production company can embellish your pitch, which might be long on pizzazz and light on the particulars. For instance, anyone lacking production experience will have little hope of providing a prospective network with a projected budget for the series, a key factor that must be addressed right away.

Best of all, since most aspiring producers are unaware of this production company approach to breaking into the business, you'll have a huge edge on the competition if you initially bypass the agents and networks and go straight to the source of all programming: the production company. It might also be in your best financial interest to secure a working relationship with a production company. For example, if you have little interest in remaining on board a particular project you've created, a production company might make a financial offer to buy the rights to your idea. Whether it ever gets picked up by a network doesn't necessarily matter. At this point, you've not only landed your first professional credit—having sold a project to a reputable production company—but you've also made a little bit of money in an industry that compensates only a select few.

Overall, there are innumerable advantages to hitching your star to a production company's wagon. This is why many celebrities start their own production companies. With their wealth, standing, and experience, they can hold on to more of the revenue from the projects they sell. Ordinarily, the creator and production company split the pot. Big shots with their own production companies play both roles and, consequently, collect all the loot.

Even if you at first encounter stumbling blocks in getting a production company to notice your project, you will probably still find the contact valuable in terms of the information you will likely acquire. Production companies, particularly those that produce reality television, maintain a watchful eye on networks to see what they are producing and, consequently, what they are looking for. A production company can tell you whether your idea is ripe for the current market or a veritable dud. Although it might hurt to hear that your concept is dead before it's even born, it's usually better to get shot down by a production company than a network. After all, you can always pitch to a production company again. Networks are less forgiving if you pitch something they find unbefitting the current market. In their view, as a producer, you should know what they want. And if you don't, that makes you appear a poor producer.

Of course, you don't need a production company to tell you what networks are eagerly and actively searching for. Auspiciously, executives often make public their wishes in a number of different ways. For example, some network suits grant interviews to the show business trade publications, where they specifically lay out everything they're looking for in the next 12 months—the veritable wish list for their network. On the other hand, some networks and cable stations consistently display poker faces and are considerably more reticent to expose their programming wishes and needs to a wide audience. They are more inclined to notify only a handful of agents or production companies who, in turn, will put the wheels in motion among their own circles to create the programming that their clients desire.

Nonetheless, the best way to determine the mood of a network at any particular moment remains to simply watch to see the types of shows they are currently broadcasting or advertising. Although monitoring the trade publicans like *Variety* and *The Hollywood Reporter* is particularly helpful to industry newcomers attempting to gauge moods and trends, ultimately there is nothing more effective than one's own eyes to provide the most discerning investigative research. Above all else, knowing what a network wants or needs is priority number one. Once you've got a sense of exactly what the network is looking for, the next step is to give them the pitch they want to hear.

DEVELOPING THE PITCH

Although developing a pitch sounds like a mighty simple task if you already have what you believe is a winning idea for a television show, in reality the process of taking your idea from a raw concept and transforming it into a compelling verbal presentation that will excite others is not a minimal endeavor. Whether there's an agent, a production company, or only your mommy standing behind you at the meeting, the burden of selling your show will always rest squarely on your shoulders, at least in terms of pitching your brainchild.

There's no single formula for a winning pitch, but when you're presenting to multiple networks, it's important to account for the diverse personalities that will be exposed to your presentation. In other words, some executives in the room might be serious and others might be goofy. Either way, you can't afford to guess which personality type will be the one vested with check-writing authority. Instead, you have to present for a general audience and convince all that your show is excellent and that you're the one who can make it all happen.

Preferably, before the meeting you should attempt to foresee any and all questions the network might have regarding your project. Although you don't want to seem overly rehearsed, your "off-the-cuff" answers should convey the same enthusiasm and precision as your canned pitch. Occasionally, however, there won't be many follow-up questions in response to your pitch, particularly if you're doing a "light pitch." In other words, you're pitching a show as nothing more than just an idea for a show. For the time being, all you have is the idea. In this scenario, though, the question that always follows is, how does this initial concept—no matter how exciting—continue as a series?

Understandably, networks are reluctant to buy a show without seeing potential for several seasons, unless, of course, your reality program is a vehicle for short-term purposes. With a light pitch, your most basic challenge then becomes explaining how your great idea can be sustained beyond one episode and endure for subsequent seasons. You have to pitch your show with emphasis on its format, a foundation—much like *Survivor*—that can persist for indefinite seasons even if you modify casts and crew. In a light pitch, the particulars aren't important. What is important is that yours is a concept that can be repeated over and over again. Like a science experiment that must be repeated multiple times to see if it proves or disproves a theory, a producer must first determine whether and how his or her format is repeatable. A project that works once or for only a limited period of time won't fly with network executives looking to solidify mainstays of their programming schedule for the next three to five years.

Essentially, when you're pitching a reality series, it's crucial to keep in mind the things for which networks are always looking. As expected, it's practically impossible to deduce all that a particular network is interested in at any given time. In some cases, they may be concentrating on filling a certain time slot, courting targeted advertisers, or testing the waters with a new demographic. What always holds true for networks, however, is that executives need to sense confidence in the producers who are pitching their ideas. What's more, no matter the type of show you're pitching, find a way to link to another hit series that somewhat resembles your own. For instance, instead of inventing your own terms to create a visual representation of how your show will play out, it's better to set the stage for further elaboration by first delivering the "high concept" or "elevator pitch," that is, saying that your project is *South Park* meets *Scrubs*," or something to that effect. Although I'm certainly not looking to undercut the intellect of the average executive, most network programming suits require simple presentations and analogies in order to facilitate an understanding of your project as you would like for it to be understood.

If all goes as intended—that is, the pitch is good, the concept is exciting, the production company is capable, the market is favorable to the launch, and you've made contact with the right person or people at the network—it's highly conceivable that your show will be among those the network purchases. To put it all into perspective, however, just because a show is "purchased" doesn't guarantee it will ever make air. For example, for the 20 or 30 shows (on average) purchased every season by a single network, fewer than a third may be piloted. And to get those 20 or 30 projects, a network might have to endure 10 times as many pitches, especially with reality programming. The industry standard remains that only about 10 percent of all shows pitched ever make it to the pilot stage. Even so, these statistics shouldn't intimidate anyone. After all, good producers realize the importance of having multiple concepts and pitches in development at all times. Eventually, one or more ideas will settle at the top of the reality show heap.

Naturally, what helps your odds of selling a show is getting in front of the most powerful executive available to take your pitch. In some cases, you might be presenting to an individual so powerful that he or she can green-light your project on the spot and almost immediately write a hefty check to pilot the program or an initial run of three to six episodes. Unfortunately, at least a majority of the time producers find themselves pitching to slightly less powerful executives. Even so, it's still a wonderful opportunity to pitch to an executive who has the means to write a check—even if it's for $100,000 instead of $1 million. The most important factor is that you're still pitching to someone with authority or influence. If they like what you're pushing, they will readily send it up the chain of command and get your show green-lit in no time at all.

The Savvy, Expedient, and Strategic Paths to Production

The *savvy* path involves working in the business, perhaps first as a low-level production assistant or intern, and eventually capitalizing on each rung of experience acquired. If you hang around the ground floor long enough, you're bound to eventually spot an opportunity for advancement. This scenario often enables an aspiring producer to forego the pitch process, particularly because producers who cut their teeth from the bottom up are regularly assigned shows to produce by executives who have watched and admired their track record.

The *expedient* path is to conceptualize a brilliant idea for a television show and team up with someone who has the experience and credibility you lack. By bringing an individual on board who knows what they are doing, you will not only have an accelerated opportunity to schedule a pitch, you'll have exponentially better odds of selling your project.

The *strategic* path is to get to know all the right people and deliver to them exactly what it is they want and need before the competition does. This strategic method largely relies on being at the right place at the right time—a fortuitous and highly uncommon situation. But for those who robustly network and introduce themselves to everyone, the strategic approach isn't nearly as far-fetched as you might imagine.

MAKING YOUR PITCH STICK

Obviously, pitching to a decision maker is ideal, but it isn't unusual for a producer without an established body of work to have to first pitch to a lower-level executive.

Overall, there is very little difference between pitching to a low-level executive than there is the president of the network. Either way, your pitch needs to be dynamite (thought-provoking, exciting, descriptive, compelling). Perhaps the only drawback to initially pitching to a less powerful executive is that you have to work harder to ensure that they understand the best points of your argument in favor of the project. After all, the person who heard your pitch now has to go upstairs and regurgitate all that they gathered from you.

Needless to say, it's important to get the person who does hear your pitch as excited about your show as possible. When they repeat it to others, their enthusiasm should be as palpable as your own. To achieve this, keep in mind during your pitch that you are not talking to the ultimate decision maker. Take your time. Low-level executives often hear dozens of pitches in a single week and don't provide their superiors with a turnaround pitch until more than a month later. Make whomever is hearing your pitch remember it—in abstract ways, if possible.

Circumventing "d-girls"—an industry term for low-level executives that applies to both sexes—and holding out for a higher-level meeting can actually be counterproductive in the long run. Making a lowly network person feel as lowly as they might actually be can result in them nixing your project before anyone higher up even learns your name. In addition, it's only common sense that making connections with junior executives is imperative, since they are likely to be promoted to higher levels of power in subsequent months or years. My own example of meeting Rachel Karzen when she was merely Leeza Gibbons' executive assistant proves the long-term value of being cordial to those who might eventually rise in the ranks.

Ironically, however, you might not realize until you arrive at the meeting who will be hearing your pitch. In fact, even during the meeting you might not actually know who the power players in the room really are. Frequently producers are told that one executive will be in the room during a pitch only to discover upon arrival that two or more will be present—some with more or less authority than anticipated. Most of the time, producers new to the industry won't even know the names of those to whom they are pitching. In this case, only titles might be known. Nonetheless, even if you know the descending levels of authority at the network, don't pitch to the most powerful person in the room. It's rude and reflects poorly on your project, which, after all, should appeal to more than just one individual. To avoid any awkward situations, though, it is wise to learn the names and titles of practically everyone in the programming department of a network prior to the meeting. This way, you will know who's who and not be distracted in the meeting trying to figure out whether the guy with the mustache is more important than the woman with the hoop earrings. If you don't take the time to do your homework, you could have a difficult time figuring out what the suits want to hear from you. But if you're educated as to who's who and who likes what, you're less likely to be thrown off your game by an unanticipated presence and more likely to successfully alter your pitch to the preferences of those in the room.

Should You Salvage a Failing Pitch?

Opinions on this quandary differ dramatically. According to some producers, if the executives in the room appear lethargic or even comatose, the person pitching should immediately regroup and find another "hook," even on the fly, if necessary. To me, however, nothing could be less favorable than leaving a room teeming with high-powered executives with the impression that you are the stereotypical used car salesman who will say whatever it takes to vend a lemon.

It has been my experience that if a room of potential buyers isn't digging your pitch from the start, you're best advised to conclude as quickly as possible, maintain consistency and confidence, and depart with your head held high. Even if they don't overtly like the pitch—and sometimes they might without your awareness—they will likely remember your professionalism and your cool-as-a-cucumber commitment to the project. Hopefully, you will earn other opportunities to pitch subsequent programming concepts. However, you're considerably less likely to be welcomed back to the sacred boardrooms of network television if your reputation to say whatever it takes to make the sale precedes you.

Hopefully, once you've pitched your show those in attendance will whoop and holler at your amazing presentation and sign you on the spot. The next step, however, isn't necessarily a national television debut. In truth, "the next step" could very well be one of any number of possible steps. For instance, the network could pay you to write a treatment for the series—specifically, how you see an entire season playing out with the particular elements of each episode (yes, even for reality TV) outlined in lucid and exciting detail. A treatment is basically an extended and more detailed version of your pitch. If your idea for a series is largely cut and dried, the next step might simply involve the network giving you and your production company a lump of money to produce tape. Although it's sometimes a good idea to work with your production company in advance to produce tape for the initial pitch, this isn't usually possible. Some feel that tape is always a helpful selling tool. Personally, I find tape a hindrance in most cases. Verbal pitching often works best because the executive's imagination should be encouraged to run free with the concept you're presenting. As expected, they will immediately imagine beautiful girls, handsome men, luscious scenery, and an enthusiastic audience. What's more, by letting an executive wrap their mind around your idea with the executive's own vision, he or she is significantly more inclined to feel committed to the series.

Of course, pitching without tape places more responsibility on the pitcher to be as descriptive and thought-provoking as possible. It's a task that certainly sounds daunting, but it's one that can reap enormous rewards if executed skillfully. To be sure, there are instances when tape is absolutely essential, usually when a particular talent is involved. Otherwise, since a video demonstration of your show is likely to be produced without adequate funding, talent, lighting, cameras, and the like, it's better to describe your show in terms of its potential rather they making a first impression with a show that is not portrayed in the best possible light.

In a perfect world, a masterful verbal pitch will result in the network ordering a pilot. With proper financial backing, the first tape shot of your idea will optimistically convey the potential it originally foreshadowed. As a rule, a pilot is simply a sample episode of your series from start to finish. Naturally, the talent, set, and other minor nuances might not be ideal, but it's understood that the pilot—which rarely ever airs as an actual broadcast—is produced solely for demonstration purposes. In most cases, networks generally begin their pilot season in early January and then mull over which shows to purchase before the middle of May.

Although it isn't common, it also isn't impossible for a network to purchase a show without a pilot. *The Michael Essany Show,* for example, was picked up for national broadcast without an official pilot being shot first. My five years on local cable, however, provided a nice demo, or "sizzle reel," for the executives at E! to consider. In the case of taking a small market show, like cable access or regional programming, and pitching it for a national launch, its helps to present a short, three- to five-minute reel of clips that best capture the heart of the show you're pitching. Even without such a demo, there are still instances of shows being purchased with a pilot. Most happen in response to a competitive pitching scenario when more than one network is champing at the bit to buy a specific show. Much of the time, in fact, this concentrated demand can be leveraged into taking the show immediately to air and bypassing the pilot stage altogether. Although it always sounds appealing for producers to take their projects directly to air, it can actually prove beneficial to pilot a program first and work out the kinks of the series before it's served for public consumption.

Of course, networks also like pilots because they illustrate how the production company in chief will execute the original vision. If satisfactory, the network will generally give the production company a considerable amount of creative control for the run of the series. Normally, however, the amount of creative control a reality TV production company gets varies from none at all to a virtual dictatorship. The issue of creative control is usually where network executives come into play. For newcomers to the business, it is often incorrectly understood that executives only play a role in the selection of which shows to purchase. In truth, network executives maintain an active and vested interest in a number of programs at any given time. Specifically, they oversee a show's budget and keep a watchful eye on its creative direction.

Of course, we're getting ahead of ourselves. Before we can worry about how much creative control a network executive will assert, the first step is to illustrate why you as a producer don't need micromanagement from the network. In other words, the more you illustrate your capable faculties as a producer, the more leeway you will be afforded during and after production.

By learning exactly what makes a good reality television producer, you'll achieve much more than mere ratings success. You'll also find yourself a trusted ally of the networks and a credible source of future projects.

In a Nutshell: How to Secure a Pitch Meeting

1. Come up with an outstanding programming idea or ideas for reality television.

2. Do your homework to ensure that the idea is actually yours. Go online and compare the originality of your concept against those have already made it to air.

3. Create a log line—a brief one- or two-sentence summary of your concept, designed to attract the interest of those who read it.

4. Draft a synopsis (four to eight paragraphs) describing your show, its general theme, characters, and so on. Attach an outline of the first 10 to 12 episodes, plotting storyline developments that bring your concept to a compelling full circle.

5. Produce a brief but gripping argument as to why your show will be profitable and popular given current audience trends and market preferences. (Research is key!)

6. Register your show idea online with the WGA and include your registration number in the written pitch.

7. Draft a single-page cover letter (called a *query letter*) introducing yourself, your relevant experience, and the attached written pitch.

8. Research networks and production companies for targeted pitching opportunities.

9. Remit your pitch via snail mail (never email) and include a self-addressed, stamped envelope. If a network is interested, they will require you to sign a release protecting them from litigation for reading your work.

10. Allow four to eight weeks for review. If you hear nothing, follow up with each contact as aggressively as you feel comfortable with.

Chapter five

The Show and Tell of Reality TV

The majority of producers who sell a reality television series do so after first working in the television industry for years, crafting a superb résumé, gaining invaluable production experience, and developing an extensive social network of everyone who is anyone in the business. Unfortunately, the overwhelming majority of aspiring producers do not enjoy the luxury of this professional pedigree. And although these "outsiders" would seem to have little hope of penetrating the seemingly impenetrable walls of show business, nothing could be further from the truth, especially today.

In the not so distant past, aspiring television producers without a foothold in the business were almost universally limited in pursuable avenues for selling a show. The only thing they could do, in fact, was the only thing that could be done: Develop a solid show concept and, coupled with the resources of an interested agent or production company, wrangle a meeting with a network executive and then give a "winning pitch." Although this approach is still the most obvious (and sometimes effective) course of action for would-be producers, there are newer, arguably more effective, and certainly more accessible potential selling opportunities than the old-fashioned route.

A few moments of scouring the Internet will reveal scores of "overnight success" stories of individuals who simply worked tirelessly to disseminate their ideas or products. That is, countless aspiring television producers, actors, writers, and musicians used the scant resources available to them—usually no more than a home video recorder or digital camera—and presented themselves, their ideas, or their talents to the world. Since then, innumerable unknowns have scored television contracts and recording deals. Yet they all made it big by first shrewdly capitalizing on the power of Internet media.

NEW PORTALS TO STARDOM

YouTube, MySpace, ManiaTV, and a multitude of other video-sharing and social networks are drawing more than just a record number of hits from the general public. At this very moment, in fact, television networks, production companies, and talent agents are, either personally or through employed proxies, combing the World Wide Web to find people like you!

In the olden days—or, you know, six years ago—it was absurd to imagine the Internet as a professional launching pad for television producers. Yet today, those with dreams of reality TV success are taking their work directly to the masses. And according to some, it's a significantly more effective approach than other available avenues.

For example, if you can't get a pitch meeting with a network, give your pitch anyway. Place a video camera atop a tripod about 10 feet in front of you—under proper lighting, of course—and dazzle your audience with your amazing concept for a show. Do everything you would have done if a network exec had been in the room at the time. In other words, do the same thoughtful research, rehearse your spiel, dress for success, and if need be record as many takes as necessary to get your pitch perfect. The nonlive element of prerecorded pitches is certainly another distinct advantage in presenting your case through digital media.

Once your presentation is complete and polished, upload the footage to YouTube and tag it "reality show pitch." If you're lucky, the same individuals you couldn't get a meeting with will still see your pitch. Some who want to break in have, in fact, even gone so far as to direct their pitch to the particular individual—by name, that is—that they couldn't get in to see. Understandably, this approach sounds a bit extreme if not outright obsessive. But it can be extraordinarily effective if handled appropriately.

Best of all, any apprehensions about having your idea stolen will be removed if you first register your program concept with the Writers Guild of America (www.wga.org). For a small online registration fee, you can catalogue your written show concept with the WGA and receive an official registration number—something you will need to secure anyway before selling your show. A WGA registration should allay any concerns about having your reality TV brainchild kidnapped.

STRAIGHT TO VIDEO

Although pitching a show directly through the PC has worked beautifully for some, a potentially more desirable alternative is to actually produce a few minutes of the project you're trying to sell. If the resources are available and such a venture is financially viable, producing a sneak peak at your series presents the possibility of your idea going "viral." If so, networks and production companies will be more willing to invest in your project if it has already tested positively among a proven fan base.

In my era, public access television was the only media outlet at my disposal for reaching the masses. In my case, the "masses" initially meant only a few thousand homes in northwest Indiana. And even though I eventually produced dozens of hours of quality television that were later distributed on VHS to countless agents and producers through snail mail, it was a consistently sluggish uphill battle trying to get noticed. Ten years ago I would have done almost anything to be able to put my best work on the Internet and then send a link to everyone in Hollywood who might be interested. It would have certainly proven faster, cheaper, and more effective than my antiquated methods.

Reaching out to the big guys in television, however, requires more than just a quick email with an attachment. You must also prepare a thoughtful—and mandatory—written presentation following the standard "query" format. For example, if I were pitching an original reality series called *Donut Island*, I would submit a query within the constructs of the following accepted template:

Author Name:	Michael Essany
Title of Show:	*Donut Island*
Format of Show:	Reality Series
WGA Registration No:	555667
Log Line:	Hollywood celebrities compete to make the best donuts while stranded on a deserted island.

Treatment:	(Insert 1/2- to 3-page series synopsis. Provide a detailed enough description of the series to give a potential buyer an exciting visual presentation of what they are evaluating.)

Once you've launched an online presentation and prepared a written query, your next step is to attract as much attention to yourself and your project as possible. Even though your YouTube video will accumulate a good number of hits without your daily involvement anyway, an important subsequent action would be to supplement your base of contacts by reaching out directly to the major talent agencies.

THE BIG FOUR TALENT AGENCIES

The William Morris Agency
One William Morris Place
Beverly Hills, CA 90212
Ph: (310) 859-4000
Fax: (310) 859-4462
www.wma.com

Creative Artists Agency
2000 Avenue of the Stars
Los Angeles, CA 90067
Ph: (424) 288-2000
Fax: (424) 288-2900
www.caa.com

International Creative Management
10250 Constellation Blvd.
Los Angeles, CA 90067
Ph: (310) 550-4000
Fax: (310) 550-4100
www.icmtalent.com

United Talent Agency
9560 Wilshire Blvd., Suite 500
Beverly Hills, CA 90212-2401
Ph: (310) 273-6700
Fax: (310) 247-1111
www.unitedtalent.com

By now, all the large talent agencies—and even some midsized ones—have developed their own reality TV departments. By contacting the agencies directly or researching them online, you can rather easily find the names of agents who represent individuals like yourself or projects like the one you're trying to sell. If truth be told, the same advice for entertainers on stage applies to aspiring producers searching for representation: Know your audience. After all, you wouldn't use George Carlin's material at a church picnic, would you? The same principle holds true for soliciting the right agent to represent your work. Find a good match.

As we've already discussed, however, finding a production company to partner with can be a more expedient plan of action. Just like scouting agents, though, you have to hit on a production company that produces your type of show. Although there are more production companies than any one individual can remember, the following are among those most recognized for their successful work in reality television.

PRODUCTION COMPANIES

Pie Town Productions
5433 Laurel Canyon Blvd.
North Hollywood, CA 91607
Ph: (818) 255-9300
Fax: (818) 255-9333
frontdesk@pietown.tv

Screaming Flea Productions
5950 6th Avenue South
Suite #109
Seattle, WA 98108
Ph: (206) 763-3383
Fax: (206) 763-3393
sfp@sfpseattle.com

Norsemen Television Productions
15422 Ventura Blvd.
2nd Floor
Sherman Oaks, CA 91403
Ph: (818) 789-2000
Fax: (818) 789-7567
generalinfo@norsemen.tv

Infinnity Productions
4028 Lamarr Ave.
Culver City, CA 90232
Ph: (310) 204-0444
info@infinnity.com

Mark Burnett Productions
640 N. Sepulveda Blvd.
Los Angeles, CA 90049

Tall Pony Productions
300 Loma Metisse Street
Malibu, CA 90265
Ph: (310) 456-7495
Fax: (310) 456-3025
www.tallpony.tv

Peter Rosen Productions, Inc.
9 East 78
New York, NY 10021
Ph: (212) 535-8927
Fax: (212) 517-5337
rosenprod@aol.com

Jag Productions, Inc.
2300 W. Sahara Ave.
#800
Las Vegas, NV 89102
Ph: (702) 222-9999
Fax: (702) 222-0949
jb@jagtv.com

Bunim-Murray Productions
6007 Sepulveda Blvd.
Van Nuys, CA 91411
Ph: (818) 756-5150
Fax: (818) 756-5140
www.Bunim-Murray.com

Mindless Entertainment, Inc.
6565 Sunset Blvd.
Suite 301

Continued . . .

PRODUCTION COMPANIES—CONTINUED

Ph: (310) 903-5400
Fax: (310) 903-5555

Los Angeles, CA 90028
Ph: (323) 466-9200
info@slmunds.com
Ph: (323) 960-4576
Fax: (323) 960-4577
www.mindlessentertainment.com

Rocket Science Laboratories
8441 Santa Monica Blvd.
West Hollywood, CA 90069
Ph: (323) 802-0500
Fax: (323) 802-0599

GRB Entertainment
13400 Riverside Drive
Sherman Oaks, CA 91423
Ph: (818) 728-7600
Fax: (818) 728-7601
www.grbtv.com

Fremantle Media Ltd.
1 Stephen St.
London W1T 1AL, UK
Ph: +44-20-7691-6000
Fax: +44-20-7691-6100
www.fremantlemedia.com

Jerry Bruckheimer Films
1631 10th St
Santa Monica, CA 90404
Ph: (310) 664 6260
Fax: (310) 664 6261
www.jbfilms.com

With regard to the notion of bypassing agents and production companies and, instead, aiming directly for the executive offices, there are two schools of thought that speak to this bold initiative.

The first maintains that pitching directly to a network as an unknown producer, either in person or by written query, is completely and utterly foolhardy. Chances are, they say, you'll never get noticed, and the time wasted chasing individuals who won't give unknowns a second glance would be better spent seducing a talent agent or production company with your idea.

The second theory, however, suggests that there is virtually nothing to lose from reaching out directly to the networks. After all, whether your idea is ignored, rejected, or ridiculed harshly, yours is just one of 1000 proposals that will pass through a network's offices on any given day. In other words, you won't be limiting your chances for success in the future by taking a shot in the dark today and falling flat on your face. In the future, the network you contacted probably won't even remember your initial entreaty.

Myself, I have always subscribed to the latter theory. When I first began producing *The Michael Essany Show* for local cable television,

I methodically reached out to every television and cable network that I thought would be inclined to launch an alternative late-night talk show. My endeavor, of course, didn't result in any networks biting. It would ultimately take my signing with Leeza Gibbons Enterprises to propel my series onto national television. Yet I still benefited enormously from cold-calling various networks. It was a process that enabled me to learn from people in the business and make valuable contacts and friendships that have lasted until now.

I have often advised aspiring television producers to hold off on pitching their best concept first. Too many mistakes are made the first time around. Instead, it can be wise to develop a show concept that is tailored to a particular network. This is what some consider reality TV baptism by fire. By concentrating, for instance, on your idea for a reality series for HGTV, you can gain precious hands-on experience pitching an idea (through online media, written query, or pounding on the network's door) that won't devastate you if it falls through—especially if it's the result of your botching the pitch or product.

Every year, new cable television channels emerge that cater to a unique market or viewing niche. Capitalize on this diverse programming field by getting your hands dirty and jumping head-first into the perilous trenches of reality television project pitching. Best of all, it's a process that can begin by simply selecting one of any readily accessible network headquarters and directly pitching an idea that is wholly created just for them.

TELEVISION AND CABLE NETWORKS

ABC
2040 Avenue of the Stars
Century City, CA 90067
Ph: (310) 557-7777
www.abc.com

CBS
7800 Beverly Blvd.
Los Angeles, CA 90036
Ph: (323) 575-2458
www.cbs.com

Fox
10201 W Pico Blvd
Los Angeles, CA 90035
Ph: (310) 369-1000
www.fox.com

NBC
3000 W. Alameda Ave.
Burbank, CA 91523
Ph: (818) 840-4444
www.nbc.com

Continued...

PBS
Steven Gray
Vice President, Program
Scheduling & Editorial
Management
PBS Headquarters
2100 Crystal Drive
Arlington, VA 22202
fax: (703) 739-5295
www.pbs.org

CW
3300 West Olive Avenue
Burbank, CA 91505
Ph: (818) 977-2500
www.cwtv.com

A&E

235 East 45th Street
New York, NY 10017
Ph: (212) 210-1400
Fax: (212) 210-9755
Homepage: www.aetv.com

About A&E

Now reaching more than 93 million homes, A&E Network offers a diverse mix of high-quality entertainment; ranging from the network's signature Real-Life Series franchise, including the hit series *Dog the Bounty Hunter*, *Intervention*, *Gene Simmons Family Jewels*, *Flip This House*, and *Criss Angel Mindfreak*, to critically acclaimed original movies, dramatic series, and the most successful justice shows on cable. A&E is the official basic cable home to the high-profile series *The Sopranos*, *CSI: Miami* and *24*.
Source: www.ncta.com

EXECUTIVES
Abbe Raven President & CEO, A&E Television Networks
Whitney Goit II Senior Executive Vice President, A&E Television Networks
Mel Berning Executive Vice President, Advertising Sales, A&E Television Networks
Bob DeBitetto Executive Vice President & General Manager, A&E Networks
David Zagin Executive Vice President, Distribution, A&E Television Networks

Steve Ronson Senior Vice President, Enterprises, A&E Television
Networks
Guy Slattery Senior Vice President, Marketing, A&E Network
Robert Sharenow Senior VP, Non-fiction & Alternative
Programming, A&E Network
Tana Nugent Jamieson Senior Vice President, Drama
Programming, A&E Network

ABC Family

3800 West Alameda Avenue
Burbank, CA 91505
Ph: (818) 560-1000
Fax: (818) 560-1930
Homepage: www.abcfamily.com

About ABC Family

ABC Family features original movies, series and specials—programming that is
reflective of today's families with all their diversity, dysfunction, humor, and passion.
Real stories. Real heart. ABC Family is an integral part of Disney ABC Television
Group, a division of the Walt Disney Company, and is advertiser supported.
Source: www.ncta.com

EXECUTIVES
Paul Lee President
Laura Nathanson Executive Vice President, Ad Sales
Ben Pyne Senior Vice President, Affiliate Sales and Marketing
Kate Juergens Senior Vice President, Original Series Programming
and Development
John Rood Senior Vice President, Brand Marketing
Annie Fort Vice President, Media Relations
Michelle Walenz Vice President, Creative
Tom Zappala SVP, Program Acquisitions & Scheduling

Adult Swim

1050 Techwood Drive
Atlanta, GA 30318
Ph: (404) 827-1700
Homepage: www.adultswim.com

About Adult Swim

Adult Swim, launched in 2001, is Turner Broadcasting System Inc.'s network offering original and acquired animated comedy and action series for young adults. Airing overnight six days a week for a total of 45 hours weekly, Adult Swim shares channel space with Cartoon Network, home to the best in original, classic, and acquired programming for children and families, and is seen in 91 million U.S. homes.
Source: www.ncta.com

The Africa Channel

11135 Magnolia Boulevard, Suite 110
North Hollywood, CA 91601
Ph: (818) 655-9977
Fax: (818) 655-9944
Homepage: www.theafricachannel.com

About The Africa Channel

The Africa Channel brings the rich and diverse perspectives of Africa and its people into U.S. homes with over 1600 hours of original and first-run English-language programming, ranging from news, music, feature films, reality, talk, and special events to soaps, travel, lifestyle, and documentaries—many of them among the top-rated and longest-running series in Africa. Virtually none of these programs have been seen in the U.S. until now. The channel is programmed to meet the broad and nationally diverse tastes of both African Americans and general American audiences who are interested in learning about the continent and its people.
Source: www.ncta.com

EXECUTIVES
James Makawa Founder & Chief Executive Officer
Jacob Arback Founder & President
Richard E. Hammer Founder & Executive Vice President, Communications
Shirley Neal Executive Vice President, Programming & Production
Bob Reid Executive Vice President & Network General Manager
Mark Walton Executive Vice President, Sponsorship & Corporate Development

Darrell Smith Vice President, Community Development &
 Marketing
Marco Williams Vice President, Marketing & Affiliate Relations
Cheryl Dorsey Vice President, Sales
Sherrice Smith Vice President, Sales

AMC

200 Jericho Quadrangle
Jericho, NY 11753
Ph: (516) 803-3000
Fax: (516) 803-4426
11 Penn Plaza, 15th Floor
New York, NY 11753
Ph: (917) 542-6200
Fax: (917) 542-6298
Homepage: www.amctv.com

About AMC

AMC is a multiplatform network that celebrates classic movies and high-quality
scripted series. Among the elite services reaching over 94 million homes, AMC
defines what it means to be a classic movie network today, creating a distinctive
viewing experience that celebrates all that is enduringly cool, personal, and
powerfully relevant about movies. AMC's comprehensive library of popular movies
strikes a meaningful chord with its audience, and its critically acclaimed slate of
originals all have a cinematic quality that allows them to stand alongside some of
the best movies of all time. AMC has garnered many of the industry's highest
honors, including four Emmy awards for its original miniseries *Broken Trail*, and
two Golden Globes for its original series *Mad Men*. AMC is "The Future of Classic."
Source: www.ncta.com

EXECUTIVES
Ed Carroll President, Rainbow Entertainment Services, Rainbow
 Media Holdings LLC
Charlie Collier Executive Vice President & General Manager, AMC
Robert Broussard President, Rainbow Network Sales, Rainbow
 Media Holdings LLC
Robert Sorcher Executive VP, Programming, Packaging &
 Production, AMC
Linda Schupack Senior Vice President, Marketing, AMC
Theano Apostolou Vice President, Public Relations, AMC & WE TV

The America Channel

120 International Parkway, Suite #220
Heathrow, FL 32746
Ph: (407) 333-3031
Fax: (801) 838-4226
Homepage: www.americachannel.us

About The America Channel

The America Channel is a new sports and lifestyle television programming network. Its mission is to combine the best in sports and community-based lifestyle programming. America Channel's *SportsLife* initiative merges life and sport, combining broadcast of nearly 600 NCAA Division I sports games and matches with real-life drama about the aspirations, achievements, challenges, adventures, community service, and lifestyles of students and student athletes. Source: www.ncta.com

EXECUTIVES
Doron Gorshein Chairman & Chief Executive Officer
Lee Sosin Senior Vice President, Business Development

Animal Planet

One Discovery Place
Silver Spring, MD 20910-3354
Ph: (240) 662-2000
Fax: (240) 662-1854
Homepage: www.animalplanet.com

About Animal Planet

Animal Planet Media Enterprises (APME), a multimedia business unit of Discovery Communications Inc., connects humans and animals with rich, deep content via multiple platforms and offers animal lovers and pet owners access to a centralized online, television, and mobile community for entertainment, information, and enrichment. Animal Planet is available in over 89 million homes in the U.S. Source: www.ncta.com

EXECUTIVES
John S. Hendricks Founder & Chairman, Discovery
Communications, Inc.

David Zaslav President & Chief Executive Officer, Discovery Communications, Inc.

Marjorie Kaplan President & General Manager

W. Clark Bunting II President, Discovery Studios

Joe Abruzzese President, Advertising Sales, Discovery Networks, US

Bill Goodwyn Executive VP, Affiliate Sales & Marketing, Discovery Networks, U.S.

Ken Dice Executive Vice President, Marketing, Discovery Networks, U.S.

Sarita Smith Senior Vice President, Research & Planning, Discovery Networks, U.S.

BBC America

747 Third Avenue
New York, NY 10017
Ph: (212) 705-9300
Homepage: www.bbcamerica.com

About BBC America

BBC America brings audiences a new generation of award-winning television featuring razor-sharp comedies, provocative dramas, life-changing makeovers, and news with a uniquely global perspective.
Source: www.ncta.com

EXECUTIVES

Kathryn Mitchell General Manager

Chris Carr Chief Financial Officer

Jo Petherbridge Senior Vice President Corporate Communications, Online & Strategy

Mary Pratt-Henaghan Senior Vice President, Operations

Richard DeCroce Vice President, Programming

Scott Gregory Vice President, Scheduling

Andrew Jackson Vice President, Creative Services

Greg Heanue Vice President, Marketing

BET

One BET Plaza
1235 W Street, NE

Washington, DC 20018–1211
Ph: (202) 608-2000
Fax: (202) 608-2631
Homepage: www.bet.com

About BET

A subsidiary of Viacom, Inc., BET is the nation's leading television network providing quality entertainment, music, news, and public affairs programming for African American audiences. BET is a dominant consumer brand in the urban marketplace with a diverse group of branded businesses, including BET.com, the number-one Internet portal for African Americans.
Source: www.ncta.com

EXECUTIVES

Scott Mills President & Chief Operating Officer

Louis Carr President, Broadcast Media Sales

Michael Pickrum Chief Financial Officer

Paxton Baker Executive VP & General Manager, BET J & Digital Networks

Stephen Hill Executive Vice President, Entertainment, Programming, Music & Talent

The Biography Channel

235 East 45th St.
New York, NY 10017
Ph: (212) 210-1400
Fax: (212) 210-9755
Homepage: www.biographychannel.com

About The Biography Channel

The Biography Channel, a 24-hour digital cable network dedicated to presenting compelling stories about the world's most interesting people, is one of the most sought-after and fastest-growing channels available today. Building on A&E Network's Emmy Award-winning series *Biography*, The Biography Channel weaves together vibrant profiles of individuals who intrigue us, plus exciting new original series, short features, and documentaries. The Biography Channel

is available nationally through all major cable and satellite distributors and can currently be viewed in more than 30 million homes.
Source: www.ncta.com

EXECUTIVES
Abbe Raven President & CEO, A&E Television Networks
John Hartinger Vice President, Marketing
Bob DiBitetto Executive Vice President & General Manager, A&E Networks
Guy Slattery Senior Vice President, Marketing, A&E Networks
Rob Sharenow Senior VP, Non-fiction & Alternative Programming, A&E Networks
Peter Tashif Vice President of Biography Channel Programming
Tom Moody Vice President of Program Planning

Bloomberg Television

731 Lexington Avenue
New York, NY 10022
Ph: (212) 617-2201
Homepage: www.bloomberg.com/media/tv

About Bloomberg TV

A sophisticated 24-hour business and financial news channel, Bloomberg Television delivers power tools for power players and serious investors via 10 networks in seven languages, reaching over 200 million homes worldwide. It builds on world-class resources to present up-to-the-minute coverage of financial news and markets, bringing journalistic expertise to its programming with the best reporters delivering news and adding perspective and analysis.
Source: www.ncta.com

EXECUTIVES
Kenneth Kohn Executive Editor
Michael Clancy Managing Editor
Russ Stein U.S. TV Ad Sales

Bravo

30 Rockefeller Plaza, 8th Floor East
New York, NY 10112
Ph: (212) 664-4444
Homepage: www.bravotv.com

About Bravo

Bravo is the cable network that plugs people into arts, entertainment, and pop culture with original programming, acclaimed drama series, movies, comedy, and music specials and by showing a whole different side of celebrities. Currently available in more than 80 million homes, Bravo is known for breaking exciting new personalities; shaking up the way we look at style, media, fame, and Hollywood; pulling back the curtain on the creative process; and making influential and inventive original programming. Its critically acclaimed original programming includes 12-time Emmy-nominated *Inside the Actors Studio*, *The Real Housewives of Orange County*, *Top Chef*, *Celebrity Poker Showdown*, and the 2004 Emmy winner for Outstanding Reality Program, *Queer Eye*, as well as the four-time Emmy-nominated hit competition series *Project Runway*. Source: www.ncta.com

EXECUTIVES

Lauren Zalaznick President, Bravo
Frances Berwick Executive Vice President, Programming &
 Production
Jason Klarman Senior Vice President, Marketing & Brand Strategy
Lisa Hsia Senior Vice President, New Media
Andrew Cohen Senior Vice President, Programming & Production
Amy Introcaso-Davis Vice President, Production & Development
Jerry Leo Vice President, Strategic Programming Planning &
 Scheduling

Cartoon Network

1050 Techwood Drive, NW
Atlanta, GA 30318–5264
Ph: (404) 827-1700
Homepage: www.cartoonnetwork.com

About Cartoon Network

Cartoon Network, currently seen in more than 91 million U.S. homes and 160 countries around the world, is Turner Broadcasting System Inc.'s ad-supported cable service offering the best in original, acquired, and classic animated entertainment for kids and families. Overnight from 11:00 P.M. to 6:00 A.M. (ET, PT) Sunday through Thursday, Cartoon Network shares its channel space with Adult Swim, a late-night destination showcasing original and acquired animation for young adults 18–34.
Source: www.ncta.com

EXECUTIVES
Michael Lazzo Senior Vice President, Adult Swim
Michael Ouweleen Senior Vice President, Development and Creative Direction
Gary Albright Senior Vice President, Trade Creative Services
Sam Register Senior Vice President, Original Animation
Bob Higgins Senior Vice President, Programming/Development
Dennis Adamovich Senior Vice President, Marketing
Jim Samples Executive Vice President/GM

Cinemax

1100 Avenue of the Americas
New York, NY 10036
Ph: (212) 512-1000
Fax: (212) 512-5637
Homepage: www.cinemax.com

About Cinemax

Cinemax is the premier movie destination on television and the second most watched pay service after HBO. Offering a wide variety of film entertainment, Cinemax combines select and broad-appeal films, from current box office to modern classics to original documentaries. Added to the more than 1200 movies shown yearly are exclusive first-to-pay box-office hits that premiere on the channel, giving viewers access to new and exclusive films.
Source: www.ncta.com

EXECUTIVES
Chris Albrecht Chairman & Chief Executive Officer

CMT

330 Commerce Street
Nashville, TN 37201
Ph: (615) 335-8400
Fax: (615) 335-8615
Homepage: www.cmt.com

About CMT

CMT, America's No. 1 country music network, carries original programming, specials, and live concerts and events, as well as a mix of videos by established country music artists and new cutting-edge acts, including world premiere exclusive videos. Founded in 1983, CMT, owned and operated by MTV Networks, reaches more than 83 million households in the United States.
Source: www.ncta.com

EXECUTIVES
Van Toffler President, MTV Networks Group
Brian Philips Executive Vice President & General Manager
Jeff Yapp Executive Vice President, Program Enterprises
James Hitchcock Senior Vice President, Creative & Marketing
Neil Holt Senior Vice President, Ad Sales
Martin Clayton Vice President of Digital Media
Paul Villadolid Vice President, Programming & Development
Sarah Brock Vice President, Production, Music & Events
Lewis Bogach Vice President, Programming & Development
Mary Beth Cunin Vice President, Program Planning & Scheduling

CNBC

900 Sylvan Avenue
Engelwood Cliffs, NJ 07632
Ph: (201) 735-2622
Homepage: www.cnbc.com

About CNBC

CNBC is the recognized world leader in business news, providing real-time financial market coverage and business information to more than 340 million homes worldwide, including more than 95 million households in the United States and Canada.

Source: www.ncta.com

EXECUTIVES

Mark Hoffman President of Operations and Programming

CNN

One CNN Center
Atlanta, GA 30303
Ph: (404) 827-1700
Homepage: www.cnn.com

About CNN

CNN Worldwide, a division of Turner Broadcasting System, Inc., a Time Warner Company, is one of the world's most respected and trusted sources for news and information.

Source: www.ncta.com

EXECUTIVES

Jonathan Klein President, CNN News Group
Sid Bedingfield Executive Vice President, CNN Productions
Rena Golden Executive Vice President & General Manager, CNNI
Susan Grant Executive VP, Newsource Sales Inc. & Interactive/
  Business Operations
Princell Hair Executive Vice President & General Manager, CNN/US
Ken Jautz Executive Vice President & General Manager, CNN
Eason Jordan Executive Vice President & Chief News Executive
Rolando Santos Executive Vice President & General Manager, CNN
  Headline News

Comedy Central

1775 Broadway
New York, NY 10019
Ph: (212) 767-8600
Fax: (212) 767-8592
Homepage: www.comedycentral.com

About Comedy Central

Comedy Central knows what's funny. And so does its more than 140 million viewers who watch every month. As the only all-comedy network, its schedule is overflowing with provocative original programming, stand-up and sketch comedy, plus offbeat comedy TV series and movies. Hits like Emmy and Peabody Award-winning series *The Daily Show with Jon Stewart* and *South Park*, along with *The Colbert Report, Mind of Mencia, RENO 911!* and *The Sarah Silverman Program*, are so popular, they've become household names.
Source: www.ncta.com

EXECUTIVES
Michele Ganeless President, Comedy Central
Lauren Corrao Executive Vice President, Original Programming & Development
David Bernath Senior Vice President, Programming
Mitch Fried Senior Vice President, Promotion Marketing
Peter Risafi Senior Vice President, Brand Marketing/Executive Creative Director

Current TV

118 King St
San Francisco, CA 94107
Ph: (415) 995-8200
Fax: (415) 995-8201
Homepage: www.current.com

About Current TV

Current is the world's first and only Emmy Award-winning peer-to-peer news and information network dedicated to young adults. Its programming consists of short, nonfiction videos (3–8 min long) in the voice and from the perspective of its audience. It covers a wide variety of topics, from pop culture to subculture, fashion to technology, careers to relationships, global issues to lifestyle. A third of its programming is made by the viewers themselves.

Source: www.ncta.com

EXECUTIVES
Al Gore Chairman
Joel Hyatt Chief Executive Officer

Discovery Channel

One Discovery Place
Silver Spring, MD 20910-3354
Ph: (240) 662-2000
Fax: (240) 662-1845
Homepage: www.discovery.com

About Discovery Channel

Discovery Channel, the United States' largest cable television network, is the nation's premier provider of real-world entertainment, offering a signature mix of compelling, high-end production values and vivid cinematography that consistently represents quality for viewers. Primetime programming features science and technology, exploration, adventure, history, and in-depth, behind-the-scenes glimpses at the people, places, and organizations that shape and share our world. Discovery is dedicated to creating the highest-quality television and media to inspire audiences by delivering knowledge about the world in an energizing way, evolving a timeless brand for a changing world.

Source: www.ncta.com

EXECUTIVES
John S. Hendricks Founder & Chairman, Discovery Communications, Inc.
David Zaslav President & Chief Executive Officer, Discovery Communications, Inc.

Joe Abruzzese President, Advertising Sales, Discovery Networks, U.S.

John Ford President & General Manager

W. Clark Bunting II President, Discovery Studios

Sarita Smith Senior Vice President, Research and Planning, Discovery Networks, U.S.

Ken Dice Executive Vice President, Marketing, Discovery Networks U.S.

David Leavy Executive Vice President, Corporate Affairs and Communications

Disney Channel

3800 West Alameda Avenue
Burbank, CA 91505
Ph: (818) 569-7500
Fax: (818) 566-1358
Homepage: www.disneychannel.com

About Disney Channel

Disney Channel taps into the world of kids and families through original series and movies plus contemporary acquired programming. Further setting Disney Channel apart is its acclaimed Disney Channel Original Movie franchise, including the No. 1 original movie on basic cable with kids 6–11 for 2006, 2005, 2004, 2003 and 2002.

Source: www.ncta.com

EXECUTIVES

Rich Ross President, Disney Channel Worldwide

Gray Marsh President, Entertainment, Disney Channel Worldwide

Tricia Wilber Executive VP, Disney Media Advertising Sales & Marketing Group

Scott Garner Senior Vice President, Programming, Disney Channel

Richard Loomis Senior Vice President, Marketing & Creative, Disney Channel

Documentary Channel

142 8th Avenue North
Nashville, TN 37203
Ph: (615) 514-2110
Fax: (615) 514-2111
Homepage: www.documentarychannel.com

About Documentary Channel

The Documentary Channel showcases innovative and inspiring work of independent documentary filmmakers from around the world. It features documentaries of all kinds and descriptions, of all lengths, and covering all categories and genres. The Documentary Channel is a one–stop–shopping location for viewers to watch interesting, high-quality documentary programs.
Source: www.ncta.com

EXECUTIVES
Thomas Neff - Chief Executive Officer
Jay Kelley Senior Vice President, Marketing
Kate Pearson Senior Vice President, Programming
Barry Rubinow Director, Creative Services

E! Entertainment Television

5750 Wilshire Boulevard
Los Angeles, CA 90036–3709
Ph: (323) 954-2400
Fax: (323) 954-2500
Homepage: www.eonline.com

About E!

E! showcases coverage of popular entertainment celebrity interviews, news, and behind-the-scenes features with today's biggest stars.
Source: www.ncta.com

EXECUTIVES
Ted Harbert President & Chief Executive Officer, Comcast Entertainment Group

Steve Dolcemaschio Executive Vice President, Finance & Business Operations

Suzanne Kolb Executive Vice President, Marketing & Communications

Lisa Berger Executive VP, Original Programming & Series Development, E!

Sarah Goldstein Senior Vice President, Public Relations, E! Networks

Jay James Senior Vice President, Development, E! Networks

Sheila Johnson Senior Vice President, Business Operations & General Counsel

John Najarian Senior Vice President, New Media

Jeff Shore Senior Vice President, Production

David Walkley Senior Vice President, Human Resources

ESPN

ESPN Plaza
Bristol, CT 06010-9454
Ph: (860) 766-2000
Fax: (860) 766-2400
Homepage: www.espn.com

About ESPN

ESPN, Inc., the worldwide leader in sports, is the leading multinational, multimedia sports entertainment company featuring the broadest portfolio of multimedia sports assets with over 50 business entities. Sports media assets include ESPN on ABC as well as six domestic cable television networks: ESPN, ESPN2, ESPN Classic, ESPNEWS, ESPN Deportes, and ESPNU.
Source: www.ncta.com

EXECUTIVES

George Bodenheimer Co-chairman, Disney Media Networks; President, ESPN, ABC Sports

Sean Bratches President, Disney & ESPN Networks Affiliate Sales & Marketing

Christine Driessen Executive Vice President & Chief Financial Officer

Ed Durso Executive Vice President, Administration
Chuck Pagano Executive Vice President, Technology
John Skipper Executive Vice President, Content

Food Network

79 9th Avenue
New York, NY 10011
Ph: (212) 398-8836
Fax: (212) 302-7896
Homepage: www.foodnetwork.com

About Food Network

Food Network is a unique lifestyle network where viewers will always be surprised and engaged by likeable hosts and personalities and the variety of things they do with food. The network is committed to exploring new, different, and interesting ways to approach food—through pop culture, adventure, and travel—while also expanding its repertoire of technique-based programs.
Food Network is one of the fastest-growing ad-supported cable networks on year-to-year subscriber growth. The E.W. Scripps Company, which also owns and operates HGTV, DIY Network, Fine Living TV Network, and Great American Country (GAC), is the managing general partner.
Source: www.ncta.com

EXECUTIVES
Brooke Johnson President
Michael Smith Senior Vice President, Marketing and Creative
  Services
Carrie Welch Vice President, Public Relations

Fox Reality

1440 S. Sepulveda Blvd.
Los Angeles, CA 90025
Ph: (310) 689-1500
Fax: (310) 689-1560
Homepage: www.foxreality.com

About Fox Reality

Fox Reality launched May 24, 2005, to become the first destination for lovers of unscripted programming. The channel offers major U.S. network favorites, exclusive international reality programming, original series, and specials. Fox Reality offers reality viewers more of their favorite reality programming with RealityRevealed in prime time with never-before-seen footage, exclusive interviews, behind-the-scenes secrets, and more reality fun. Fox Reality distribution is set to propel past 35 million subscribers in its second year, becoming one of only four new networks to achieve that feat. Its programming is available on television, broadband, cellular phones, and other leading mobile devices.
Source: www.ncta.com

EXECUTIVES
David Lyle President
Bob Boden Senior Vice President, Programming, Production and Development
Lorey Zlotnick Senior Vice President, Marketing and On-Air Promotions

Fuse

11 Penn Plaza, 17th Floor
New York, NY 10001
Ph: (212) 324-3400
Fax: (212) 324-3445
Homepage: www.fuse.tv

About Fuse

Fuse is the music television network, featuring music videos, exclusive artist interviews, live concerts, series, and specials. Fuse reflects the rapidly changing interests and attitudes of its 12- to 34-year-old audience by uniting the media platforms at the center of their communication and entertainment—TV, web, mobile technologies, and interactive gaming—and by incorporating their opinions and suggestions into the network's on-air and online programming.
Source: www.ncta.com

FX

P.O. Box 900
Beverly Hills, CA 90213
Ph: (310) 369-1000
Homepage: www.fxnetworks.com

About FX

FX is a flagship general entertainment basic cable network from Fox. The diverse schedule includes a growing roster of distinctive original series and movies; an impressive roster of acquired hit series; an established film library with box-office hits from 20th Century Fox; and marquee sports such as NASCAR.
Source: www.ncta.com

EXECUTIVES
John Landgrafe President & General Manager, FX Networks
Lee Bartlett Senior Vice President, Business & Legal Affairs, FX Networks
Chuck Saftler Senior Vice President, Programming, FX Networks
Chris Carlisle Executive Vice President, Marketing & Promotions, FX Networks
Lindsay Gardner President
Michael Hopkins Executive Vice President
Michael Biard SVP, Affiliate Sales & Marketing

G4

12100 West Olympic Boulevard
Los Angeles, CA 90064
Ph: (310) 979-5000
Fax: (310) 979-5100
Homepage: www.g4tv.com

About G4

G4, the fastest growing network on television for 2006, launched in April 2002 and is now available in 61 million cable and satellite homes nationwide. The #1

Continued...

About G4—continued

podcasted cable network in America and a leader in VOD, G4 embraces the male 18–34 audience and their fascination with video games, the Internet, broadband, technology, comics, and animation. Additionally, G4 provides breaking news and insider opinions on these topics as well as the broader culture young men are interested in. The company is headquartered in Los Angeles and is owned by Comcast Corporation.
Source: www.ncta.com

EXECUTIVES
Neal Tiles President
Dale Hopkins Chief Operating Officer

Galavisión

605 Third Avenue, 12th Floor
New York, NY 10158
Ph: (212) 455-5300
Fax: (212) 986-4731
Homepage: www.univisionnetworks.com

About Galavisión

Galavisión is the leading Spanish-language cable network for U.S. Hispanics in both distribution and viewership. The network averages over 50 hours of news, sports, and entertainment programming each week.
Source: www.ncta.com

EXECUTIVES
Tim Krass Executive Vice President, Affiliate Relations
Deanna Andaverde Regional Vice President – Central
John Heffron Regional Vice President – Eastern
Timothy Spillane Vice President
Jasmine Rezia Vice President, Affiliate Marketing

The Golf Channel

7580 Commerce Center Drive
Orlando, FL 32819

Ph: (407) 345-GOLF
Fax: (407) 363-7976
Homepage: www.thegolfchannel.com

About The Golf Channel

The Golf Channel is the first and only television network devoted exclusively to golf. It offers in-depth coverage of more than 100 tournaments including the PGA Tour, Champions Tour, Nationwide Tour, LPGA, European Tour, Sunshine Tour, and PGA Tour of Australia. Also featured is private instruction from golf's top teaching professionals plus up-to-the-minute golf news and stats each day. Source: www.ncta.com

EXECUTIVES

Page H. Thompson President

Jeffrey Dilley Chief Financial Officer

Don McGuire Senior Vice President, Programming, Production & Operations

Kevin Byrnes Senior Vice President, Sponsorship Sales

Gene Pizzolato Executive Vice President, Sales, Marketing & Business Development

Shannon O'Neill Senior Vice President, New Media & Business Development

Christine Sullivan Senior Vice President, Marketing & Brand Management

GSN (Game Show Network)

2150 Colorado Avenue, Suite 100
Santa Monica, CA 90404
Ph: (310) 255-6800
Fax: (310) 255-6810
Homepage: www.gsn.com

About GSN

GSN is an industry-leading, game content provider distributing competition programming through its 66-million subscriber cable television network and its

Continued...

casual and skill-based online games portal, GSN.com. As the premier television network for games, GSN produces some of the most popular original casino and game show series on TV today. GSN.com features all types of game play: flash games for fun, skill cash game tournaments, and free downloadable games. GSN is distributed throughout the U.S. and Canada by all major cable operators, satellite providers, and telcos. The company is jointly owned by Sony Pictures Entertainment and Liberty Media Corporation.

Source: www.ncta.com

EXECUTIVES

David Goldhill President & Chief Executive Officer

Steve Brunell Executive Vice President of Operations and Chief Financial Officier

Christopher Raleigh Senior Vice President, Advertising Sales

Michael Kohn Senior Vice President, Business Affairs

Jamie Roberts Senior Vice President, Programming

John P. Roberts Senior Vice President, Interactive & Online Entertainment

Dennis Gillespie Senior Vice President, Distribution

The Hallmark Channel

12700 Ventura Boulevard
Studio City, CA 91604-2463
Ph: (818) 755-2400
Fax: (818) 755-2564
1325 Avenue of the Americas, 22nd Floor
New York, NY 10019
Ph: (212) 445-6600
Fax: (212) 445-5395
Homepage: www.hallmarkchannel.com

About The Hallmark Channel

Hallmark Channel is the quintessential 24-hour television destination for family-friendly programming and a leader in the production of original movies. The network launched in 2001 and brings to audiences a brand with a 50-plus-year legacy that resonates with consumers. Hallmark Channel is

the fastest-growing major ad-supported cable network since its launch, and its strong ratings consistently rank the channel in the top 10 in prime time. Hallmark Channel is seen in 84 million homes across the U.S. and has developed a stellar reputation for keeping viewers engaged and entertained.
Source: www.ncta.com

EXECUTIVES
Henry Schleiff President & Chief Executive Officer
William J. Abbott Executive Vice President, Ad Sales
David Kenin Executive Vice President, Programming
Laura Masse Executive Vice President, Marketing
Brian Stewart Executive Vice President & Chief Financial Officer
Janice Arouh Senior Vice President, Network Distribution & Service
Barbara Fisher Senior Vice President, Original Programming

HBO

1100 Avenue of the Americas
New York, NY 10036
Ph: (212) 512-1000
Fax: (212) 512-5637
Homepage: www.hbo.com

About HBO

The No. 1 premium channel is the place for some of the best programming on TV. Each month HBO offers more than 80 theatrical motion pictures, including new movies on Saturday night, as well as groundbreaking and award-winning original series, films, documentaries, comedy, family shows, sports specials, and championship boxing. On Sunday nights, HBO delivers year-round premiere showings of its critically acclaimed original series.
Source: www.ncta.com

EXECUTIVES
Bill Nelson Chairman & CEO
Michael Lombardo President of Programming
Richard Plepler Co-President

Eric Kessler Co-President
Hal Akselrad Co-President

The History Channel

235 East 45th Street
New York, NY 10017
Ph: (212) 210-1400
Fax: (212) 907-9409
Homepage: www.history.com

About The History Channel

The History Channel is one of the leading cable television networks featuring compelling original, nonfiction specials and series that bring history to life in a powerful and entertaining manner across multiple platforms. The network provides an inviting place where people experience history in new and exciting ways, enabling them to connect their lives today to the great lives and events of the past that provide a blueprint for the future. The History Channel reaches more than 91 million Nielsen subscribers.
Source: www.ncta.com

EXECUTIVES

Nancy Dubuc Executive Vice President & General Manager, The History Channel

Mel Berning Executive Vice President, Advertising Sales, A&E Television Networks

David Zagin Executive Vice President, Distribution, A&E Television Networks

Charlie Maday Senior Vice President, Programming

Mike Mohamad Senior Vice President, Marketing

Libby O'Connell SVP, Corporate Outreach AETN, Chief Historian

HGTV

9721 Sherrill Boulevard
Knoxville, TN 37932
Ph: (865) 694-2700
Fax: (865) 694-4392
Homepage: www.hgtv.com

About HGTV

At HGTV, home is more than a house with four walls and a roof. Home means communities, workplaces, and shared spaces. As the leading lifestyle television network, HGTV invites viewers to imagine, create, and enjoy where they live. Its wide variety of programming features expert information, practical advice, and human drama, so whether it's decorating, designing, landscaping, or buying a house, HGTV tells the stories that start at home!
Source: www.ncta.com

EXECUTIVES
Jim Samples President, HGTV
Lori Asbury Senior VP Marketing, Creative and Brand Strategy
Audrey Adlam Vice President, Communications and Partnership Marketing

IFC (Independent Film Channel)

200 Jericho Quadrangle
Jericho, NY 11753
Ph: (516) 803-3000
Fax: (516) 803-4616
11 Penn Plaza, 15th Floor
New York, NY 10001
Ph: (212) 324-8500
Fax: (917) 542-6298
Homepage: www.ifc.com

About IFC

The Independent Film Channel (IFC) is the first and most widely distributed network dedicated to independent film 24 hours a day, uncut, uncensored, and commercial-free. The network is part of IFC Companies—the only brand to operate in every area of independent film to include television, production, financing, distribution, digital, on-demand, and exhibition.
Source: www.ncta.com

EXECUTIVES

Evan Shapiro Executive Vice President & General Manager, IFC Network

Robert Broussard President, Rainbow Network Sales, Rainbow Media Holdings LLC

Alan Klein Senior Vice President, Partnerships & Licensing, IFC Network

Debbie DeMontreux Senior Vice President, Original Programming, IFC Network

George Lentz Vice President, Scheduling & Acquisitions, IFC Network

Kent Rees Vice President, Marketing, IFC Network

Elektra Gray Vice President, Consumer Publicity, IFC Network

INSP (Inspiration Network)

7910 Crescent Executive Drive, Fifth Floor
Charlotte, NC 28217
Ph: (704) 525-9800
Fax: (704) 525-9899
Homepage: www.inspnets.com

About INSP

The Inspiration Channel (INSP) blends ministry programs with family-oriented movies, dramas, music, children's shows, and specials.
Source: www.ncta.com

EXECUTIVES

David Cerullo Chairman & Chief Executive Officer
Bill Airy Chief Operating Officer
Rod Tapp Executive Vice President, Sales & Marketing
Mark Favaro Senior Vice President, Ad Sales
Tom Hohman Senior Vice President, Affiliate Relations
Ron Shuping Executive Vice President, Programming

TLC (The Learning Channel)

One Discovery Place
Silver Spring, MD 20910-3354

Ph: (240) 662-2000
Fax: (240) 662-1854
Homepage: www.tlc.com

About The Learning Channel

TLC is the only television network dedicated to lifelong learning for viewers who want to grow up, not old. Featuring programming that explores life's key transitions and turning points, TLC presents high-quality, relatable, and authentic personal stories. TLC connects more than 97 million homes in North America to the human experience with life's lessons you can't learn from books. Source: www.ncta.com

EXECUTIVES

John S. Hendricks Founder & Chairman, Discovery Communications, Inc.

David Zaslav President & Chief Executive Officer, Discovery Communications, Inc.

Angela Shapiro-Mathes President & General Manager

Clark Bunting II President, Discovery Studios

Bill Goodwyn President, Affiliate Sales & Marketing, Discovery Networks, U.S.

Sarita Smith Senior Vice President, Research & Planning, Discovery Networks, U.S.

Edward Sabin Chief Operating Officer

Lifetime

309 West 49th Street
New York, NY 10019
Ph: (212) 424-7000
Homepage: www.lifetimetv.com

About Lifetime

Lifetime is the leader in women's television and one of the top-rated basic cable television networks. A diverse, multimedia company, Lifetime is committed to

Continued...

offering the highest-quality entertainment and information programming and advocating a wide range of issues affecting women and their families. Lifetime Television, Lifetime Movie Network, Lifetime Real Women, Lifetime Home Entertainment, and Lifetime Online are part of Lifetime Entertainment Services, a 50/50 joint venture of The Hearst Corporation and The Walt Disney Company. Source: www.ncta.com

EXECUTIVES

Andrea Wong President & Chief Executive Officer

James Wesley Executive Vice President & Chief Financial Officer

Lynn Picard Executive Vice President & General Manager, Lifetime Television

Louise Henry Bryson Executive Vice President, Distribution & Business Development

Tim Brooks Executive Vice President, Research

Richard Basso Senior Vice President, Pricing & Planning

Gwynne McConkey Senior VP, Operations, Information Systems & Technology

LOGO

1633 Broadway, 5th Floor
New York, NY 10019
Ph: (212) 654-3005
Homepage: www.logoonline.com

About LOGO

Logo is the ad-supported network targeted to lesbian, gay, bisexual, and transgender (LGBT) viewers, launched by MTV Networks. LOGO provides a mix of original and acquired entertainment programming that is authentic, smart, inclusive, and open-minded. LOGO joins Viacom's roster of popular and highly targeted cable networks, which include MTV, Comedy Central, BET, and Spike TV. Source: www.ncta.com

EXECUTIVES

Brian Graden President

Lisa Sherman Senior Vice President and General Manager

The Military Channel

One Discovery Place
Silver Spring, MD 20910-3354
Ph: (240) 662-2000
Fax: (240) 662-1854
Homepage: http://military.discovery.com

About The Military Channel

The Military Channel brings viewers compelling, real-world stories of heroism, military strategy, technological breakthroughs, and turning points in history. The network takes viewers "behind the lines" to hear the personal stories of servicemen and women and offers in-depth explorations of military technology, battlefield strategy, aviation, and history. As the only cable network devoted to military subjects, it also provides unique access to this world, allowing viewers to experience and understand a world full of human drama, courage, innovation, and long-held military traditions.

Source: www.ncta.com

EXECUTIVES

John S. Hendricks Founder & Chairman, Discovery Communications, Inc.

David Zaslav President & Chief Executive Officer, Discovery Communications, Inc.

Joseph Abruzzese President, Advertising Sales, Discovery Networks, U.S.

Bill Goodwyn President, Affiliate Sales & Marketing, Discovery Networks, U.S.

Clark Bunting II President, Discovery Studios

Ken Dice Executive Vice President, Marketing, Discovery Networks U.S.

Sarita Smith Senior Vice President, Research & Planning, Discovery Networks, U.S.

MSNBC

One MSNBC Plaza
Secausus, NJ 07094

Ph: (201) 583-5000
Fax: (201) 583-5179
Homepage: www.msnbc.com

About MSNBC

MSNBC is a program service of NBC Universal Cable, a division of NBC Universal, one of the world's leading media and entertainment companies in the development, production, and marketing of entertainment, news, and information to a global audience.
Source: www.ncta.com

EXECUTIVES

Steve Capus President, NBC News

Phil Griffin Senior Vice President, NBC News & Executive-in-Charge, MSNBC

Dan Abrams General Manager, MSNBC

Susan Sullivan Vice President, News, Daytime Programming, MSNBC

Bill Wolff Vice President, Primetime Programming, MSNBC

Val Nicholas Vice President, Advertising & Promotion, MSNBC

Jeremy Gaines Vice President, Corporate Communications, MSNBC

MTV

1515 Broadway
New York, NY 10036
Ph: (212) 258-8000
Fax: (212) 258-8100
Homepage: www.mtv.com

About MTV

MTV is Music Television. It is the music authority where young adults turn to find out what's happening and what's next in music and popular culture. MTV reaches 412 million households worldwide and is the No. 1 media brand in the world. Only MTV can offer the consistently fresh, honest, groundbreaking, fun,

and inclusive youth-oriented programming found nowhere else in the world. MTV is a network that transcends all the clutter, reaching out beyond barriers to everyone who's got eyes, ears and a television set.
Source: www.ncta.com

EXECUTIVES
Judy McGrath Chairman & Chief Executive Officer, MTV Networks
Van Toffler President, MTV Networks
Christina Norman President
Brian Graden President, Entertainment, MTV Networks Music Group
Tina Exharos Executive Vice President, Marketing, MTV/MTV2
Dave Sirulnick Executive VP, MTV Multi-Platform Production, News and Music
Amy Doyle Senior Vice President, MTV Music & Talent

National Geographic Channel

1145 17th Street, NW
Washington, DC 20036
Ph: (202) 912-6500
Fax: (202) 912-6603
Homepage: www.nationalgeographic.com/channel

About National Geographic Channel

National Geographic Channel (NGC) is the network for adventures all over the world and amazing journeys on land, under sea, in the sky, and beyond. With unique access to the most respected scientists, journalists, and filmmakers, NGC offers innovative and contemporary programming of unparalleled quality that pushes the boundaries and takes viewers as far as they can go. NGC has carriage with all of the nation's major cable and satellite television providers, making it currently available to more than 66 million homes.
Source: www.ncta.com

EXECUTIVES
David Haslingden Chief Executive Officer
Steven J. Schiffman Acting General Manager

John Ford Executive Vice President, Programming
Mike Hopkins Executive VP & General Manager
Kiera G. Hynninen Senior Vice President, Marketing
Richard Goldfarb Senior Vice President, Media Sales
Michael Cascio Senior Vice President, Special Programming
Juliet Blake Senior Vice President, Production
Russell A. Howard Senior Vice President, Communications
Mike Beller Senior Vice President, Business & Legal Affairs
Steve Burns Executive VP of Content

Nickelodeon

1515 Broadway
New York, NY 10036
Ph: (212) 258-8000
Fax: (212) 258-6284
Homepage: www.nick.com

About Nickelodeon

Nickelodeon, in its 27th year, is the number-one entertainment brand for kids. It has built a diverse, global business by putting kids first in everything it does. The company includes television programming and production in the United States and around the world, plus consumer products, online, recreation, books, magazines, and feature films. Nickelodeon's U.S. television network is seen in almost 92 million households and has been the No. 1 rated basic cable network for almost 12 consecutive years.

Source: www.ncta.com

EXECUTIVES
Judy McGrath Chairman & Chief Executive Officer, MTV Networks
Cyma Zarghami President, Nickelodeon & MTVN Kids and Family Group
Tom Ascheim Executive Vice President & General Manager, Nickelodeon Television

Nick at Nite

1515 Broadway
New York, NY 10036

Ph: (212) 258-8000
Fax: (212) 846-1775
Homepage: www.nickatnite.com

About Nick at Nite

Nick at Nite is currently the No. 1 basic cable network among women 18–49, women 18–34, women 25–54, and African-Americans 18–49. It is also the home to hit sitcoms *The Cosby Show, The Fresh Prince of Bel-Air, Who's the Boss?, Full House, Murphy Brown,* and *Roseanne.* Though these modern sitcoms will always be the lifeline of Nick at Nite, the network recently began contemporizing its schedule with fresh originals that meet the "Four Fs" criteria: family-friendly, funny, and familiar.
Source: www.ncta.com

EXECUTIVES
Larry W. Jones President, TV Land & Nick at Nite
Cyma Zarghami President, Nickelodeon
Keith Cox VP, Programming

Oxygen

75 9th Avenue, 7th Floor
New York, NY 10011
Ph: (212) 651-2070
Fax: (212) 651-2099
Homepage: www.oxygen.com

About Oxygen

Oxygen, the only cable network owned and operated by women, is currently available in over 74 million homes. The network was launched in 2000 to fill a void in the television landscape, creating a network targeted to younger women.
Source: www.ncta.com

EXECUTIVES
Todd Schwartz Vice President of Programming

Playboy TV

2706 Media Center Drive

Los Angeles, CA 90065
Ph: (323) 276-4000
Fax: (323) 276-4500
Homepage: www.playboytv.com

About Playboy TV

Mature original series, racy reality, live interactive call-in shows, and exclusive
director's cut movies from the best-known adult entertainment provider.
Source: www.ncta.com

EXECUTIVES
Bob Meyers President of Media
Todd Schwartz Vice President, Programming – Playboy TV
Gary Rosenson Senior Vice President, Sales & Affiliate Marketing

Sci-Fi
30 Rockefeller Plaza
New York, NY 10112
Ph: (212) 664-4444
Fax: (212) 703-8533
Homepage: www.scifi.com

About Sci-Fi

Sci-Fi Channel is a television network where "what if" is what's on. Sci-Fi fuels
the imagination of viewers with original series and events, blockbuster movies,
and classic science fiction and fantasy programming, as well as a dynamic
website and magazine. Launched in 1992 and currently in 86 million homes,
Sci-Fi Channel is a network of NBC Universal, one of the world's leading media
and entertainment companies.
Source: www.ncta.com

EXECUTIVES
Bonnie Hammer President, Sci Fi Channel
David Howe Executive Vice President & General Manager

Mark Miller President, Ad Sales
Mark Stern Executive Vice President, Sci Fi Original Programming
Thomas Vitale Senior Vice President, Programming & Original Movies
Sallie Schoneboom Senior Vice President, Publicity

Showtime

1633 Broadway, 17th Floor
New York, NY 10019
Ph: (212) 708-3200
Fax: (212) 708-1212
Homepage: www.sho.com

About Showtime

Showtime features an average of 200 titles a month, including Hollywood hits no one else has, award-winning original pictures, series and championship boxing.
Source: www.ncta.com

EXECUTIVES
Mathew C. Blank Chairman & Chief Executive Officer
Robert Greenblatt President, Entertainment
Melinda Benedek Executive Vice President, Business Affairs & Production
Matthew Duda Executive Vice President, Program Acquisitions & Distribution
Len Fogge Executive Vice President, Creative & Marketing
Ray Gutierrez Executive Vice President, Human Resources & Administration
Gary Levine Executive Vice President, Original Programming
Pancho Mansfield Executive Vice President, Original Programming
H. Gwen Marcus Executive Vice President, Operations & General Counsel
Michael Rauch Executive Vice President, Production
Jerome Scro Executive Vice President & Chief Financial Officer

Spike TV

1775 Broadway
New York, NY 10019
Ph: (212) 767-8705
Fax: (212) 846-2560
Homepage: www.SpikeTV.com

Spike TV is available in 96.1 million homes and is a division of MTV Networks.
Source: www.ncta.com

EXECUTIVES
Doug Herzog President – MTVN Entertainment Group
Kevin Kay President – Spike TV
John Cucci Chief Operating Officer – Spike TV
Sharon Levy Senior Vice President, Alternative Programming
Robert Friedman Senior Vice President, Programming
Casey Patterson Senior VP, Talent Development & Event
    Production – Spike TV
Niels Schuurmans Senior Vice President, Creative Director – Spike
    TV
Dario Spina Senior Vice President, Marketing – Spike TV
Brian Diamond Senior Vice President, Sports & Specials
Bill McGoldrick Vice President, Programming

TBS

1050 Techwood Drive, NW
Atlanta, GA 30318
Ph: (404) 827-1700
Homepage: www.tbs.com

TBS, a division of Turner Broadcasting System, Inc., is television's top-rated
comedy network. It serves as home to such original comedy series as *My Boys*,

The Bill Engvall Show, Tyler Perry's *House of Payne*, *10 Items or Less*, and *Frank TV*; hot contemporary comedies like *The Office*, *Sex and the City*, *Everybody Loves Raymond*, *Family Guy*, *King of Queens*, *Seinfeld*, and *Friends*; specials and special events such as *Funniest Commercials of the Year* and The Comedy Festival in Las Vegas; blockbuster movies; and hosted movie showcases.
Source: www.ncta.com

EXECUTIVES
Mark Lazarus President, Turner Entertainment Group
Steve Koonin President, Turner Entertainment Networks
Jonathan Katz Senior Vice President, Program Planning & Acquisitions
Ken Schwab Senior Vice President, Programming, TNT and TBS
Michael Wright Senior Vice President, Content Creation Group, TBS, TNT & TCM
Sandra Dewey Senior Vice President, Original Programming
Michael Borza Senior Vice President, On-Air Creative, TBS, TNT and TCM

Telemundo

2290 West 8th Avenue
Hialeah, FL 33010
Ph: (305) 889-7900
Fax: (305) 889-7205
Homepage: www.telemundo.com

About Telemundo

Telemundo, a U.S. Spanish-language television network, is the essential entertainment, news, and sports source for Hispanics. Broadcasting unique national and local programming for the fastest-growing segment of the U.S. population, Telemundo reaches 93 percent of U.S. Hispanic viewers in 210 markets through its 16 owned and operated stations, 36 broadcast affiliates, and nearly 700 cable affiliates. Telemundo is wholly owned by NBC Universal, one of the world's leading media and entertainment companies.
Source: www.ncta.com

EXECUTIVES

Don Browne President, Telemundo

Carlos Bardasano Executive Vice President, Entertainment

Peter Blacker Senior Vice President, Digital Media

Derek Bond Executive Vice President, Studios

Mildred Carrasquillo Senior Vice President, Research

Jorge Hidalgo Senior Executive Vice President, Sports & Network News

Alexandra McCauley Senior Vice President, Human Resources

Lynette Pinto Vice President, Affiliate Marketing Telemundo

Alejandro Pels General Manager, Mun2

Alfredo Richard Senior Vice Communications & Talent Development

TNT (Turner Network Television)

1050 Techwood Drive, NW
Atlanta, GA 30318
Ph: (404) 827-1700
Homepage: www.tnt.tv

About TNT

Turner Network Television (TNT), television's destination for drama and one of cable's top-rated networks, offers original movies and series, including the acclaimed and highly popular detective drama *The Closer*. TNT is also home to powerful one-hour dramas such as *Law & Order*, *Without a Trace*, *Cold Case*, *ER*, *Charmed*, and *Judging Amy*; broadcast premiere movies; compelling prime-time specials such as the Screen Actors Guild Awards®; and championship sports coverage, including NASCAR and the NBA.
Source: www.ncta.com

EXECUTIVES

Mark Lazarus President, Turner Entertainment Group

David Levy President, Turner Ad Sales & Marketing and Turner Sports

Steve Koonin President, Turner Entertainment Networks

Jonathan Katz Senior Vice President, Program Planning & Acquisitions

Ken Schwab Senior Vice President, Programming, TNT & TBS
Michael Wright Senior Vice President, Content Creation Group, TBS, TNT & TCM
Sandra Dewey Senior Vice President, Original Programming

Travel Channel

One Discovery Place
Silver Spring, MD 20910
Ph: (240) 662-2000
Fax: (240) 662-1854
Homepage: www.travelchannel.com

About Travel Channel

The Travel Channel is the only television network devoted exclusively to travel entertainment. Capturing the fascination, freedom, and fun of travel, Travel Channel delivers insightful stories from the world's most popular destinations and inspiring diversions.
Source: www.ncta.com

EXECUTIVES
John S. Hendricks Founder & Chairman, Discovery Communications, Inc.
David Zaslav President & Chief Executive Officer, Discovery Communications, Inc.
Patrick Younge President & General Manager
W. Clark Bunting II President, Discovery Studios
Joseph Abruzzese President, Advertising Sales, Discovery Networks, U.S.
Ken Dice Executive Vice President, Marketing, Discovery Networks U.S.
Sarita Smith Senior Vice President, Research & Planning, Discovery Networks, U.S.

TV Guide Channel

1800 North Highland Avenue
Los Angeles, CA 90028

Ph: (323) 817-4600
Home Page: www.tvguide.com

About TV Guide Channel

TV Guide Channel reaches over 80 million homes and is the premiere television entertainment network for viewers seeking the latest information on the best programs, hottest stars, and latest trends on television. Headquartered in the heart of Hollywood at its TV Guide Studios, the network combines original programming with comprehensive program listings information, all of which deliver on viewers' need for an entertaining and easy guide to what's on TV. Backed by a brand with more than 50 years of television history and authority, TV Guide Channel's programming is dedicated to the omnipresent world of television, offering compelling celebrity interviews, talk shows, television news and previews, behind-the-scenes specials, and comprehensive coverage of industry award shows.
Source: www.ncta.com

EXECUTIVES

Rich Battista Chief Executive Officer, Gemstar-TV Guide International, Inc.

Tonia O'Conner Executive Vice President, Distribution

Matthew Singerman Senior Vice President, Programming & Production

Richy Glassberg Senior Vice President, Advertisement Sales

Doug Yates Senior Vice President, Consumer Marketing

Leslie Furuta Vice President, Communications, TV Guide Television Group

USA Network

30 Rockefeller Plaza
New York, NY 10112
Ph: (212) 664-4444
Fax: (212) 413-6509
Homepage: www.usanetwork.com

About USA Network

USA Network is cable television's leading provider of original series and feature movies, sports events, off-net television shows, and blockbuster theatrical films. USA Network is seen in over 88 million U.S. homes. USA Network is a program service of NBC Universal Cable, a division of NBC Universal, one of the world's leading media and entertainment companies in the development, production, and marketing of entertainment, news, and information to a global audience. Source: www.ncta.com

EXECUTIVES
Bonnie Hammer President, Sci-Fi Channel & USA Network
Jeff Wachtel Executive Vice President, Original Programming
Chris McCumber Senior Vice President, Marketing & Brand
 Strategy
Jane Blaney Senior Vice President, Program Acquisitions &
 Scheduling

VH1

1515 Broadway
New York, NY 10036
Ph: (212) 846-6000
Homepage: www.vh1.com

About VH1

VH1 connects viewers to the music, artists, and pop culture that matter to them most with series, specials, live events, exclusive online content, and public affairs initiatives. VH1 is available in 90 million households in the U.S. Source: www.ncta.com

EXECUTIVES
Brian Graden President, Entertainment, MTV Networks Music Group
Tom Calderone General Manager, VH1

Rick Beispel SVP, Advertising Sales, VH1

Nigel Cox-Hagan SVP, Creative Group and Consumer Marketing, VH1

Richard Gay Senior Vice President, Strategy and Business Operations, VH1/CMT

Tina Imm VP, Digital Media, VH1

Rick Krim Executive Vice President, Talent & Music Programming, VH1

Ben Zurier Senior Vice President, Programming Strategy, VH1, VH1 Classic

WE tv

200 Jericho Quadrangle
Jericho, NY 11753
Ph: (516) 803-3000
Fax: (516) 803-4398
Homepage: www.we.tv

About WE tv

WE tv is the only cable network dedicated to helping women connect to one another and the world around them. With quality original programming including the hit series *Bridezillas*, unique movie packages like Cinematherapy, topical specials, and its public affairs initiative WE Empowers Women, the network supports women and appeals to their interests in pop culture, relationships, and personal style. WE tv is a division of Rainbow Entertainment Services.
Source: www.ncta.com

EXECUTIVES

Ed Carroll President, Rainbow Entertainment Services, Rainbow Media Holdings LLC

Kim Martin Executive Vice President & General Manager, WE tv

Robert Broussard President, Rainbow Network Sales, Rainbow Media Holdings LLC

Steve Cheskin Senior Vice President, Programming, WE tv

Kenetta Bailey Senior Vice President, Marketing, WE tv

Theano Apostolou Vice President, Consumer Public Relations, AMC & WE tv

The Weather Channel

300 Interstate North Parkway
Atlanta, GA 30339-2404
Ph: (770) 226-0000
Fax: (770) 226-2950
Homepage: www.weather.com

About The Weather Channel

The Weather Channel has more than 100 meteorologists and state-of-the-art technology to provide 24-hour-a-day coverage of local, regional, and national weather; 10-day forecasts; severe weather coverage; on-location updates; travel; and a schedule of education productions and original series.
Source: www.ncta.com

EXECUTIVES

Decker Anstrom Chairman, The Weather Channel Companies
Debora Wilson President, The Weather Channel Companies
Wonya Lucas General Managaer & Executive Vice President
Becky Powhatan Executive Vice President, Distribution & Business
  Affairs
Lynn Brindell Senior Vice President, Marketing
Terry Connelly Senior Vice President, Programming & Production
Marla Hoppenfeld Vice President, Affiliate Marketing & Public
  Relations
Carter McGuire Senior Vice President, Distribution

DITCHING THE DISCLAIMER

It's important to note that almost every cable and television network explicitly states on their website that unsolicited ideas are not accepted, either "at this particular time" or simply never. Ignore such warnings altogether. I have found a tremendous deal of work in my career (in television, radio, and now publishing) by paying absolutely no heed to such meaningless admonitions as "all unsolicited materials will be returned unopened."

I always called their bluff. To be sure, sometimes I was wrong. But if I shied away from every production company, television network, or publisher that boldly purported to disregard all unsolicited queries, I would still be an unknown punk from Indiana who never made it past local cable.

As a youngster attempting to break into the business, I had developed quite a penchant for contacting anybody and everybody. By the time I was 14 years old I had already written well over 1000 handwritten letters to Hollywood celebrities, musicians, athletes, politicians, and recording artists. Whether I was attempting to book guests for my show or just requesting a little helpful advice, I never did only what I was advised to do when it came to contacting the rich and famous. Most celebrities, after all, employ well-paid publicists to handle such requests. Conversely, it is expected that one in my peon position would respect those established avenues of contact and restrict my advances to those proper channels.

To be sure, I always went through publicists when trying to arrange an interview or schedule a meeting with a particular famous person. Of course, when the publicist was a jerk and wouldn't return phone calls—or worse, would hang up on me—I didn't relent or restrict my efforts to the publicist track. If need be, I would contact everyone from the desired celebrity's neighbor to their gardener if those were my only options. In most cases, I would only relent when the individual I was trying to contact personally turned me down. Otherwise, I wasn't going to let anyone speak on behalf of the person I needed to get in touch with. As a result, some called me overzealous. But I've always maintained that persistence and determination are the ultimate equalizers in life.

By now, you might be wondering how my guest-booking strategies apply to your production aspirations, particularly if you're not even interested in selling a talk show.

My point—and I do have one—is that you can't go by the book, even this one, when it comes to trying to break into the business. You have to think outside the box, travel into uncharted territory, and consistently find new ways to make connections, pitch your work, and get noticed in a business that doesn't notice many.

In short, one of my frequently criticized "radical ideas" is that aspiring television producers should send a letter of introduction, if not an actual project pitch, to as many production companies as possible, particularly those owned and operated by film and television stars.

The majority of these production companies, understandably, produce only films for theatrical release. Then again, a production company is a production company. Sandra Bullock's business, Fortis Films, for example, ostensibly existed only to produce feature films. That was, of course, until she bucked the trend and helped launch George Lopez's popular self-titled sitcom. By the time *George Lopez* reached syndication, Bullock's Fortis Films had earned a reported $10 million from its involvement in the sitcom business.

It's an obvious long shot, but nobody knows which celebrity's production company will be the next to follow Sandra's lead and produce more original television programs, scripted or unscripted. Fortunately, there are myriad production companies out there who might be persuaded to dabble in a new medium if the idea is right and potentially profitable.

CELEBRITY PRODUCTION COMPANIES

Tim Allen
Boxing Cat Productions
11500 Hart Street
North Hollywood, CA 91605
Ph: (818) 765-4870
Fax: (818) 765-4975

Brad Grey
Plan B Entertainment
9150 Wilshire Boulevard, Ste. 350
Beverly Hills, CA 90210
Ph: (310) 275-6135

Tom Arnold
Clean Break Productions
14046 Aubrey Road
Beverly Hills, CA 90210
Ph: (818) 995-1221
Fax: (818) 995-0089

Alec Baldwin
El Dorado Pictures
725 Arizona Ave., Ste. 100
Santa Monica, CA 90401
Ph: (310) 458-4800
Fax: (310) 458-4802

Melanie Griffith &
Antonio Banderas
Green Moon Productions
3110 Main Street, Ste. 205
Santa Monica, CA 90405
Ph: (310) 450-6111

Drew Barrymore
Flower Films
9220 Sunset Blvd., Ste. 309
Los Angeles, CA 90063
Ph: (310) 285-0200
Fax: (310) 285-0827

Kim Basinger
Skyfish Productions
725 Arizona Ave., Ste. 100
Santa Monica, CA 90401
Ph: (310) 458-9002

Pierce Brosnan
Irish Dreamtime
2450 Broadway, Ste. E-5021
Santa Monica, CA 90404
Ph: (310) 449-3411

Continued...

CELEBRITY PRODUCTION COMPANIES— CONTINUED

Sandra Bullock
Fortis Films
8581 Santa Monica Blvd, Ste. 1
West Hollywood, CA 90069
Ph: (310) 659-4533
Fax: (310) 659-4373

Nicholas Cage
Saturn Films
9000 Sunset Blvd., #911
West Hollywood, CA 90069
Ph: (310) 887-0900

George Clooney
Smoke House
4000 Warner Blvd.
Bldg. 15
Burbank, CA 91522
Ph: (818) 954-4840

David Arquette &
Courteney Cox Arquette
Coquette Productions
8105 W. 3rd St.
West Hollywood, CA 90048
Ph: (323) 801-1000

Billy Crystal
Face Productions
335 N. Maple Dr., Ste. 135
Beverly Hills, CA 90210
Ph: (310) 285-2300
Fax: (310) 285-2386

Danny De Vito
Jersey Films
10351 Santa Monica Blvd, #200
Los Angeles, CA 90025
Ph: (310) 203-1000

Michael Douglas
Furthur Films

Gabriel Byrne
Plurabelle Films
10125 Washington Blvd., #205
Culver City, CA 90232
Ph: (310) 244-6782

Tia Carrere
Phoenician Films
8228 Sunset Blvd., Ste. 311
Los Angeles, CA 90046
Ph: (323) 848-3444

Sean Connery
Fountainbridge Films
8428 Melrose Place, Unit C
Los Angeles, CA 90069
Ph: (323) 782-1177

Tom Cruise
C/W Productions
5555 Melrose Ave.
Hollywood, CA 90038
Ph: (323) 956-8150
Fax: (323) 862-1250

John Cusack
New Crime Productions
555 Rose Ave.
Venice, CA 90291
Ph: (310) 396-2199

Robert De Niro
Tribeca Productions
375 Greenwich Street, 8th floor
New York, NY 10013
Ph: (212) 941-4040

Robert Duvall
Butchers Run Films

100 Universal City Plaza
Building 1320/4E
Universal City, CA 91608
Ph: (818) 777-6700
Fax: (818) 866-1278

Emilio Estevez
Estevez Productions
3000 W. Olympic Blvd
Building 5, Ste. 2215
Santa Monica, CA 90404
Ph: (818) 789-5766

Jodie Foster
Egg Pictures
5555 Melrose Ave
Jerry Lewis Building
Los Angeles, CA 90038
Ph: (323) 956-8400
Fax: (323) 862-1414

Mel Gibson
Icon Productions, Inc.
5555 Melrose Ave
Los Angeles, CA 90038
Ph: (323) 956-2100
Fax: (323) 862-2121

Tom Hanks
Playtone Productions
100 Universal City Plaza
Universal City, CA 91608
Ph: (818) 777-1000

Dustin Hoffman
Punch Productions
1926 Broadway, #305
New York, NY 10023
Ph: (212) 595-8800

Ron Howard
Imagine Entertainment

100 Universal City Plaza
Building 507, Ste. 2D
Universal City, CA 91608
Ph: (818) 777-7333

Mike Farrell
Farrell Minoff Productions
14011 Ventura Blvd., Ste. 401
Sherman Oaks, CA 91423
Ph: (310) 712-9510

Morgan Freeman
Revelations Entertainment
301 Arizona Ave., Ste. 303
Santa Monica, CA 90401
Ph: (310) 394-3131

Danny Glover
Carrie Productions
4444 Riverside Dr., Ste. 110
Burbank, CA 91505
Ph: (818) 567-3292

Goldie Hawn
Cherry Alley Productions
225 Arizona Ave., Ste. 350
Santa Monica, CA 90401
Ph: (310) 458-8886

Lauren Holly
Hollycould Productions
10202 W. Washington Blvd
Culver City, CA 90232
Ph: (310) 244-3314

Helen Hunt
Hunt-Tavel Productions

Continued...

CELEBRITY PRODUCTION COMPANIES— CONTINUED

9465 Wilshire Blvd., 7th Floor
Beverly Hills, CA 90212
Ph: (310) 858-2000
Fax: (310) 858-2020

Diane Keaton
Blue Relief
301 N. Canon Drive
Ste. 205
Beverly Hills, CA 90210
Ph: (310) 275-7900

Denis Leary
Apostle Pictures
The Ed Sullivan Theater
1697 Broadway, Ste. 906
New York, NY 10019
Ph: (212) 541-4323

David Letterman
Worldwide Pants Inc
1697 Broadway, Ste. 805
New York, NY 10019.
Ph: (212) 975-5300

Madonna
Maverick Films
331 N. Maple Drive
3rd Floor
Beverly Hills, CA 90210
Ph: (310) 276-6177

Penny Marshall
Parkway Productions
10202 W. Washington Blvd
Astaire 2210
Culver City, CA 90232
Ph: (310) 244-4040
Fax: (310) 244-0240

Demi Moore
Moving Pictures

10202 W. Washington Blvd.,
Astaire 2410
Culver City, CA 90232
Ph: (310) 244-3144

Martin Lawrence
You Go Boy Productions
10202 W. Washington Blvd
Hepburn East, 1st Floor
Culver City, CA 90232
Ph: (310) 244-6332

Jay Leno
Big Dog Productions, Inc.
P.O. Box 7855
Burbank CA 91510

Barry Levinson
Baltimore/Spring Creek Pictures
4000 Warner Blvd.
Burbank, CA 91522
Ph: (818) 954-1210

John Malkovich
Mr. Mudd
5225 Wilshire Blvd., Ste. 604
Los Angeles, CA 90036
Ph: (323) 932-5656

Bette Midler
All Girl Productions
c/o CBS Studio Center
4024 Radford Ave., Bung. #20
Studio City, CA 91604
Ph: (818) 655-6000

Eddie Murphy Productions
152 W. 57th Street 47th Floor

1453 Third St., Ste. 420
Santa Monica, CA 90401
Ph: (310) 576-0577

Nick Nolte
Kingsgate Films, Inc.
18954 W. Pico, 2nd Fl
Los Angeles, CA 90035
Ph: (310) 281-5880
Fax: (310) 281-2633

Edward James Olmos
Olmos Productions, Inc.
2020 Ave. of the Stars, Ste. 500
Century City, CA 90067
Ph: (310) 557-7010

Bill Paxton
American Entertainment Co.
5225 Wilshire Blvd. #615
Los Angeles, CA 90036
Ph: (323) 939-6746
Fax: (323) 939-6747

Julia Roberts
Red Om Films
145 W 57th St, 19th Floor
New York, NY 10019
Ph: (212) 243-2900

Alicia Silverstone
First Kiss Productions
468 North Camden Dr., Ste. 200
Beverly Hills, CA 90210
Ph: (310) 860-5611

Barbara Streisand
Barwood Films
330 W. 58th Street
New York, NY 10019
Ph: (212) 765-7191

New York, NY 10019
Ph: (212) 399-9900

Chris O'Donnell
George Street Pictures
3815 Hughes Ave. Ste. 3
Culver City, CA 90232
Ph: (310) 841-4361
Fax: (310) 204-6310

Bill Pullman
Big Town Productions
6201 Sunset Blvd., #80
Los Angeles, CA 90028
Ph: (323) 962-8099

Robert Redford
South Fork Pictures
1101 Montana Ave., Ste. B
Santa Monica, CA 90403
Ph: (310) 395-7779

Meg Ryan
Prufrock Pictures
335 N. Maple Drive, Ste. 315
Beverly Hills, CA 90210
Ph: (310) 285-2360

Ben Stiller
Red Hour Films
193 North Robertson Blvd.
Beverly Hills, CA 90211
Ph: (310) 289-2565
Fax: (310) 289-5988

Will Smith
Overbrook Entertainment
100 Universal City Plaza, Bldg. 6111
Universal City, CA 91608
Ph: (818) 777-2224
Fax: (818) 866-6206

Continued. . .

CELEBRITY PRODUCTION COMPANIES— CONTINUED

Jean-Claude Van Damme
Long Road Productions
1801 Avenue of the Stars
6th Floor
Los Angeles, CA 90067
Ph: (310) 535-6466

Sigourney Weaver
Goat Cay Productions
P.O. Box 38
New York, NY 10150
Ph: (212) 241-8293

Oprah Winfrey
Harpo Studios
1058 W. Washington Blvd
Chicago, IL 60607
Ph: (312) 591-9222

Jon Voight
Jon Voight Entertainment
1901 Ave. of the Stars
Ste. 605
Los Angeles, CA 90067
Ph: (310) 843-0223

Robin Williams
Blue Wolf Prods., Inc.
725 Arizona Ave., St. 202
Santa Monica, CA 90401
Ph: (310) 451-8890

Henry Winkler
Fair Dinkum Productions
2500 Broadway St., Bldg. E-5018
Santa Monica, CA 90404
Ph: (310) 586-8471
Fax: (310) 586-8469

Lily Tomlin once likened the maturity level of most television executives to that of the average kindergartener. If that's true, pursue your quest for reality television success by constantly remaining mindful of what classroom activity many kindergarteners enjoy most: show and tell.

Good producers are good storytellers. Bad producers fail to realize that they have to be good storytellers even before their project is green-lit. To gain a sure foothold in this highly competitive genre, you must capitalize on—or invent—every opportunity conceivable to deliver the best show-and-tell presentation of a proposed reality television series.

Some prefer to be selective about where they distribute their ideas, for fear of seeming "too desperate for attention or work." Those, however, with the best chances for success maturely and masterfully exploit every available avenue for both networking and becoming an acceptably ubiquitous presence. Until the ink on that first contract has fully dried, every day should be "show and tell" for those looking to sell a series and produce for reality television.

Chapter | six

Producing Reality

Despite common misperceptions, producers in reality television are just as important to the quality and outcome of unscripted programming as they are to its scripted counterpart. Like the storytellers behind dramatic and comedic television, reality producers often need to plot and point an entire season of "storylines" before network executives will so much as green-light a simple pilot. Naturally, this trend begs the obvious question: If reality television is so "real," how can a producer outline an entire season's worth of storylines and cliffhangers?

Understandably, television executives are reluctant to purchase projects without a clear trajectory of evolving storylines throughout an initial run of episodes. Consequently, once the go-ahead is given, the first goal of every savvy reality television producer is to find a cast inclined to facilitate the actions and outcomes his show needs to both execute the original vision and satisfy the executives who doled out buckets of money.

As we've already explored, reality television is only real to a limited extent. Beyond casting individuals who will nominally play themselves and communicate openly on camera—at least a majority of the time—without the aid of scripted dialogue, most other elements of the series are carefully planned to elicit specific reactions from the real people placed in these contrived situations.

For example, the bulk of verbal quarrels and physical encounters on reality television are legitimate. However, the producers and their casting wizards behind the scenes knowingly inspired such spats by strategically juxtaposing oil-and-water personalities within uncomfortably close quarters. Like setting off fireworks on the Fourth of July, once you have the proper materials, it doesn't require much effort to provoke colorful explosions.

Unless your project involves only a few individuals already cherry picked and approved by the network, you will likely require a full cast of individuals you have yet to have in the fold. Luckily, if you've already reached the point of preproduction, there's an excellent possibility that your production company can help set you up with an experienced casting producer.

The casting needs for each reality show differ, yet the genre regurgitates similar qualities (or flaws) in cast members:

Personality	Likeability
Docility	Intelligence
Attractiveness	Arrogance
Athleticism	Strong sex appeal
Sense of humor	Naiveté
Energy	Emotiveness

Although casting involves little more than interviewing potential subjects who otherwise have no background in television or the performing arts, a good casting director can skillfully project how particular individuals will behave or react in myriad situations on camera. A casting director who lands his or her finger on the pulse of a reality TV subject will provide you or other producers with valuable insight as storylines develop during production. Knowing, for example, who "the emotional one" is will help you figure out how to best utilize this individual cast member for the specific objective you might be trying to achieve with a particular segment or perhaps even a season-long storyline.

Essentially, any program's production calendar begins with casting. Most believe that casting is so integral to the outcome of a project that it demands more time and energy than any other aspect of production. Indeed, many unoriginal concepts for programming have flourished on the backs of exceptional cast members. However, just as many programs, if not more, have suffered due to poor casting. So if you're fortunate to find a casting producer who gets the overall vision of your brainchild and its objectives, then half the battle is already won.

Once your cast is in place, the most pressing of production responsibilities is selecting suitable locations for filming. Since most reality shows aren't exclusively confined to one sound stage or simple set, reality show producers often experience enormous headaches in terms of scouting production locations. Unfortunately, a good number of production novices typically worry the most about gaining permission, securing liability coverage, or even just getting the proper release forms signed.

On the other hand, an experienced producer knows that the selection process itself should be the hard part. In most cases, gaining consent and covering the technical aspects of remote shooting aren't as cumbersome as they initially seem. As a producer, your first objective is finding a locality that is conducive to your production objectives. For instance, if you plan to shoot your cast volunteering to work in a neighborhood restaurant, take more into account when scouting restaurants than just how much space the kitchen affords or the quality of lighting in the dining area. Instead, focus on the feel you get from the place. Chances are that what you feel and experience on location is exactly what viewers at home will also feel and experience. What's the atmosphere of the restaurant? How amiable and camera friendly are the staff who could also appear on air? There are many questions to ask and factors to consider when you're scouting locations. But as long as you can maintain the "overall mood" of your series, or even just this one particular episode, few other things are worth getting bent out of shape about.

PLANNING "UNPLANNED" TELEVISION

At the beginning of almost any reality TV show production, producers often get a little nervous just in light of how "unplanned" it all seems. Obviously, to a degree, reality shows are designed to create story arcs on the fly. As we've already said, however, the early stages of pitching and preproduction often demand that you plot out the major story points of a whole season. Although it's almost requisite to hold steadfast at least to an original vision, it's also vital to proceed without a totally rigid format. In other words, during the course of filming, certain characters might develop that add a little something extra, and unforeseen, to the project. What is important is to hold true to the overall story structure (beginning, middle, and end) that you sold to the network. In effect, you've only sold the frame to the portrait. You are still in charge of painting your masterpiece.

Although it varies from project to project, casting can take anywhere from two weeks to two months. Typically, preproduction—which involves assembling a team, scouting locations, and briefing your crew—takes considerably less time. The physical production phase itself, however, is a whole other story.

Some series film one episode per day. Others take weeks to crank out a single episode. The turnaround time is only important to the extent that your network or production company needs—or sometimes just wants—a finished product or sample episode. In general, it's best to find a happy medium between a rushed scheduled and a relaxed one. You don't want to sacrifice the quality of the product by cranking it out too fast. Of course, on the other hand, you don't want to drain the fresh spark from your cast (not to mention your likely constrained budget) by letting the energy of your show fizzle out from too many consecutive days of production.

PUTTING THE PIECES TOGETHER

Although most editing takes place as soon as the physical production wraps and the tapes come back to the edit bay, a popular trend today is to have shows airing while the tail end of the season is still being produced or edited. This allows for network and audience feedback to either emphasize or curtail certain storylines or characters for the rest of the season. Though this approach could ultimately work to the benefit of the series, producers should also be mindful of the problems it can present. Cast members, for example, who now see themselves on TV might begin acting differently on camera based on how they perceive themselves to appear. This is why many top producers demand that shows delivered to the network are held back from broadcast until production is complete.

An enormous advantage given to contemporary reality television producers is the advent of the story development department. Essentially, people who comprise the story development department watch the raw footage of your project as soon as the tape is ejected from the camera. From there, they scrutinize the various characters and conflicts as they emerge. Although you might also have a keen sense of interesting stories as they develop, the folks in this handy-dandy little department—usually two or three individuals either on location or back at the network or production company—sift through the tape to get a sense of what the final product needs. They look for strengths, weaknesses, and gaps. As a result, by the time production wraps, all necessary pieces for a complete and entertaining puzzle will be available in the edit bay. In short, they find what's most compelling and what promises to extend viewer interest and, consequently, the lifespan of the series.

On the surface, of course, it sounds as though the story development department is actually producing the show. In truth, they are merely an advisory body. Essentially, the department is a production aid that is used frequently, but not on every show. To be sure, producers generally welcome these departments because if the footage they return to the edit bay is pitiful, the network or production company will ordinarily place the blame squarely on that producer.

Nonetheless, whether you have a story development department or not, one helpful tip for avoiding gaps in storylines or ensuring that you get the character developments you need for a desired finish is to shoot hours of interviews with cast members and other show participants. Dubbed "testimonials," these interviews, either formal or on the fly, can prove veritable lifesavers to a particular episode or even an entire series. Even though there is no predetermined length of time allotted for each interview, producers typically have to continue prying until they get the comments or reactions they want. This is why such questions as, "Can you tell me about your day?" are never asked. Instead, producers incite particular reactions by asking more pointed questions. For example, "What was your reaction when Mabel slapped your boyfriend and insulted your mother?" In short, anything that elicits emotion, anger, humor, or suspense will make it to air. These sound bytes would be enormously difficult to come by without the assistance of testimonials.

The executive producer for the second season of *The Michael Essany Show* filmed extensive interviews with everyone on our show, including myself, at the conclusion of each day of production. Much of it was grueling, redundant, and sometimes personal. In the final analysis, though, I understood the need for this process and appreciated the purpose it served.

Arguably the biggest mistake producers make during production is failing to shoot enough testimonials. This is the easiest way possible to get an editor frustrated with you. From their perspective, testimonials simplify the often laborious challenge of expanding or shortening crucial segments, highlighting incidents not captured, recapping integral developments, clarifying particular happenings or exchanges, and, perhaps most important, providing an up-close and personal look at the stars of the program. Testimonials remove the need for narration, which can utterly kill the spontaneous feel that reality programming warrants.

Interviewing the cast, guest stars, and even production staff about anything and everything is enormously time consuming but the best possible tool for ensuring the desired outcome.

Production Basics for Reality TV

- Set a firm production schedule and meet all corresponding deadlines.
- Go into production with a complete vision for a finished product.
- Facilitate frequent communication among all levels of production to avoid confusion, frustration, and production-related errors.
- Formulate a backup plan for almost every aspect of production (e.g., if one shoot location falls through, what's the second best and most expedient option?) Don't wait for a disaster to think up a solution.
- Operate within budget at all times. Don't anticipate "cutting corners later."
- Treat production crew and cast with respect and understanding.
- Allow twice as much time for location shoots as you presently anticipate. And don't forget to include location info and directions (if necessary) on the call sheet.
- Realize that Murphy's Law and reality TV production go hand in hand. Expect things to go wrong. Respond positively and decisively when they do.
- From double-checking lists to ensuring the crew has enough tape and batteries, perform the "dummy check" frequently.

- Don't try to do everyone else's job. Trust those working with you to do their jobs just as you trust yourself to do yours.

- Invite the crew (and the cast, if not detrimental to the project) to share your vision. If they're only shooting tape without a clear understanding of what is to come of it all, they can't perform as well as you need and expect them to.

- Purchase aspirin. A *lot* of aspirin.

PRODUCTION BASICS

From staffing your project to utilizing the proper tools of the trade, the term *production basics* means something different to every producer. Based on the complexity and scope of the shoot, each reality show requires a dissimilar number of cameras. Many programs, however, use a combination of fixed and robotic cameras. In most cases, four to six cameras are sufficient. On the other hand, if you're producing a series on the scale of *The Amazing Race*, you could be dealing with dozens of cameras and a comparable number of crew members.

Though shows like *Survivor*, *The Amazing Race*, and *Big Brother* necessitate an enormous number of cameras and audio sources, many programs are filmed in a "run-and-gun" shooting style. Much of the time, in fact, *The Michael Essany Show* was shot in this style. Essentially, run-and-gun shooting means programming is filmed with handheld cameras—usually no more than two—that are rarely if ever affixed to a tripod. The coverage plan is based solely on keeping the spontaneous action in frame. In almost all cases, a run-and-gun crew is simply one camera operator and an audio engineer.

Although the video component of production seems paramount at all times, recording audio is actually significantly more complicated than video on reality shows, particularly if a sizable cast is involved. Incredibly, most professional digital or Beta cameras have only two clean audio inputs. Naturally, this creates the need for a separate audio receiver when more than two people are featured on screen. When there are a multitude of subjects, the audio engineer is in charge of miking everyone and combining the feeds into one centralized recorder that in most cases can accommodate up to 64 separate channels or audio tracks.

For an audio engineer, separating the tracks into individual channels is the easy part. Troubleshooting, however, is infinitely more complicated. With video, for instance, one can easily establish a bank of television monitors and quickly detect upon first glance a signal error or video feed interruption. With audio, each channel has to be meticulously listened to individually to detect a problem. Since every wireless mic operates at its own radio frequency, interference can result from one of any localized transmission blockages. Consequently, if you have 12 audio inputs, the audio engineer must isolate each channel while visually monitoring the mic's corresponding subject's movement and sound. This is the only way to correct a signal or transmission problem, discover a weak or faulty battery, or reposition a mic that might otherwise be rubbing against one's clothing.

If time is limited, however, and shooting must begin without an adequate opportunity to remedy a wireless microphone transmission, a boom microphone could be used as a suitable alternative. In essence, a boom mic is a special shotgun mic with a narrow pickup pattern, so it will work farther away than a conventional mic. It's affixed to a retractable pole that a sound man hoists above a single subject or group of individuals. At all times, the boom mic remains out of frame, usually two to three feet above the cast's heads. Although most reality programs utilize both lavaliere (wireless lapel) mics and boom mics, for the cleanest possible audio, boom mics should only be used in situations when wireless mics simply cannot be attached to their subjects (for example, four barely dressed friends playing volleyball on the beach).

Of course, though the audio and visual aspects of physical production are enormously important to the viability of a series, just as critical to the outcome is the rapport among producers and participants, not to mention the symbiotic relationship between producers and production crew.

On every reality series, relationship dynamics quickly emerge among show producers, cast, and crew and then evolve over the duration of production. Skilled producers not only realize the value of these relationships, they also come to depend on them to achieve a successful product. For reality show super-producers like Mark Burnett, producing is a collaborative process: "A good producer realizes he must collaborate with his customer—the network—whether he wants to or not." Having a common vision realized is the goal.

"But because everyone in television has an independent mind, you want to take the best ideas from every creative source involved and avoid micromanaging the project as though it's exclusively your own," Burnett advises.

Apart from the network's relationship with the producer, a more complex and frequent interaction takes place between the cast and production crews. This, too, can pose difficult problems, specifically if camera crews grow too friendly with a particular cast member. On some programs, like *Survivor*, camera crews are routinely swapped to cover different tribes so that crew members don't become too friendly with certain participants. The reason, of course, is that even the most faint and delicate of factors can influence the behavior of cast members. The camera and sound crews are expected to be an almost invisible, nonexistent presence. Indeed, the more "present" and friendly the crew gets to be with the cast, the more likely it is that cast members will ham it up to the cameras and, consequently, remove the fly-on-the-wall voyeuristic element of production.

After all, the goal of reality programming is to capture the relationships among people who, to the furthest extent possible, will behave naturally, as though there are no cameras in range. Professional distance should be consistently imposed or enforced to guard against any participants growing too comfortable with the crew or beginning to think that either the crew loves them or hates them. Both scenarios could be detrimental to the show. Now, on the other hand, if you examine what constitutes a healthy relationship between cast members and producers, a close relationship is absolutely vital. Why? Because a major responsibility of producers is to facilitate a production atmosphere that makes cast members feel relaxed and willing to communicate openly on camera—as though no camera exists at all.

Needless to say, learning to facilitate—or prevent—relationships among individuals on a reality show set is key to executing the desired vision for a project. Of course, unlike using the proper tools of the trade (cameras, microphones, etc.) in sensible complements that represent the more conspicuous aspects of reality television production, the relationship dynamics among cast members, producers, and crew represent the more latent components of this production genre. But as any newcomer to the industry will readily learn, a multitude of other equally latent production factors should—or must—be considered during production. From managing conflicts on set to addressing the inherent ethical dilemmas of reality television production, producers have much, much more to concern themselves with than just the lights, cameras, and action.

Chapter | seven

Where Ethics and Reality Collide

In early 2002, when I signed with E! Entertainment Television to launch *The Michael Essany Show*, the concept of reality TV as it is understood today was still very much in its infancy. No one knew exactly how reality television would eventually play out. At the time, of course, I was too much concerned with the future of my own series to lose sleep over the entire genre of reality programming.

For several months prior to and after the series premiere, appearing on morning talk-radio programs in major markets around the country became a rewarding but exhausting part of my daily routine. As expected, some of the on-air personalities were hyperactive, sarcastic, and eager to unload their arsenal of tacky, juvenile humor. But others consistently made the grind considerably more enjoyable.

At the top of that very short list was Danny Bonaduce, the former child actor and star of *The Partridge Family* who became known as an adult for his tumultuous personal life. Without a doubt his morning show in L.A. was absolutely electric. And he was as nice to me as he was to my show. Danny plugged it constantly, in fact. Whether he was really a fan or just trying to help a young guy get started, I'll never know. No matter the reason, Danny boosted our Pacific ratings, and the suits at E! noticed.

As I recall, one morning I found myself on the air with Danny chatting about the occasionally invasive rigors of filming a reality television show. In no uncertain terms he claimed that he would never subject himself to an omnipresent reality lens. I had not reflected on those words, of course, until VH1 premiered *Breaking Bonaduce*.

The show, which chronicles Danny's failing marriage, substance abuse, and psychological turmoil, features Bonaduce and his now ex-wife undergoing counseling from a Dr. Phil wannabe whose face has seen more brushes of vanity than the *Mona Lisa*.

As Bonaduce has even admitted himself, *Breaking Bonaduce* provides an unsettling look at a man with unsettling problems. As a reviewer for *Variety* wrote, "... It's hard to imagine a shower long enough to wash away the experience of simply viewing the show, much less having produced, programmed, or participated in it."

To date, the public has largely responded to *Breaking Bonaduce* with undeniable interest and impunity. My reaction has long remained one of deep concern. Having experienced the reality of reality television, I know how producers readily manipulate reality for the sake of ratings. Some, in fact, have begun to wonder when reality TV will see its first on-air casualty. Most expect a stunt on *Fear Factor* to go horrifically awry. I don't. After all, such a fiasco could provoke a costly lawsuit, and networks won't take a slapdash risk. A person perishing at the hands of his own demons, on the other hand, would be much more cost-effective to document and present fewer liabilities in production.

Although there is no telling what will ultimately happen with Danny Bonaduce—a veritable paradox of both strength and weakness—I suppose it's this very element of uncertainty that provides the lure of the series and the goal of production. Of course, the greater consequence is the precedent *Breaking Bonaduce* sets for future reality programming.

With audiences continuing to display a voracious appetite for a voyeuristic exploitation of human frailties, many producers have similarly continued to grow devoid of basic compassion and respect for the well-being and privacy of reality television subjects. Although reality television offers great potential to entertain and inspire millions, in the last few years this genre has traveled down the lowest and most perilous of roads. And, in most cases, it's the producers who are driving.

WALKING THE REALITY TV PLANK

A friend of mine who once executive-produced a series for A&E revealed to me some time ago that for every one star of reality television seen crying on screen, there are usually two more production staff bawling just as hard, if not harder, off camera. To be sure, most of the time it isn't a producer. Producers are the ones, after all, doing everything imaginable to elicit these emotive responses from their reality subjects.

In recent years, A&E has drawn both unparalleled praise and unrivaled criticism for its admittedly captivating original series entitled *Intervention*. Each episode chronicles a different participant afflicted by an addiction to drugs, alcohol, and almost any other substance or behavior imaginable. Although the subjects are initially told that they are being filmed for a documentary about addictions, the footage is actually shot as a prelude to an intervention premeditated by family or friends.

Although in one sense *Intervention* provides a tremendous service by offering an amazing and startling examination of how addictions destroy lives, it is also based on misleading the individuals who have almost unimaginable emotional and psychological afflictions. No matter how gripping the episode, the element of deception is difficult for many to put aside while watching this enormously popular series.

To be sure, in many instances the program succeeds in helping a troubled individual find treatment and comfort on the road to recovery. Other times, however, happy endings are markedly more elusive.

But because both negatives and positives are generated by the series, *Intervention* has polarized audiences, particularly after a 2007 episode that wholly illustrated the perilous types of ethical quandaries in which a producer can find himself during the production of a reality TV series.

The episode in question featured a woman with a severe alcohol addiction driving while visibly intoxicated. The on-site producers did little (according, at least, to the footage broadcast) to prevent a potentially fatal situation other than to offer a ride. She refused, of course, and proceeded to leave, although not without a final pick-me-up drink from an open bottle of vodka. Within moments, the woman had tottered to her Pontiac Sunfire and drove off—as expected, with the film crew eagerly tagging close behind to capture their subject struggling to operate her vehicle.

While some viewers later claimed that the producers of this episode should be held accountable or guilty for allowing this fragile individual to drive while under the debilitating influence of alcohol, in the eyes of the law, producers, like witnesses, are under no legal obligation to stop reckless behavior.

Ironically, the regrettable incident was powerfully reminiscent of the episode of *Breaking Bonaduce* where an intoxicated Danny Bonaduce took his camera crew for a drive, proposing that a car crash would make for great television. Although many producers are unthinkingly willing to take such foolish risks for the sake of exalted ratings, some have found themselves inactive eyewitnesses to dangerous, illegal, and potentially life-threatening behavior without cogently reacting to hinder or halt the conduct.

These types of rare yet increasingly common situations are not only beginning to put the lives of reality TV subjects and producers in jeopardy, they are also setting horrendous examples for what are acceptable ratings ploys.

At some point in the career of every reality show producer, ethics will square off against ratings during the course of production. And although many producers have seemingly crossed the line of what is morally acceptable television content, the choice to stop tape always remains evenly on the producer's shoulders.

BAPTISM BY FIRE

Unfortunately, no production class, reality TV seminar, or how-to guide can ever fully prepare a producer for dealing with these types of situations. However, one of the most important lessons to learn for producers new to the industry is to be wary of the ways in which the presence of a video crew can seemingly diminish the serious peril of some real-life situations.

It is quite common, in fact, for a producer to worry *less* about the well-being of a reality TV subject when a camera crew is present rather than if the producer was alone with the subject being chronicled. The presence of cameras can easily lend a misleading aura of protection that is strictly a disingenuous illusion. It also fosters an incredibly dangerous sense of false confidence to everyone involved. For many producers, this is where the line between fantasy and reality blurs. Reality television in its purest form, like *Intervention*, might still seem like just another project for producers who, over time, come to carelessly view reality subjects in the same light as trained, professional actors doing their jobs to spike ratings.

Though it's certainly much easier said than done, producers must consistently be mindful of the human elements at stake in the production of reality television. It's so easy to become engrossed in the real-life movie unfolding before the lens that one could effortlessly forget that the drama taking place isn't born of a script. Instead, real people in highly vulnerable emotional situations are revealing legitimate frailties that demand more attention from producers than whether or not their painful meltdown is transpiring in frame.

Since the modern reality TV boom apparently consumed the globe overnight, many believe, and with truly compelling arguments, that countless personal tragedies have transpired as a result of experiences in front of or behind the scenes of a reality television series.

Frequently referred to as the first U.S. casualty of reality TV, 23-year-old Najai Turpin sustained a fatal self-inflicted gunshot wound after losing a critical boxing match on *The Contender*, a sports reality series produced by Sylvester Stallone.

A few years earlier, 34-year-old Sinisa Savija killed himself by jumping beneath a moving train after getting booted off a Swedish reality series called *Expedition: Robinson*. Savija's widow said her late husband was struggling to cope with his nationally broadcast humiliation.

Thirty-five-year-old Cheryl Kosewicz, a deputy district attorney in Reno, Nevada, took her life in the summer of 2007 after being eliminated from the now-cancelled CBS reality series *Pirate Master*. In a MySpace message she wrote just prior to her death, Cheryl revealed the strain that her reality television stint had placed on her relationship with her longtime boyfriend, who had also recently committed suicide.

An equally tragic fate befell 17-year-old May Carina Stephenson, who hung herself after four months of shooting *The Colony* in Australia. Having revealed herself as a lesbian on the popular reality series, Stephenson reportedly became withdrawn while in a glaring and invasive national spotlight.

Although countless deaths have been attributed, directly or indirectly, to involvement in reality television, the truth remains that it's not the medium itself but those who produce it that actually create the emotionally and psychologically hazardous environments conducive to suicide or, even more common, post-production nervous breakdowns.

THE ETHICS CHECKLIST

Without exception, the five most vital ethical objectives for all reality television producers are as follows:

1. Remember that reality TV subjects, in most cases, are not trained professional performers and should be treated equitably, gently, and compassionately.

2. A solid, mature psychological state for potential cast members should be of equal or greater importance than any other ancillary criteria when selecting series participants.

3. At all times trust between producer and cast member must be firmly established and entrenched.

4. Every conceivable rational step must be taken to help prime and prepare participants for anything and everything that may and probably will happen to them—before, during, and especially after the show.

5. Though incredibly controversial and enormously unpopular with many television networks and production companies, a skilled and ethically conscious producer does little, if anything, to synthetically alter how one appears on the program, either in mind, body, or spirit. If a cast member has to be tweaked in the edit bay, it's no one but the producer's fault for not finding the right participant, preparing interesting scenarios, or solving this critical problem before wrapping production.

Producers who follow these guidelines and, of course, still deliver a timely product of quality that meets client expectations are the gold standard in show business. Needless to say, there are also producers of the gold-plated variety that loosely follow similar guidelines but for different reasons altogether.

To this other breed of ubiquitous producer, ethical concerns are incidental. In such instances, ethical dilemmas are usually avoided mostly as the result of producers protecting themselves from the myriad liabilities born of exploiting, endangering, or embarrassing others. Nonetheless, all calibers of producer, from gold to rust, almost universally guard against the three most common threats to the survival of their projects, not to mention their careers:

- *Violation of privacy.* Innumerable television producers have found themselves in hot water after supposedly violating the privacy of others. From failing to secure personal and location release forms to prying beyond acceptable boundaries of personal inquiry and exploration, producers must be careful at all times to not cross any line that the show's participants would adamantly oppose.

- *Defamation of character.* Reality television, to a lesser degree, resembles the essential nature of tabloid journalism. That is, an entire program or series can be built around little more than rumor and insinuation rather than fact and truth. However, when potentially slanderous mistruths are spoken in specific reference to others, producers must take great care to suspend their gluttonous thirst for compelling sound bytes in return for avoiding potential legal action from those whose reputations were wrongfully sullied. Without question, professional accountability on the part of producers and their staff is a fundamental component of reality television production.

- *Encouragement of unlawful behavior.* Encouraging, promoting an environment for, or capturing illegal activities on film are never good ideas, no matter the ideal dramatic circumstances. What might at first appear a sure-fire opportunity for ratings gold could very rapidly deteriorate into a potentially tragic or destructive outcome that could forever impact the lives and careers of others, including, to say the least, your own.

PUSHING AND SHOVING THE LIMITS

It's certainly no exaggeration, then, to state that reality television pushes almost every limit conceivable to provide a steady stream of drama. Accordingly, producers are under constant barrage from network superiors to create and implement innovative ways to heighten the compelling elements of established or emerging reality programs. As an understandable but unfortunate consequence of such growing pressure, the invaluable but difficult-to-capture production gem that is creativity is frequently overlooked in favor of a much easier artifice used to enhance reality TV excitement: deception.

Without a doubt, the almost dictatorial network demands for reality TV drama seriously influence the subsequent ethical standards upheld or ignored by producers. With conflict absolutely essential to production, many producers will resort to roughly anything to obtain it. Beyond, of course, casting a potentially explosive and incongruent blend of cast members, producers have been known to severely alter the otherwise "natural" living conditions of the cast to help facilitate drama. And when that doesn't work and all else seems to fail, a good number of producers are certainly not above making alcohol readily available on the set.

Hang around the business long enough and you're bound to hear at least one producer refer to his or her set as "the lab." No medical research is conducted on reality television, yet human experiments take place all the time. And unlike human guinea pigs in a legitimate medical laboratory who must provide their wholly informed consent, the often unwitting souls who find themselves in the reality TV lab have usually given only a partially informed consent. That is, they sign a release form allowing producers to do whatever they want so long as it remains within the law. But, as many have discovered the hard way, that's an awful lot of leeway.

Almost certainly, no network or production company will ever tweak their standard release forms purely for liability purposes. Nonetheless, some producers—presumably those with a conscience—have begun instituting their own production doctrine by which all subordinate staffers must abide. Such guidelines, for example, regularly speak to the circumstances in which the cameras must stop rolling. The implication, of course, is that just because the footage ostensibly serves to entertain, the responsibility to treat individuals respectfully is not eliminated.

Not surprisingly, it's difficult to gauge whether these scant on-set ethical decrees have proven effective. But they have almost certainly helped to at least foster a greater awareness of the human element of reality television production. By thoughtfully and vigilantly outlining what is and isn't acceptable conduct for production staff, these ethical doctrines are yet another tool for ensuring the well-being of participants who might legitimately have no idea what they have gotten themselves into.

By now, perhaps, you could easily infer from such repeated encouragement for the proper treatment of reality stars that I view such program subjects as "victims waiting to happen." Naturally, I understand that a great many, if not the majority of, reality show cast members know *exactly* what they're getting themselves into. After all, by today, much of the danger associated with reality television stardom or failure is widely known. Still, hundreds of thousands of charismatic, intrepid individuals submit their audition tapes to reality shows every year, all in search of fame, fortune, or the pure adrenalin that comes from such an incredible experience.

Although the ratio of those who survive reality TV unscathed compared to those who don't might suggest that my harsh admonitions about reality TV are grossly exaggerated, at some point or another in almost every life, we either bite off more than we can chew, attempt a feat we think we can conquer but can't, or agree to something that ultimately turns out to be unlike anything we had expected. So for those to whom reality TV is a similar experience, we must be careful to guard against any damage beyond that which we couldn't control from the get-go.

On more than one occasion during production of *The Michael Essany Show*, I butted heads with producers who had employed a wildly popular production technique known as "Frankenbyting," or stringing together unrelated audio clips to produce originally unintended but more "entertaining" dialogue. Undeniably, mixing and matching words is a commonly employed method of delivering the drama, conflict, and intrigue producers desperately want. Skilled editors who can pull off this difficult but desirable technique are in big demand and earn even bigger bucks for their deceptive editing skills.

According to Daniel Shriver, a story producer for *Big Brother 2*, it would seem that Frankenbyting is quickly becoming a prerequisite talent for reality TV editors.

"There's a real art to it," says Shriver. "Because of the inflection of the voice, some things just don't cut together, so you can't just look at a transcript. You actually have to watch tapes, cut them together, and see how they work."

Even though many arguments directed toward reality television's frequent ethical peccadilloes are easily dismissed as extreme or impractical, few can defend the practice of creating artificial Frankenbyting sentences with a straight face. Yet it's just one of many production quandaries that raise ethical questions for reality television producers when they're trying to deliver the goods and still remain good people.

Like death, taxes, and William Shatner, some things in life are simply unavoidable. But for novice producers who believe that reality television and humiliating deception are an unavoidable coupling for superlative programming, nothing could be further from the truth.

I realize, however, that for some programs, the crux of the entire series is deception. Yet even when deception is "mandatory" for the project at hand, the ways in which such deceptions are revealed, flaunted, or forced on reality subjects is what really makes this integral element of deception humiliating and harmful. Again, it isn't the concept of the program or the reality genre itself that does the damage. It's the producers who routinely fail to value human emotion and psychological frailties and who push the boundaries of what is tolerable ethical conduct.

But before you freak out and regret not having declared behavioral psychology as a second major, you're in luck. Depending on the nature of the project, many production companies and networks have begun budgeting for an on-set psychologist during production. This also bodes well for potentially unstable contestants without the means or desire to seek needed counseling after their reality show participation ends. Since most emotional and psychological breakdowns occur in the immediate hours and days after leaving these shows, an on-set psychologist can offer this vital post-production counseling.

Unfortunately, the presence of a "psychological protector" occasionally gives producers the wrong idea. In effect, psychologists aren't brought in to clean up the fallout from a producer doing whatever he or she wants to the cast and crew. Instead, the on-set psychologist observes physical production and regularly speaks with cast members. For an increasing number of programs, psychologists are becoming a veritable reality show safety net.

MEETING MR. MURPHY

Sooner or later, all reality television producers grow intimately acquainted with Murphy's Law. That is, in terms of potential ethical dilemmas, anything that could go wrong usually does and on many different occasions. The producers in charge, though, will ultimately have difficult choices to make. And, sadly, many side with their ethically suspect options only to please the networks for which they work. To be fair, many producers have been fired—or "reassigned"—for trying too hard to protect the talent and, consequently, failing to deliver every square inch of dramatic footage possible. On the other hand, working to remove a potential ethical disaster and, as a result, spare the network or production company expensive litigation, public embarrassment, or the collapse of a project could also draw a considerably more favorable network response. But at the end of the day such choices lie with each individual producer. Hopefully, with time, all will recognize the immense value of refusing to allow reality television to thrive as a callous medium that exists almost at the exclusive expense of others. Taking a higher road in reality television production will ultimately do a greater service to the genre and the thousands of people affiliated with it than any one project you could ever produce.

Nonetheless, whether it's establishing an ethical code of conduct, carefully screening potentially unstable cast members, or even orchestrating the on-set services of a professional psychologist, contrary to popular belief there are many bulwarks that can be applied to help cushion the inevitable impact that results when ethics and reality collide.

Chapter | eight

The Ugly Reality

According to folklore, a "deal with the devil" is understood as a pact between an ordinary person and Satan himself. In exchange for one's soul, the devil provides a form of diabolical nepotism, usually evidenced by newfound power or wealth.

For most of my life, I had virtually no conception of what the contract proposed by the devil might actually look like. That was, of course, until I saw the performance contract offered to participants on *American Idol*.

The notoriously restrictive agreement has rarely been seen by anyone not directly involved with the show's production. My first reaction to this aggressively binding document led me to believe that even Satan himself would likely feel sorry for the signatories. When it comes to flagrant examples of a performance agreement stepping beyond what may be considered ethically acceptable, the *AI* contract is truly in a league of its own.

According to an attorney with whom I reviewed the document, "The contract is about as one-sided as they come. When you sign the agreement, you give away the whole store. And the producers are essentially free to do whatever they wish with you or *to* you. It's actually very dangerous."

Of course, the lucky few who manage to receive this holy grail of reality television are typically so overjoyed that they sign on the dotted line, completely oblivious to the rights they've unknowingly tossed—including the right to protect themselves from being embarrassed on national television. The *AI* contract, in fact, specifically refers to public humiliation and embarrassment as a potential outcome for which signatories will not hold Fox or *American Idol* accountable or responsible for any subsequent damages.

THE DANGEROUS DOTTED LINE

In the entertainment business, you're not going to produce, write for, or appear on any program without first signing *something*—a standard release, production agreement, performance contract, or the like. And since most aspiring producers and performers work so diligently to secure that first *real* contract, almost anything seems worth signing initially, even if it's a deal with ... well, you know who.

Regrettably, since enough "innocent" reality television participants and producers have found themselves victims of the genre, the nature of Hollywood negotiations is straying from old-school practices and blending with the mainstream trend. In other words, it's difficult to find a smart producer in Los Angeles today who doesn't seek legal counsel before deciding which flavor to select for his triple-shot, caffeine-free, low-fat, grande frappuccino. Although the industry standard largely remains that every producer and performer should at all times be signed with a reputable talent agent, a skilled entertainment or copyright attorney is ultimately the best representation to employ during contract talks. A bumper sticker puts it best: "Agents save careers. Lawyers save asses."

In early 2002, a friend of mine who worked on *Access Hollywood* was offered a contract by Sony Pictures to produce three new game shows to be filmed on the lot. He let his agent from CAA negotiate the deal from start to finish. Despite the established agent's "experience," he misunderstood the language of one contractual provision on exclusivity. When his client began consulting work outside his contractual game show responsibilities, Sony fired him from his multimillion-dollar deal. And it was all because of a simple misunderstanding that an agent is exponentially more inclined to make than an attorney.

When I received my 36-page contractual offer from E! Entertainment Television, my impatient heart said, "Sign it now, read it later" while my rational brain said, "Don't even open the damn envelope without an attorney present." Ultimately, my instincts sided with my brain and I was able to negotiate knowledgably with the network executives. Unfortunately, some contracts—like the standard *American Idol* deal—aren't so conducive to "tweaking." In fact, they're completely nonnegotiable. If you want to be on *American Idol*, you have to sign the agreement as is, just like everyone else does. And because it's such a hugely popular series, the producers behind the program can get away with doing this, whereas most others could not. Of course, that certainly doesn't stop others from trying.

Indeed, every conceivable variety of production or performance agreement is out there *somewhere*. If you're really serious about making it in reality television, sooner or later you'll need to sign one. And even though performers are the most obvious victims of all-powerful and all-controlling contracts, that doesn't mean producers can't be victims too. Most of the time, however, it's the *lack* of a contract and not the existence of one that facilitates the biggest professional calamities for producers, specifically as they pertain to plagiarized intellectual property.

FEAR FACTOR

Several years ago, during an interview with the self-proclaimed pioneer of late-night talk, Steve Allen, the first host of *The Tonight Show* observed that one hasn't truly succeeded in show business until one has had at least one really good idea brazenly usurped by an "individual of lesser talents." Allen's perspective clearly belongs to one of two very different schools of thought regarding the value of one's intellectual property and the importance of protecting it.

The first maintains that no unsecured idea should be risked on the open market. That is to say, if you have a script or even a well-developed concept for a television series, conceal the idea from everyone until it is copyrighted—a process we'll explore in a bit. Every single day in Hollywood—and this is not an exaggeration— "producer pickpockets" steal and claim other people's ideas. Even if there are particular individuals you believe would be trustworthy keepers of your intellectual property, it simply isn't worth the risk to share it with them.

Sometimes, however, producers don't even recognize the inherent danger of sharing ideas because they are so wholly consumed (or obsessed) by their endeavor that they fail to keep in the forefront of their minds that show business is far more about the business than it is about the show. In Hollywood, all business is big business. And there are plenty of unscrupulous producers who will claim your work as their own if given the right opportunity.

During an interview several years ago with film director Harold Ramis, the former *Ghostbusters* star talked about the lengths to which one faux screenwriter went to get "his" idea made into a feature film. "I came into the office one morning," Ramis recalled," and there was a pretty package wrapped like a Christmas present on top of my desk. When I opened it, there was a screenplay inside with a note attached urging me to make this guy's movie. But the name on the note didn't match the name on the script.

"So I looked up the guy who *did* write the script, and guess what? He didn't send it to me."

Unfortunately, not every concept crook is caught red-handed. This is precisely why sticklers for borderline-paranoid idea protection urge anyone with a viable television or film project to copyright their intellectual property before distributing it to anyone or showcasing it anywhere.

Intellectual property, or IP as it is recognized in law, encompasses the ownership entitlements to written or conceptualized ideas, recorded media, and the like. Those who hold such entitlements possess exclusive rights to the subject matter, which is their "intellectual property." Ideas in and of themselves cannot be protected, but the expression of an idea in the form of a tangible product, or even a name for the product, *can* be.

According to well-defined practices and procedures, most legal experts agree on the initial steps one can and should take to guard their ideas from plagiarists. Collectively, these helpful strategies could be appropriately labeled the Ten Commandments of Intellectual Property.

The Ten Commandments of Intellectual Property

1. *Use nondisclosures.* If you have a time-sensitive project that could potentially sell before the idea is copyrighted, it is possible to pitch your work under a cloak of secrecy. An increasingly popular and common tool for such an arrangement is made possible through a nondisclosure agreement (NDA). The contractual equivalent of the "Cone of Silence" from *Get Smart,* an NDA precludes those who will hear your idea from sharing or disseminating any sensitive information to which they are made privy. Because a violation of this trust is tantamount to a breach of contract, nondisclosure forms are very effective; blank forms can be easily downloaded from the Internet and personalized, in most cases without any further legal assistance.

2. *Obtain legal protection.* Although NDAs are helpful, they can be insufficient under certain circumstances. Eventually, your idea could require legal protection to be safeguarded to the fullest extent possible. Fortunately, intellectual property laws vary to accommodate different forms of subject matter. In the entertainment business, however, the *copyright* is what most commonly applies to intellectual property manifested in movies, music, and television. In most cases, a copyright holder possesses the exclusive control of his or her works for a period spanning somewhere between 10 and 30 years. It's a process that begins by contacting the U.S. Office of Copyrights (www.loc.gov/copyright). If nothing more, a copyright proves that you possessed the idea for a particular project by a certain point in time. To be sure, a copyright can't prevent your work from being stolen, but if it is, you will at least have an opportunity for recourse. By demonstrating that the idea was originally yours, you can seek and obtain proper credit and potentially vast financial compensation, particularly if your idea proved enormously profitable for someone else.

3. *Do your homework.* Although an attorney should always be consulted prior to negotiating or signing any contract, there are times when consultation is a needless expense. Simply brushing up on a few books relevant to intellectual property will help you identify red flags, recognize situations and people to avoid, and uncover useful ways to protect your work until you're ready or able to copyright it.

4. *Don't get ahead of yourself.* Just because you've done your homework doesn't mean you're ready for the exam. When it comes time for contract talks, invest in prudent legal counsel. Not only will this arrangement help secure the deal you want, you will also benefit enormously from the increased knowledge that results from working with a legal expert.

Continued...

5. *Play fair.* Many producers quickly grow frustrated by having their work plagiarized or discovering that they cannot have their IP copyrighted for one reason or another. In response, many opt to "fight fire with fire," so to speak, and consequently sully their own good names. However, just because someone won't respect your work does not mean that you shouldn't respect theirs.

6. *Copyrighting is the beginning, not the end.* Once your idea is copyrighted or trademarked, the work is not done. Many mistakenly assume that if their idea survived the legal gauntlet that is the copyrighting process, it will thrive and sell in the marketplace with very little effort. How anyone reaches this illogical conclusion is beyond me, but it happens time and time again. Similarly, just because an idea is copyrighted does not mean you can now afford to be less than circumspect with the distribution of your project idea, materials, and presentations. Ideas can always be stolen and modified to appear different but still similar enough to weaken your brand if the knock-off is sold first.

7. *Flaunt it.* Television executives, potential investors, performers, producers, and almost anyone else established in the industry will take your idea more seriously if you make it patently clear that your idea is a copyrighted one. This emphasis coupled with a comprehensive, entertaining pitch exponentially increases your chances of selling a project, particularly since it bears little risk of proving fraudulent or plagiarized months later.

8. *Record your activities.* Start a journal with a collection of your ideas, graphs, charts, progress reports, drawings, findings, and copious dictations of your idea's birth and subsequent development. Have the book signed, notarized, witnessed—essentially whatever it takes—to maintain a serious running account of your project development. Though not as effective as a copyright or patent, this approach is faster and cheaper and provides compelling evidence of your ownership of an idea.

9. *Don't make assumptions.* Let's say you develop an idea for a reality show about training cows to cook Chinese food. Sounds ridiculous, right? But if 10 years from now science finds a way to convert cows into Chinese culinary experts, your show will be on the cutting edge of mainstream television. The point, of course, is that any original idea warrants protection, whether you intend to capitalize on it or not.

10. *Have faith, prudence, and patience.* You probably know by know, albeit grudgingly so, that success doesn't happen overnight. Moreover, if you've reached the stage where you have a viable concept for broadcast television, it's important to hold tight to your faith as you endure the lengthy process of protecting your idea to producing it for profit. It takes considerable time and resources to license a patent or obtain a copyright. For the time being, consistently and stealthily build on your idea. Sooner or later, you'll be ready to showcase it to the world.

After such a compelling and comprehensive argument in favor of taking every precaution imaginable to protect one's intellectual property, it might be quite difficult to mount an equally compelling argument for the second school of thought alluded to earlier, one that harks back to the mentality of Steve Allen. It's a perspective that holds that ideas are bound to be stolen and you can't afford to slow an aggressive campaign just to avoid what could very well happen anyway.

As a major proponent of pursuing success with more faith than fear, I never advise aspiring producers to restrict their exposure in any capacity. Exposure and experience are the collective lifeblood of new producers. If you've really got the goods, you'll hopefully have more than one decent show idea in your career. Just make sure you *have* a career. The best way to ensure your foothold in the field is to disseminate your work and prove to anyone who will listen that you have what it takes to conceptualize television projects and then produce them brilliantly. Eventually, if you convince enough people of your talents, you'll have a way in. Ideas can be stolen; genuine talent and experience cannot. In the end, these are the most integral components of a long, successful career.

To be sure, this approach only endorses more liberal risk taking as it pertains to the distribution of your intellectual property. In no way does the second school of thought differ from the first in its subscription to the value of legal counsel when necessary. By no means should any contract be entered into without adequate consultation from a legal expert. Nor should any reasonable measure to protect your IP—such as the use of nondisclosure agreements—be shunned where legitimately applicable.

Ironically enough, the increasing prevalence of attorneys patrolling the board rooms of networks and production companies provides yet another significant argument *against* excessive legal measures to secure your IP. If someone steals your idea, for instance, it will likely require more money than you have to spend to convince a judge that you, the new guy in town, got screwed, particularly since false claims litter the courtrooms of Southern California on an hourly basis.

Incredibly, the victims of idea theft aren't limited to lowly producers trying to make their way in the reality TV world. Shortly after Fox executives' announcement of their intention to launch a reality competition boxing show called *The Next Great Champ*, Mark Burnett Productions and DreamWorks, joint producers of NBC's competing series of a strikingly similar nature, *The Contender*, sued Fox and *Champ* producers to prevent the show from airing as scheduled.

Although Burnett and his partners were not granted their request for a temporary restraining order to prevent *The Next Great Champ* from seeing broadcast daylight, they *were* given extraordinary access to network documents relevant to the production of *Champ*—known as the right of "discovery" in legalese. In addition, they were even granted a hearing in response to their request for a preliminary injunction due to alleged "unfair business practices."

For weeks and months prior to the scheduled premiere of *The Next Great Champ*, the warring parties traded barbs and asserted their claims of originality. In the final analysis, though, it was altogether unclear what, if anything, was gained—or by whom—in taking the matter to court, except maybe increased publicity for both *competing* programs.

For established and amateur producers alike, even with ample measures already taken, it can remain almost inconceivably onerous to prove that an idea was originally yours. Most of the time, in fact, lawyers won't take such cases on contingency for this particular reason. Chances are, the studio or network you're up against has a team of well-paid lawyers eager and ready to squash you and your reputation like a bug. In many cases, it would take everything short of DNA evidence and fingerprints on the stolen script to validate your claim and win the suit. Simply put, due to the growing emphasis on powerhouse legal teams, the "average Joe" producer has little or no chance at the start of his career to successfully fight to regain what is wrongfully stolen from him. Worst of all, the tremendous time and resources squandered on what may very well amount to a losing battle similarly results in lost time and effort you could expend on other projects that could still do for you what your stolen idea did for someone else.

PERSONALIZED PROTECTION

Every producer ultimately goes his or her own way regarding the best approach to protecting their work while proactively advertising their goods. Most reach a happy medium by distributing their work without abandon, but only after first registering the show idea with the Writers Guild of America or joining the Screen Actors Guild (SAG). Auspiciously, SAG offers a comprehensive registry of scripts to which its members can contribute. SAG's legal staff safeguards all registered works. That, of course, is the upside to joining SAG. On the other hand, becoming a SAG member costs a cool two grand. But if you're going to be in show business making millions anyway, I suppose a small investment is worth a big return, right?

Of course, once you finally do sell a project after dwelling for months or years in a neighborhood of concept kleptos, you're still not out of the woods by any stretch of the imagination in terms of legal concerns. In fact, soon after a producer signs his big contract, he must make others sign theirs. In other words, good producers remain vigilant about their responsibilities pertaining to rights and releases forms. Though the process of protecting intellectual property adds up to a helpful top 10, field production always demands attention on the top five: the five essential releases that can kill a project or a career if not properly obtained. Conveniently enough, however, many of these forms, not to mention numerous others, can be obtained (albeit for a small fee) from www.filmtvcontracts.com.

The Top Five Essential Release Forms

1. *General release.* All non-actors or nonperformers (those who are not members of SAG, AFTRA, EQUITY, or the like) must sign a general release to have their name, likeness, voice, or image used for broadcast. If a person is filmed and broadcast without signing a general release, they could sue you, your network, your production company, or all of the above.

Continued...

The Top Five Essential Release Forms—continued

2. *Talent release.* Ostensibly serving the same function as a general release, the talent release is a form to be signed by participants who *are* professional actors and models (i.e., members of AFTRA, SAG, EQUITY, etc.). Since payment can be mandated for their involvement, a general release is not applicable to professional performers.

3. *Minor release.* Any child considered a minor within the jurisdiction of the video production must have a parent or legal guardian sign a minor release form.

4. *Materials release.* The general release equivalent for inanimate objects, a materials release form is used to acquire permission for the use of various media, film, video, or photographs that are copyrighted or owned by an individual or group.

5. *Location release.* The most frequently forgotten release form of all is the location release, which is used to secure permission to record video or capture photographs of any property owned by someone else.

Several years ago, while struggling to enjoy an overpriced beverage at a trendy Los Angeles eatery, I overheard a woman at the adjacent table confide to her lunchmate that if she had known how much legal BS was involved in TV production she would have stuck with her original dream to design fashion. The more I thought about her comment, however, the better I understood the obvious similarity between designing clothes and producing television: both demand covering one's ass—one literally, the other figuratively.

Luckily, the burdensome worries about nondisclosures, copyright procedures, release forms, and the endless pageantry of legal drivel associated with television production will subside with time. To be sure, they will never go away, but after a while, they become an expected and more easily accepted part of the business, which, incidentally, is still a vastly rewarding creative workshop for talented producers with the heart to ride out the rough patches.

Just reminding you, that's all.

Chapter | nine

Fit for Reality

Aspiring producers spend a considerable amount of time in the early part of their careers trying to find a "good fit" for almost everything relevant to their work. Is your location a good fit for the mood you're trying to create? Are the personality types you've cast a good fit for your series? Is your pitch a good fit for NBC? Is your outfit a good fit for the pitch meeting?

Time and time again, producers obsess over these and myriad other "good fits." Sadly, however, many fail to explore the most important "fit" of all. Since we've already come this far together, there's no sense in delaying the inevitable any further. It's a nasty little question that begs to be asked but one that no one wants to answer. In short, it's the question of whether or not you as a person are a good fit for reality television itself. To be sure, this question has no pertinent connection to your talents as a producer. I'm of the school of thought that practically anyone can learn to produce reality television. Not everyone can be Mark Burnett, but it doesn't take a genius to produce a typical reality series. As we've seen, a heap of creativity, a resilient mindset, and the aptitude to learn the art of television production are the essential ingredients of a basic reality show producer. However, just because one *can* do something doesn't mean that one *should*. Reality television is a difficult medium to negotiate and survive if you're not the type of person the industry needs you to be.

FIT FOR DUTY

In his forward to this book, Emmy-award winning producer, writer, and author Charlie White puts it best: "You might want to consider if you're really cut out for this competitive industry. Are you thin-skinned, resistant to change, bruised with any criticism and a loner, shunning any teamwork and going solo? Then maybe you're considering the wrong line of work."

Deciding whether or not one is well suited for the reality television business begins with an introspective journey and a cogent understanding of the nasty underbelly of this exceedingly competitive industry. If you fear rejection, are stubborn, can't play well with others, lack focus and communication skills, wear your heart on your sleeve, offend easily, or discourage quickly, there's an excellent possibility that reality television isn't what your guidance counselor would have recommended as suitable work.

Of course, lots of producers working steadily in television today contend with many of these potentially hindering traits on a daily basis while still succeeding admirably in their craft. That said, you won't be outright disqualified for reality television production just because you are generally stubborn or unable to cope with rejection. The ultimate test of "viability" is whether you, as an individual, are aware of both your weaknesses and the weaknesses the medium will exploit. Consequently, if you manage to go into work every morning fully conscious of the inner foibles and exterior forces that could hastily derail your chances for achievement, you are still a feasible candidate for reality television success.

Some time ago I had the privilege of interviewing television producer Caroline Stack. A veteran of scripted and unscripted programming, Caroline has amassed an impressive body of work that includes a slew of projects with HBO, NBC, CBS, ABC, Fox, and a sprinkling of other cable networks and production companies. Like Charlie White, Caroline understands the inner workings of this complex industry—one that frequently seduces individuals who are otherwise talented but altogether ill suited for the world of reality television.

THE RIGHT STUFF FOR REALITY TV

Me: An often ignored but sobering fact is that reality television simply isn't for everyone. From a new or aspiring reality television producer's standpoint, which elements of the reality genre may initially prove most frustrating or difficult to contend with?

Me: What personal traits or characteristics do you find to be most conducive to success as a reality television producer?

Caroline: In my experience, the two keys to production are preparation and flexibility. Everything turns on a dime. You might have an entire day of interviews set up and something comes up and your day is cancelled. It starts raining so you need the rain gear you packed after all, or you need to go to your backup indoor location. A whole segment you've been researching for months gets cut. All your preparation is thrown out the window, and you need to start prepping again from scratch. Production is not work for people who like to know what's going to happen from day to day. You'll even find that each production company does the same task slightly differently, so it never hurts to ask what the procedure is when starting at a new company. Fortunately, I find a challenge exhilarating, so this aspect of production is something I enjoy—most of the time.

Caroline: People who express themselves well and communicate clearly make really good reality producers. When good communicators also know how to ask good questions that result in stellar interviews, they're golden.

Producing also requires sales skills. For a few days in college, I worked on a political campaign where I walked door to door and another temp job where I was basically a telemarketer, and I was surprised how much producing relied on the cold-calling skills I had picked up. You need to be persuasive on the phone and know how to recruit talent and resources for your programs. This is another reason to feel good about what you are working on.

Good producers also don't take criticism personally. You will get notes from higher-ups, studios, and networks, and you need to learn to take any suggestions in stride whether you act on them or not.

Me: Just as one with unsteady hands could never be a skilled surgeon, what type of person should not attempt to be a producer in reality television?

Caroline: I've known all kinds of people and personalities in reality television. This industry casts a wide net. I guess most good reality television producers work really well with other people. If you're a loner, this might not be a good industry for you. But who knows? Maybe someone will come up with a video blog show that's self-produced. It could happen.

You also have to have incredible tenacity. All the good producers I know don't take no for an answer. They negotiate. They throw in incentives. They try to find workarounds. They try different routes to the same end. And when everything they think of doesn't work out, they try one last thing because you never know. What's the worst that can happen? They already said no.

Reality Hits Home

Producers new to the reality genre learn very quickly that their work doesn't remain in the studio every night when the soundstage goes dark. For as much as it is an obsession for the general public, a number of prominent producers have reportedly become "reality addicts" in the sense that they cannot emotionally divorce themselves from their projects. Unfortunately, as a plethora of producers came to realize in the wake of reality TV-related deaths or similar tragedies, the production process can devastate those who are unable to emotionally detach themselves from their work in this format of real-life dramatic entertainment.

Me: As one who has worked in many facets of production for both network and cable television, would you speculate that the barriers to entry in reality television production are growing or diminishing?

Caroline: The barriers for entry into reality television are about the same as when I started out. I see new faces all the time. The biggest difference I've observed is that the volume of nonfiction television produced has increased, so there's a lot more work out there, but at the same time, the pressure to cut costs and keep budgets low has made producing nonfiction television more challenging than when I started out.

Me: What question(s) should any aspiring producer ask himself or herself before plunging into the murky but unfailingly alluring

Caroline: Are you passionate about making television? More important, are you passionate about reality television? People who are passionate about what they are doing tend to rise to the top. Second, are you willing to waters of reality television production?

make the sacrifices necessary to succeed? Production isn't a 9-to-5 job. You'll most likely end up working extremely long hours, and if you are working on your own projects, you may not see results for a long time.

Me: What have you learned from your success in both scripted and unscripted programming that you wish you had known at the beginning of your career?

Caroline: I wish I'd known the "cocktail party rule," which is if I can't imagine enthusiastically talking up whatever program I'm working on at the time to a stranger at a party, I don't take the job. Even if you're a PA or an intern, you need to feel great about what it is you are a part of. It makes it much easier to work hard, make an impression, and most important, feel good about yourself and what you are doing. Sometimes this can seem like a luxury because there's not a lot of work in the offing, but the more you work on projects that just plainly fascinate you, the more likely you are to succeed.

Off to the Reality Races

Upcoming producers are routinely shocked by the "run-and-gun" pace of the reality television production process. Unlike the medium's scripted counterpart, reality TV regularly presents a more hurried and less polished production trajectory. For many producers who anticipated a thoughtful pace to suit their methodical nature, the reality format has jolted their system with a rude reality awakening.

Me: There are many ways to break into the business as a producer. Which did you experience and which would you advise?

Caroline: It's all about relationships. When you're starting out it's easy to get resentful because you don't "know someone in the industry."

Once you're "in," the fact that this is a people business starts to work in your favor. Some people know you and want to work with you. It just takes one or more breaks to establish a reputation, and you may find that you start getting calls to see if you are available to work on your former employer's new project, and you may start to get referrals from colleagues you've worked with in the past.

I found getting that first break in reality television the most challenging. In my case after a few years living in Los Angeles, I met a reality producer who helped me get my first entry-level job as a transcriber. I transcribed interviews up to 30 hours a week for a few months before I was promoted to assistant at the same documentary production company.

As a side note, I met the reality producer through a group I was a member of at the time. Networking is really important and usually misunderstood. Most of your networking efforts will not pan out, but joining an unofficial or official group of like-minded people will get you closer to your goals because you never know where that first or second break will come from. Also, because this business is chock full of people who like people, there are a lot of organizational options out there even for those who are just starting out. For instance, a student can join the Academy of Television Arts and Sciences. Do your research and ask around, and you might be surprised at the groups you'll find.

Getting back to what to do once you break in, everybody's story is different, but the usual route is someone starts out as an intern, a runner, or a PA. When you get those first jobs, make a good impression: be punctual, work really hard, anticipate what people will need before they even ask, and when you can, work your way up by doing the next level of work to show people that you can do it. A good way to do this is to offer to help your boss with some of the tasks on his or her plate.

Me: For a producer, how does the nature of work primarily differ between scripted and unscripted programming?

Caroline: There a few big differences between scripted and unscripted shows I've worked on. The first is the union status of projects. Scripted shows have union rules that affect schedules, hours worked, and the type of work people do and are allowed to do. Unscripted shows tend to have fewer crew members and to ask those people to wear a lot of different hats. An exception to this is the scripted pilot, which tends to have a smaller bare-bones staff. Scripted television also has a specific schedule where pilots are produced in the winter and spring and rolled out for advertisers in New York in May at events called the Upfronts. (Like everything else in television, this seems to be changing. More and more pilots are being produced and premiered year round.) Once the shows are picked up by networks, there's a mad scramble to get crewed up, and unless you already worked on the pilot, you end up being part of an industrywide game of musical chairs for the remaining slots.

A Grim Reality

Although to my knowledge no medical study has been conducted to compare, for instance, the average blood pressure of reality television producers in relation to those toiling in other genres, it has been my experience that a good number of reality TV producers look awful behind the scenes. Typically, they're exhausted, drawn, and stressed to the point of craving substances, legal or otherwise, that they should really avoid at all costs. Reality television takes a physical toll (as well as a mental one) on some of its most dedicated (or obsessed) producers. Regrettably, not enough take adequate steps to keep their bodies and minds as healthy as possible. Even though it's difficult to convince a sleep-deprived, overworked producer to leave the studio for an hour to catch a nap or hit the gym, I've learned that it's easier convincing a producer friend to take better care of himself or herself if you first indicate that their work is starting to suffer in response to their own personal deterioration.

Me: What do you believe to be the biggest drawback to the reality TV industry that new producers may have difficulty confronting or overcoming?

Caroline: The biggest drawback to reality TV is the same thing that makes it so attractive to networks: the smaller, tighter budgets, especially on cable. This makes it especially important to be working on something you feel strongly about because it makes it easier to ask for what you need again and again, even when you don't have a lot of resources to get it.

Me: Given where the reality TV format has been and where it is now going, what skills, education, or experience should an

Caroline: First of all, do not wait until you graduate to gain experience in the field of your choosing. Over the years, I've known a number of students from aspiring producer seek today in order to thrive in the genre tomorrow?

as far away as Canada and Virginia who came to work as summer interns at production companies I worked for at the time. These students had a huge advantage over others seeking entry-level jobs coming out of school.

In general, I would say that a four-year degree seems to be a prerequisite for most entry-level jobs that are listed, but I think this is mostly to weed out candidates.

To answer the skills part of the question, the most important ability a person should demonstrate is an aptitude for picking things up quickly. Don't know how to use a camera? Learn. Don't know how to edit? Figure it out. Ask a lot of questions. Be curious about everything. More and more, producers are expected to know an awful lot about the technical aspects of the job. Learn as much as you can whenever and wherever you can about the art and craft of making TV.

Me: What do you think differentiates a long-lasting career as a television producer from one that never really gets off the ground?

Caroline: Remember to pace yourself. People burn out in this industry every day. When I first came to Los Angeles, I knew a lot of people who gave themselves two years or less to "make it." Most of them live back home now. I took a much longer view. From the beginning, I had a 20-year plan, and since I've been out here 13 years, I guess I will need to expand it by another 10. In short, you really need to be in it for the long haul. But in the meantime, be sure you have a life—good friends and other interests. Having a life is really important for two reasons. The first reason is even if you don't "make it," your life is that much better; second, it often ends up helping your career because people hiring smell desperation a mile off, and nothing feeds desperation like a barren life.

Me: What have you found to be the most burdensome aspects of producing for reality television?

Caroline: The entertainment industry seems to thrive on uncertainty. In other words, "nothing is certain until it's certain," and a lot of "hurry up and wait" is required. You have a project in the works that you are attached to work on, but the production company is waiting for the green light from the client or studio or network and is delayed for many weeks. You meet with a producer to work on a project that starts shooting in a few months, and the job never materializes because it's determined that your role isn't necessary or affordable after all. You begin working for a startup or even an established company, and your first paycheck bounces. So in a sense, circumstances require you to be a mercenary.

This is really difficult in those early lean years when you are working entry-level jobs that don't pay much at all. My first entry-level job was as a receptionist at a film production company, and I had three other part-time jobs just to afford the job I really wanted and still pay my bills. I learned some important lessons from the lean times. Save your money, keep your overhead low, pay for your health insurance, and it will be a buffer against the uncertainty.

Another difficult aspect of the job is you say goodbye a lot. You develop really close ties with a group and then you all move on like leaves in the wind. I know for some people jumping from project to project as a freelancer is really personally difficult, whereas I tend to thrive on new situations. What I like about mobility is that it encourages a group to focus on the work, and it's all about the work. You're brought together to put something together, and you disband when it's done. In the meantime, you end up meeting and working shoulder to shoulder with some of the most creative and fascinating people you'll ever meet in your entire life. And it's in your best interests to stay in touch with those colleagues with whom you formed genuine ties.

Me: What's the greatest misconception about the work or lifestyle afforded by reality television production?

Caroline: When I went to my 10th high school reunion, I won an award for having the most fascinating job of anyone there. But what people don't understand is that, like any job, producing has a lot of aspects that aren't pleasant or glamorous. Getting back to someone with bad news about their prospects for getting on the show, having interviewees drop out and having to replace them, making time for the talk with someone who's not working out in their job, finding out a b-roll shot is unusable and needs to be replaced immediately, and just the sheer slog of finding new and interesting stories for a series that requires a constant diet of different but the same. It can be really, really hard work, but it's really satisfying to see tangible results at the end of it all. To watch your work on TV, see your name in the credits, and know that you were a part of bringing that program to fruition brings me great satisfaction.

There's No Crying in Baseball . . . I Mean, Reality Television

One of the most difficult aspects of pitching and producing in this competitive landscape is coping with rejection. After reading the trades to learn who sold what project to whom, it's especially difficult to confront the industry that is yet to afford you similar opportunities. Ultimately, however, the producers who sell the most projects and engender lasting bodies of work are those who absorbed the most consistent rejection throughout their careers. In fact, some of the greatest hitters ever to play baseball hold strikeout records most would never expect. Of course, it didn't matter to those players. They were only concerned with swinging as hard as they could every time they stepped up to the plate. Reality television producers, particularly those who have traditionally failed to cope well with rejection, are advised to approach their work in the same bullheaded manner.

Me: Can you think of any experience you had at the beginning of your career that would be particularly instructive to those currently in your shoes?

Caroline: William Goldman coined a famous saying in his book, *Adventures in the Screen Trade*, that went, "Nobody knows anything." The biggest lesson I learned early on that reminds me of Goldman's saying is, "Don't assume anything." If you don't know, ask. It's better to ask three times and get it right than to assume something and possibly cost the production money. If you cost the production too much money, they might just let you go. This is especially important when you are negotiating with someone for something that involves some kind of payment. As much as possible, get email confirmations of agreements made on the phone and keep a log of your telephone conversations because you never know when there will be a discrepancy between what was agreed to and what was understood.

Me: Looking into your reality TV crystal ball, what do you anticipate for the future direction of reality programming and the industry of unscripted programming itself?

Caroline: Television producers are in the intellectual property business, and the landscape is being transformed by the Internet. I see a future where your computer will be your television and your television will broadcast what's on your computer. Sites like YouTube are making everyone into a producer and distributor. This is a very exciting time because if you find a way to earn money from your Internet content, you have it made, but few people have cracked the code. It's a little like Levi Strauss during the California gold rush; he made all his money selling jeans to the miners rather than panning for gold himself. Similarly, a few companies are making an awful lot of money on the back of Internet distribution, which often does not trickle down to those who are providing the content. Fortunately, history has shown that each technology goes through some growing pains before people figure out how to make money from it, and with the Internet, it's only a matter of time.

Chapter ten

Living Reality

On even the most ordinary of days in Los Angeles, one can easily identify more than a few Hollywood moguls enjoying lunch in a chic café, shopping on Rodeo Drive, or dodging paparazzi around every imaginable corner. But though those who command such unremitting attention frequently lead flamboyant lifestyles that render anonymity impossible, one of the entertainment industry's biggest players blends surprisingly unnoticed into the casual flow of "ordinary folk" traffic. Reality TV super-producer Mark Burnett, namely, ranks chief among such extraordinary ordinaries.

I first met the iconic creator and executive producer of *Survivor* and *The Apprentice* after unknowingly standing beside him for 15 minutes in the lobby of the Hollywood Renaissance Theatre in early 2003.

With my junior reporter's notepad in tote, I was systematically interrupting as many power lunches as I could in hopes of landing interviews for an exclusive entertainment blog I was launching at the time.

Although Burnett was arguably the most important person in the room, I found him among the most relaxed. A soft-spoken and markedly unhurried presence, Mark Burnett doesn't strike the casual observer as precisely what he is: one of the busiest and most prolific powerhouse executives in show business, a status attained through his always emulated but never duplicated mastery of the reality genre.

FIGURE 10.1   Mark Burnett and Michael Essany.

Despite a laundry list of afternoon meetings awaiting him, Burnett still took time to thoughtfully answer my questions—a task perceptibly less important than the other scheduled items on his teeming agenda.

Me: Conventional wisdom holds that achieving status in show business—particularly as a producer—is among the most challenging and unlikely goals one could possibly undertake. How did you manage to endure and thrive?

Mark: Ten years ago I was with the first American team to compete in the French extreme races called Raid Gauloises. We were in the Middle East doing all these crazy things—riding camels and horses, mountaineering for days, really extreme sorts of activities. And our team needed sponsors. And the sponsors, naturally, would want exposure in return. So I decided to go and make a show of it all, but in a unique way. I called on the French organizers to provide me with the footage from their multiple camera teams in return for exposure in the United States. I got a local reporter and cameraman out of L.A. involved and together we assembled a 90-minute television special. I wasn't paid a cent, but KCAL-TV Channel 9 in Los Angeles agreed to air the show, with the rights reverting to me after broadcast. The whole thing went great and I was able to take the project and make a deal with ESPN. I told them "if you give me half the commercials, I'll give you a free show." So I sold the commercials at a profit and satisfied our sponsors by getting them the exposure they wanted. Once you reach the point where you realize how the business behind the art works, you're golden. Once that savvy sets in, you can do a lot.

Although most careers in show business aren't born in the Middle East or quite so straightforwardly, Burnett's creative maneuverings prior to becoming one of Hollywood's elite producers illustrate a vital example to those aspiring to Burnett's lofty league: Don't limit your creativity to the *art* of reality television. The *business* demands it even more.

Me: Your body of work not only reflects innovative television programming but also innovative ways of having your work produced. What lessons can up-and-coming producers learn from your example?

Mark: Reality television has broken a lot of molds, particularly in the way that shows are financed. To a degree, the standard television commercial is dying. This is why today producers and advertisers are working in concert—totally unheard of in the past. Because TiVo alone is making it difficult for advertisers to maximize their investment, producers now have to work directly with sponsors in organic, creative ways to integrate their brand or product *into* the programming—of course, in a nondistracting sort of way for the viewer. Alternative financing forms are just as important to producers like me as they are to newcomers to our business because, bottom line, they get shows produced.

And getting shows produced is exactly what Mark Burnett has been doing since the launch of the culture-impacting CBS reality series *Survivor* in the summer of 2000. For Burnett, however, fame and fortune were once far removed from his humble beginnings across the pond.

An only child, Burnett was born in London in the early 1960s and later served with the British Army. In 1982, he relocated to the U.S. and settled in Southern California, where he held an assortment of odd jobs until the early 1990s. From serving as a "professional nanny," starting his own credit card marketing company, and even vending T-shirts on Venice Beach, Burnett has always had his sights trained on the vast rewards of entrepreneurship, a passion reflected in his creation of *The Apprentice*.

Me: Are your ideas for reality programming primarily born of your own interests or whatever you think audiences are in the mood for?

Mark: Both. I mean, timing is critical in reality television. There's no denying it. But you definitely have to have passion for your work, not just a suspicion that a project will resonate with viewers. In fact, it almost certainly *won't* be a success unless you as a producer have the passion to make it so. And you can't summon that passion without a genuine interest in the nature of your series. You almost have to *live* reality television in order to produce it.

Living the reality TV experience is indeed what ultimately separates the amateurs from the pros and continues to place Burnett at the creative forefront of the reality programming industry. According to Burnett, it's the fear of wholly investing oneself behind the viability of a project that prevents many aspiring producers from getting their work produced and broadcast.

Me: Every day in the trade papers you read about a producer who is either surprised by a project's unexpected success or staggered by its unexpected failure. Can a producer—established or upcoming—ever truly be confident in his or her project?

Mark: Before *Survivor* debuted, I was scared to death. I had no idea if it would work. People in the business much smarter than me said it wouldn't. But I've learned to trust my gut feeling, even through disappointments. And I think that's the key. I'm never certain. I don't know anyone who is. You just have to execute your original vision. To play around with a concept until you are *certain* of something is foolish. It's procrastination, really. When you're inspired, you have to seize that moment. And if it doesn't work, move on as quickly as you moved forward.

Me: A lot of producers speak of the juggling act—having so many responsibilities that it's difficult to focus on the creative tasks at hand. As

Mark: By design, I'm rarely in the office. My cell phone keeps me tethered to work. Otherwise I have a brilliant team who micromanages someone busier than the typical producer, how do you manage it all?

and allows me to be hands-on where I feel I'm most needed. Actually, a lot of feature-film people work for me. Even though they haven't spent a great deal of time in television, their experience is phenomenal. The same goes for our production staff. All of my line producers, for example, were accountants before coming on. And because they can manage a budget, that means I don't have to. I'm very proud of my team. I would estimate that 90 percent of the people I've hired in 10 years are still with us. That's a rarity on the production side. But that's what happens when you trust people to do their jobs and trust yourself to do yours.

BEWARE OF THE ENERGY-SUCKING IDIOT

On meeting Mark Burnett for the first time, I was impressed by his immense positive energy—the invaluable quality, as it turns out, that he similarly looks for in others, particularly those employed at Mark Burnett Productions. According to Burnett, those with whom you surround yourself in work *and* play have considerably more to do with an eventual success or failure than any show concept ever could.

Mark: Let's assume you fill a bathtub full of crystal-clear, clean water. And let's say that this tub of water represents your energy for the day. You get up, have breakfast, take the kids to school, and go to work. This represents the start of your day. And with the start of your day, the water starts to

Now let's consider another day, when you're surrounded by energy-sucking idiots. People who get in your way, complicate your progress, and fail to work cohesively with you and others on your team. Collectively, these energy-sucking idiots drain your tub drain slowly from the tub. Once the water starts to drain, the plug can't go back in and you can't add more water. Each hour of your busy day empties your tub further. And by the time you go to sleep, after a 14- or 16-hour day, the last drop goes out of the drain.

faster than anything else could. The only way to prevent it is to surround yourself with people who will keep your tub as full as possible. This is why it's so important to choose your teammates before you choose your journey. Having a goal and a corresponding business plan is great, but it will only work if the right people are there with you. It's all about the people, really. I mean, I don't think up great shows and then go it alone. If I didn't have people around me to make me better, I would not be here today.

Like Burnett, *American Idol* executive producer and fellow British bigwig Nigel Lythgoe doesn't waste time, energy, and talent on secondary tasks. According to Lythgoe, "A lot of green producers want to master every aspect of production, which can be a colossal mistake. At some point, you have to let others do their job. In reality television, the producer should be concerned primarily with compelling ways of conveying the human element. Extraordinary producers are extraordinary storytellers. They are explorers of the human mind. On *Idol*, we introduce the audience to the kids, showing what makes them tick and what makes them want to sing. A pure talent show would have never become what *Idol* has."

Although there are four basic categories of reality programming (talent competition, slice of life, the social experiment, and the game show) and multiple subcategories, the common denominator linking even the most diverse categories is human drama. Talent and good looks among participants certainly help, but ultimately there is nothing like a poignant, inspiring, embarrassing, illustrative, or comical personal story to better motivate an audience to repeat viewing.

Mark: I don't know why they call it reality TV, actually. It really is unscripted drama. For me, that's exactly what it is. I like to tell stories—good, dramatic stories that offer compelling ideas and situations that transport viewers to places they've never been.

For Mark Burnett, however, developing a new show concept and working it through to launch begins with one of the most important actions any producer can take: reaching a decision and standing by it. Although it's incredibly simple in theory, Burnett regards indecision among the greatest threats to promising careers in television producing

Mark: In Europe we have to learn Latin, the very root of all language. In Latin, *decision* means *to cut off*. And that's how I like to think of decisions. A decision is like the scene from *Indiana Jones*; you go along a bridge and then you cut the rope ladder behind you. Now you have no choice but to go forward. That's how you must produce for television. A lot of producers aren't bold enough to follow through on the course they've set. At the first sign of resistance they question their project, their vision, even their own self-worth. You can't be like the people at Starbucks who step out of line to rethink the order they intended to place when they walked in. Most of the time your first idea or plan proves to be the right one over time. Whether you're right or wrong, just make a decision and see it through. What you accomplish won't matter more than what you learn from the overall experience.

Indeed, learning is the most important process for anyone hoping to produce reality television. And as both Burnett and Lythgoe agree, there are several key lessons to be learned about reality television that are as vital to a career as they are to the genre itself.

BEND IT LIKE BURNETT

Those who marvel at Burnett's ability to wield a full plate with a perpetually relaxed demeanor are often baffled at how he manages to reconcile two seemingly opposed qualities: determination and flexibility. "Flexibility," says Burnett, "means monitoring your own behavior. The inept salesman has only one way of presenting. He doesn't understand that there are different types of people who would respond to a different kind of pitch." Time and time again, Mark Burnett's determined efforts to sell a project have come to fruition only after molding his pitch, responding to feedback, and critically monitoring what does and does not work. In Hollywood, plastic isn't hard to come by. In some producers, however, plasticity is a surprisingly uncommon and sorely needed trait.

Mobilize Your Marketing

If Mark Burnett retired from show business today, by tomorrow he would be one of the highest-paid marketing consultants in the world. Without question, Burnett is a PR wizard whose marketing genius has generated billions in advertising dollars and personal wealth.

According to his shining example, anyone interested in producing television should take an equal interest in the fundamentals of marketing. "The greatest idea is meaningless," says Burnett, "if its value isn't convincingly communicated. Learning to market your vision and yourself should be high priorities for those looking to produce." Astonishingly, textbook examples of basic marketing strategy are all that's needed in many cases to "outwit, outplay, and outlast" the competition gunning for the success you can capably claim for yourself.

Avoid Derivatives

To Nigel Lythgoe, imitation is more than just the sincerest form of flattery. It's also the reason so many producers with genuine potential end up employed in their fallback careers. "A great misconception in reality television," says Lythgoe, "is that if you derive a program concept from a similar but established series that's already a hit all over the world, you should have no trouble selling the derivative and capitalizing on a proven formula. That is completely false!" Since the advent of modern reality television revolutionized mainstream broadcasting in early 2000, appetites have changed drastically in the ivory network towers. Five years ago, the idea for any reality series, just for being one, could catch the ear of a network executive. Today, although programming might not ostensibly reflect it, the unscripted genre is strikingly more mature. The broadcasting landscape has grown more competitive in the wake of networks scrambling for reality programming unlike anything previously seen. As a result, Mr. Newcomer Producer is best advised to abandon any concept that resembles another identifiable model and, instead, create something—anything, in fact—that is dazzlingly original, even if outright absurd on first examination.

Expose Yourself

There's an excellent possibility that a project you couldn't sell in a grueling yearlong campaign would have been effortlessly sold by Burnett—with a less impressive pitch, I might add—in a five-minute teleconference with network executives who still don't know you even exist. How does he do it? Apart from having natural talent, he's internationally famous. Mark Burnett is every bit as celebrated as the reality genre itself.

Fortunately, reaching a similar—albeit considerably less impressive—perch of recognition is also possible for you, even if you have yet to sell your project number one. How so? By repeatedly exposing your enthusiasm, passion, and expertise to anyone who will listen. Pitching early and often is a good way of getting all the right people to grow familiar and, most important, comfortable with you. Repetitively impressing executives with your zeal and chutzpah, even if the projects don't sell, will still help you succeed in selling yourself. And, eventually, this form of positive exposure will reap greater benefits than you can ever imagine today.

Cherry-Pick 'Em

Listen to any series of interviews with Mark Burnett and you're bound to notice a familiar pattern. Time after time, he speaks of his "team" with as much adulation as he does frequency. Mark Burnett, like few of his contemporaries, has placed considerable emphasis on the delegation of responsibility. And although the fledging producer may have difficulty assembling and compensating a large team dedicated to his or her far-fetched vision for a television program, the time will eventually arise in any persistent producer's life when a production team is needed. Following Burnett's example, cherry-pick those who exert positive energy, share and appreciate your vision, and balance out your or your team's collective strengths and weaknesses. No one goes it alone in producing television. And for producers striving to literally survive in the reality TV business, building strong alliances is far more important than it will ever be on a remote island halfway across the world.

Chapter | eleven

Reality Baggage

What comes with success in reality television? What comes with failure? No matter how you slice it, reality television comes with substantial baggage, whether you ultimately succeed or fail. Merely toiling in the genre itself will result in others perceiving you in a different way. But how that "different way" is interpreted, of course, depends on the beholder's opinion of reality television—a format that in many ways divides as much as it unites.

To be honest, a lot of folks, including numerous heads of studios and major production companies, berate the reality genre as a malicious, trivial, and altogether worthless entity that taints its producers and participants by association alone. Others, conversely, view reality TV as an artistic wonderland that, though silly, provides quality entertainment that is consistently bankable and elevates the status of producers who excel in the medium.

Perhaps the most compelling evidence of reality television's ability to stain even the most beloved or wholesome of icons resulted from the nightmarish publicity fallout from *Oprah's Big Give*, a 2008 reality series that, according to *The Hollywood Reporter*, is "a profoundly hyperkinetic and unwieldy adventure in product placement, in Oprah-as-Messiah hype and, ultimately, in what's so utterly fake and insidious about reality television itself."

Though I have no doubt that Oprah's intentions were genuine and legitimately directed toward helping others, the reality television platform itself likely corrupted the valid sincerity behind the series concept. The unintended consequence, of course, was Oprah getting smeared as a wannabe savior seeking every opportunity possible to glorify her almighty benevolence. "Shallow as a birdbath," the scathing article continued, "the program would appear to exist less as a true philanthropic exercise than yet another self-aggrandizing vehicle in Oprah's divine quest to become synonymous with all that is virtuous and good on Earth. We might well refer to this as 'Touched by a Talk Show Host.'"

In retrospect, Oprah actually got off easy. Since she is one of the most adored and respected personalities and humanitarians of our time, even reality television's nefarious aftertaste couldn't long impede Oprah and her sundry multimedia endeavors. Others, though, have been less fortunate. From former reality show contestants subsequently losing their jobs back in the real world to producers having difficulty finding decent work after a reality series went down in flames, there are indeed potentially serious consequences to associating yourself with this industry.

Even though I had aspired to host my own television series since I was old enough to possess any aspiration at all, there was certainly more to my human existence than that well-publicized desire. While in college at Valparaiso University, for example, I studied public administration in the department of political science, graduated with high honors, and was inducted into several political science honors societies. Since childhood, I had also hoped to follow the community-minded lead of my immediate family and one day serve my neighborhood, start a nonprofit organization, or maybe even run for local public office if the inspiration and opportunity ever arose.

Four years after domestic production of *The Michael Essany Show* wrapped, I was heavily involved in low-profile community politics in my relatively quiet hometown of Valparaiso, Indiana. As a college graduate, a newlywed, and a successful nationally published writer, I decided to run for City Council in Valparaiso.

Although the position I sought was largely of limited responsibility and provided a scant $5,000 annual salary, I passionately fought for the issues I had publicly championed for years. And despite my local popularity and political credentials, my opposition blasted me as that "kid from reality television" who had no business ever doing anything of serious importance. The supposed "mark of disgrace" resulting from my work on and association with unscripted television was relentlessly thrust upon me.

Although the election was one of the closest in Valparaiso history, I missed winning a seat by only 138 votes out of more than 9,000 votes cast. To be sure, I'm not blaming reality television for my loss, but it certainly didn't help. Even though it conflicts with the notion that name recognition means everything in politics, anonymity would have likely afforded me a greater opportunity to talk without distraction about the issues and ideals that motivated my campaign in the first place. Unfortunately, my run was clouded by images from my youthful but otherwise harmless escapades on reality TV.

As I learned the hard way, reality television comes not without unavoidable baggage, particularly when you're trying to secure a foothold in a new field or industry. And despite common misperceptions, those behind the scenes are just as likely as on-camera talent to find reality TV a veritable albatross later in life.

No Immunity in Real Life

Preventing reality television from impairing your dignity, credibility, or future professional or personal opportunities is an enormously perplexing quandary. The first step in the process is to realize that there is a guilt-by-association rule in this business. Similar to assessing whether or not you're a good fit for the reality TV business, it's important to ask yourself where you want to be personally and professionally in five, 10, or even 25 years. If your ultimate goal is related to the television industry, you can afford to proceed less cautiously (but still guardedly) in the projects you pitch and produce. If your ultimate goal, conversely, is unrelated to show business, your chances could very well be spoiled by your short-term work in reality television. At all times, apply great caution when working as a producer or performer in this business. Unfortunately, there is no immunity from association with a reality TV series or "incident" gone wrong.

REALITY TELEVISION: THE FLAPDOODLE OF MODERN BROADCASTING

Since early 2000, pop culture in the United States and Great Britain has been robustly dominated by reality television. Emerging along with the popularity of reality television has been its corresponding canon: an unofficial but widely accepted dogma that anything connected to or associated with reality television is inherently frivolous.

As both an adjunct professor in the department of communications at Valparaiso University and one of the most respected entertainment journalists in the Midwest, Phil Potempa is exceptionally familiar with the frivolity of reality television, including the ramifications of success and failure in the world of unscripted programming.

"The most noted of reality stars I've interviewed over the years," recalls Potempa, "include Tammy Faye Baker and Vanilla Ice (*The Surreal Life*), Reichen Lehmkuhl (*The Amazing Race*), Richard Hatch (*Survivor*), and Jeri Manthey (*Survivor: Africa 2001*)."

Me: What potentially harmful consequences do you perceive to be chiefly associated with involvement in reality television?

Phil: There's a definite perception than any association with reality television is "lowbrow." And, depending on the particular show (*Joe Millionaire, Boy Meets Boy*, etc.), even the word *trashy* might be a better fit.

Me: Are there any producers or participants that stand out in your mind for having skillfully used the reality genre to their advantage without being harmed by the inherent dangers posed by this often cruel format?

Phil: The world of reality television has given many new TV personalities a chance to capture their 15 minutes of fame. What they ultimately do with this gift depends on their own strengths, talents, and ambitions. So someone like Jeff Probst, the host of CBS's widely successful *Survivor*, has fared very well from his connection to reality television and has managed to not only become a household name but also be very well compensated for his duties. Other identities, like CNN's Anderson Cooper, have opted to use reality television as a stepping stone for experience and exposure to move on to more challenging and satisfying opportunities. Cooper, now one of the most respected and watched names in news, began in 2001 as the host of ABC's *The Mole*. And of course, from a producing standpoint, there's "the father of reality television," Mark Burnett, the man who has capitalized on and profited the most from introducing the entire world to reality shows with his 2000 summer season hit *Survivor*. He's moved on to become one of the most sought-after producers in television, crossing the line to more traditional programming, such as producing Martha Stewart's successful syndicated daytime TV talk show.

Me: Who has reality TV helped? Who has it harmed?

Phil: Reality TV has helped a few various groups. It's helped anyone who could be classified as someone without the benefit of talent or training (e.g., the lousy singer cut during early auditions for *American Idol* or the social misfit who doesn't fit in on *The Bachelorette*, gets dismissed from the show early on, and becomes the topic of water-cooler chat in offices the next day and makes the morning talk show rounds), to be seen and heard by a wide broadcasting audience, while often also allowing these same people to usually make a little money from the opportunity. On the other end of the spectrum, it's also helped a few "diamonds in the rough," those few people like *American Idol* Clay Aiken or *The Apprentice* Bill Rancic to take their already proven success and abilities and expand those virtues and talent to even greater levels. As for who has been harmed by reality television, it's hurt any on-air participant who's not careful to guard and protect their own identity and reputation. Depending on careful editing and the whims of producers, anyone's image can be portrayed in a way that's far from flattering. In the broadest sense of reality television's impact, it has also hurt television viewers starved for imaginative writing, plots, characters to remember and identify with for generations to come, and the art of storytelling and compelling

Me: As someone who has comprehensively covered the entertainment business for many years, how do you think reality television has influenced show business as a whole?

scripts for programming with a purpose other than just momentary mild diversion.

Phil: I've worked as a full-time newspaper entertainment reporter (*The Times* of Northwest Indiana) for 15 years, beginning right after I graduated from college in 1992. So the earliest programming concept for reality television, or at least what we define reality TV to be today, was just launching with the first season of MTV's *The Real World* in 1992. For the first time, everyday people could suddenly launch careers in an industry that previously demanded far more work, experience, and talent before tasting fame and notoriety. From the viewer's line of vision, I believe reality television can be likened to chewing a piece of bubble gum in place of ingesting a nutritious meal. In the duration, reality TV doesn't really leave audiences very satisfied or fortified.

WHAT'S SO BAD ABOUT REALITY TV?

Although most will argue that there is nothing inherently bad *about* reality television, they will also concede that reality television can do some pretty bad things *to* people.

Apart from the ethical quandaries born of the genre and the exploitive tendencies it encourages, the abstract baggage associated with reality television can be comparably detrimental, even to producers.

It's been my experience that reality television's baggage is perpetuated by two distinct factors: the myth and the legacy.

The Myth

An acquaintance of mine, a former reality television star who shall remain nameless for his own good, recently shared with me the reason a potential employer opted not to bring him on board his law firm: "I was told that my professional background in reality television—notwithstanding my law degree—was unbecoming of one expected to provide sober counsel to clients within the field of family law. The managing partner was concerned that if word got out that an attorney for his firm once worked in reality TV, current and potential clients may be turned off. I got the feeling they were concerned that a hidden camera might be escorting me around the office all day."

Numerous individuals either in front of or behind the cameras have been burned by the reality television business. From those who dabble in new arenas to others trying to leapfrog into more "traditional" broadcasting formats, the unscripted genre of television programming has produced many cases where the ghost of reality TV past came back to haunt future endeavors.

Speaking to the prevalence and power of rumors and myths, Winston Churchill once observed, "A lie can make it all the way around the world before the truth can even get its pants on." Although it's unlikely that the former British Prime Minister had reality television in mind when articulating this memorable observation, the biggest myth that harms former producers or performers trying to embark on a new professional enterprise is that people who have worked in reality television are supercilious buffoons incapable of commanding respect and typically worthy of scorn. It's likely that the managing partner of the firm to which my friend was applying had eagerly bought into this broadly absorbed theory.

At the end of the day, however, we must at least acknowledge the substantive morsels of truth that hastily inspired the origins of this universal presumption. In other words, we have to face the fact that a few truly bad apples have rapidly spoiled the whole orchard. Let's face it: The "talent" of many reality show participants is suspect. In some cases, obviously, such suspicions are warranted. In others, genuinely gifted performers are incorrectly lumped into the vast pool of supposedly talentless "reality show bums."

As a former reality television star, I learned early on that the masses don't wholly correlate legitimate talent with reality television participants. Remarkably, in fact, I have also attended more than a few cocktail parties in Los Angeles where upcoming producers within the reality realm cringed when asked what they do for a living. Apparently for some at the bottom of the reality show food chain, simply being linked to the medium has already placed negative baggage on their professional carousel.

Though a distant and largely irrelevant memory today, there was a time in a bygone era when people working in the film industry looked on television actors with utter contempt and blistering disdain. In its infancy, the medium of television was viewed by some in show business as inherently lowbrow and beneath the standards of legitimate entertainers. In an ironic twist of circumstances, it can now be difficult to separate the film stars from the television stars. The mediums have traded so much talent in recent years that it's safe to presume that television is no longer the redheaded stepchild of show business. Strangely enough, it could now be said that some within the mainstream world of scripted television cast the same aspersions on the reality television genre that the film industry once cast on television. Naturally, some are hoping that reality television will grow into a more respectable medium in the years to come and ultimately be recognized for its quality work, talented participants, and indispensable producers. For the time being, though, if you have a lot of talent— as a producer, a writer, or even an entertainer—reality television might not be an appropriate forum for you if you consistently need to be told just how talented you really are.

Unfortunately, the words *talent* and *reality television* are rarely if ever used in the same sentence. The enduring myth that anyone can be on or produce reality TV has diluted an appreciation for the myriad skills and time-honored talents that the format consistently demands and would surely founder without.

Overall, the "myth" alluded to has actually inspired many people to never toil in reality television alone. As a result of the subsequent professional ramifications illustrated by some, a growing number of aspiring producers are branching into scripted television, film, and even theatre to offset the potential long-term consequences of being linked solely to reality television.

The Legacy

Despite every positive aspect of reality television's existence—including, to no small extent, providing big-break opportunities to singers, actors, comedians, and others who otherwise might have never gotten that opportunity—the "legacy" of reality TV or its recognized body of work and cultural influence is not widely regarded in high esteem.

For the most part, the legacy of reality television is perceived as an expansive collection of flash-in-the-pan programs and participants that did remarkably little to enlighten or inspire the masses.

Just as one would receive immediate respect and adulation for revealing that one works as a scientist for NASA, the opposite can sometimes be true for those who reveal their exploits in reality TV. Instead of being hailed as a brilliant, innovative pioneer of technologies enabling humankind to reach new worlds and explore uncharted frontiers, they'd probably be regarded as one of the lowbrow types who introduced the world to *Joe Millionaire*. Congratulations.

Although I've always told students of film and television to ignore the tenuous legacy of reality television and instead work to create their own, it's important to know what has spoiled the respectability of reality television in the eyes of many people. As we've seen in recent years with the reduction of sleaze-oriented reality and the emergence of more intellectually appealing reality programming, a coalition of producers is increasingly working to elevate the status of its beloved genre. And in this worthwhile endeavor, there's always room for more helping hands. You just have to be willing and able to endure what *is* for the sake of what could ultimately *be:* a reality television empire that is respected in return for respecting others.

Too idealistic? Perhaps. But there's an excellent possibility that the genre won't ascend to greater heights unless it embraces a more mature and sophisticated posturing in the years ahead.

CARRY-ON BAGGAGE

Though it's unfortunate that we should need to approach the reality television industry with a guarded if not cynical mindset, it's imperative for aspiring producers to take necessary precautions, particularly if they ever plan to practice law, run for office, or embark on any endeavor unrelated to show business that could eventually be fatally impaired by their experience in this genre.

Without question, there are many worthwhile reasons to pursue a career in this exciting and infinitely rewarding business. There are, however, substantial reasons to avoid it at all costs. Regrettably, most books serving as a primer to reality television production assume that your path has already been set in stone; come hell or high water, you *are* going to work in reality television in some capacity. My hope is that this book will, if nothing else, remind you that despite the momentum you might already have built, you still have a choice. To be sure, there's no shame in deciding *not* to pursue a career in reality television, either as a producer or a performer. It doesn't make you a quitter or a coward. In fact, if an honest assessment of your future goals and personal traits reveals that reality television might not be worth the potential baggage you'll acquire along that road, you could very well be making the smartest professional decision of your life in opting out.

Despite my occasionally dreary outlook, I am certainly not advancing the notion that reality television is a zero-sum game. There are, indeed, outcomes from working in this business other than simply making it big or failing miserably. You could very well fall somewhere in between those two extremes. Perhaps you'll produce quality work, earn a substantial living, and never be injured, embarrassed, or professionally limited by the reality television genre. Many, after all, have managed to do so. How? For starters, they never picked up any more "baggage" than they could, or should, handle.

Those best equipped to survive and thrive in reality television employ a quasi-Socratic approach to the business—that is, they never stop asking the right questions. Producers inclined to protect themselves as well as their work analyze potential projects like a butcher selecting the finest cut of meat for his favorite patron. The reality television novice takes what's available. "Any work is good work," proclaims the rookie, who believes that his or her career will be furthered by experience wherever it is gained. Although this is the quickest way to the climb the reality TV ranks, it certainly isn't the safest.

Before creating, pitching, or jumping on board any project, try to see the big picture. Are you working on a *Temptation Island* or an *Apprentice*? Both became internationally famous, but only the latter is "respectable." Trying to hold out for projects that serve a greater purpose than to shock and awe is one of the savviest ways of protecting your professional credibility and reducing the baggage born of reality television.

Needless to say, however, shows like *Temptation Island* are easier to find than *The Apprentice*. And even though it could be powerfully tempting to tackle an island-based series featuring an assortment of sexy cast members, it's important to remember that "no" isn't a dirty word. You *can* and *should* be selective. Will doing so initially limit your opportunities for work? Probably. But if you're trying to play it safe, it is better to limit your work than it is to limit your future.

In the final analysis, no matter how well you fare or which projects you produce, the business comes with certain unavoidable baggage, at least in the minds of those with preconceived notions about reality television. And even though there is no guaranteed method to ensure a clean break from the business if and when you ever opt to pursue a new professional course, being aware of the baggage that comes with reality television is a healthy first step to ensuring it never becomes too unwieldy to manage.

Chapter twelve

Random Secrets of the Reality Trade

Given the open-book nature of reality television, it is hard to imagine that there are any secrets whatsoever associated with this industry. Incredibly, though, there are scores of random secrets—or should I say, little-known tricks of the trade—scarcely underused and certainly underappreciated by those looking to labor in this unique business.

Some of the following tips might seem brainless, obvious, amateur, and juvenile. But then again, sometimes reality TV itself can be described the same way. Of course, you might already be way ahead of the game and not require any of these beginner steps. If so, please feel free to bypass this chapter. No hard feelings. Otherwise, you might pick up a helpful lesson or two that could pay invaluable dividends down the line.

SKIP THE "WHERE." GET TO WORK

One of the biggest mistakes young producers make is wasting time on all the wrong quandaries, particularly where, geographically speaking, to start their careers. No matter how you slice it, an important key to remember is that where you start your career is always less important than starting your career.

In the past, a great debate raged on (and still does) over whether it is better to get your start in New York City or Los Angeles. This struggle, to be sure, was born of the show business catch-22 that to get a job in television, you need experience, but the only way to get that experience is to first land a job.

Since "first jobs" are still difficult to come by in both L.A. and New York—even though they would be considered plentiful when compared to, say, Lincoln, Nebraska—the best jobs through which to acquire experience are often those you create for yourself. And, yes, you can put that experience on a résumé.

As one who created and launched a national television show from the cornfields of Indiana, I learned firsthand that New York and L.A., though still very important, are markedly less important than they once were, particularly since the advent of web-based entertainment, in terms of both content and employment opportunities.

With few exceptions, figuring out where to live and work is never worth a monumental struggle or investment of time, a precious commodity at the beginning of any new professional venture. Countless aspiring producers, actors, writers, and the like spend years bouncing back and forth between New York and L.A. looking for the "right" opportunity or big break. If truth be told, the big break will take place wherever you want it to, so long as you invest your energies into creating it for yourself. The general consensus among my former producer colleagues at E! Entertainment Television, for example, is that the best ideas and, subsequently, the best producers come from all across the country, not just the coasts. Illustrating this point, teleconferencing pitches now comprise a considerable chunk of all the pitches taken in the boardrooms at E!, not to mention a slew of other cable and television networks. Most agree that one of the biggest secrets of the reality trade is to limit your time worrying about logistics and instead focus on creating the projects and pitches that deserve attention. With any luck, your work will ultimately take you to where you need to be and are supposed to be, whether it's New York, Los Angeles, or someplace in between.

Of course, if you're a traditionalist, the odds of gaining employment will always be in your favor if you live near the coasts. Although Los Angeles boasts the greatest number of production companies and television-related job opportunities, in the last 15 years New York has welcomed a veritable tidal wave of film and television production companies setting up shop in the Big Apple. As a result, some now argue that New York and L.A. offer an equal number of employment opportunities.

BUY LOW. SELL HIGH

Before I personally knew Leeza Gibbons, I certainly knew *of* her. I had been a fan of her work as both a television personality and a producer. An incredibly likable person, Leeza also made a fantastic talk show guest. In fact, the first time I recall watching Leeza interviewed on television, she was giving advice to new show business blood on how they could break into the business. Looking back, one phrase in particular never left me: "No job is beneath you," said Leeza. "Put your ego aside."

As one who has encountered many individuals in possession of what some might call "healthy egos," I have firsthand experience with the temptation to believe that you're somehow "above" a certain position or responsibility. Over the years I have met countless aspiring producers and entertainers, young and old, who boldly professed their budding talents but condemned the notion of breaking into show business through lowly channels only because they "shouldn't have to do that."

Not surprisingly, I still have yet to turn on the television and see these supremely talented individuals anywhere. In retrospect, it might have very well been their cocksureness more than anything else that ultimately held them back from realizing their professional aspirations. To be sure, having an ego (but only a tiny one) isn't an inherently bad thing. After all, you have to have a great deal of self-confidence to survive in this business. Networks and production companies smell diffidence like sharks detect blood in open water. So though it's vital to maintain absolute confidence in yourself and in your professional vision, you can't afford to let that confidence interfere with your chances for eventual success. Some of the most talented people in the world will never make it into the business because they didn't do what they needed to do: start from the ground up.

The concept of buying low and selling high is particularly important in this regard. By buying into the business low (for example, starting out as a production intern) and then eventually selling high (that is, cashing in your ground-level experience and contacts to reach an elevated plateau), you're managing your career the way a savvy speculator trades commodities. Starting "low" in show business isn't necessarily a secret. But for many truly talented aspiring producers, you would think it's the biggest secret in the world, because so few actually want to start at the nadir instead of the apex.

BECOME A PRODUCTION INTERN

The internship opportunities offered by major colleges, universities, and corporations are well known. Lesser known, however, are the internship opportunities available with most major film and television production companies. Without fail, internship programs are repeatedly available in almost every facet of TV production. And even though production interns acquire vast reserves of experience and credibility, production companies offer these opportunities by the boatload for two distinct, self-serving purposes. First, they benefit from the inexpensive or free manpower. Second, they are able to scout talent for future projects or positions within the company. Overall, this is mostly a win-win situation for everyone involved.

The downside, of course, is that production internships are typically unpaid positions. Yet the experience gleaned and the opportunity to meet the movers and shakers who could end up hiring you one day are well worth the gratis servitude. Some industry players even advance the notion that being a production intern comes with certain privileges or perks few paid employees enjoy. Primarily, an intern has a considerable degree of workplace flexibility and will often float from one department to another while simultaneously soaking up precious experience.

Simply put, I've met very few *bored* production interns. Furthermore, novice producers without the background as production interns often find themselves drowning in a new world of unfamiliar responsibilities and red tape common to working full time at a network or production company. Contrary to what you might have heard, production interns are treated surprisingly well—at least in most cases—and afforded the patience and guidance to acquire the necessary training for their future careers.

Most auspiciously, if you screw up at first, you're "just a production intern." Gaffes are expected of you. But if you make the same rookie mistakes as a full-time producer or employee, such errors will typically not be dealt with in such a nurturing manner. Needless to say, if you know your stuff as a production intern and shine through like a pro, your skills will be amplified that much more.

If you're sold on the obvious advantages inherent in starting your career off as a production intern, there are a number of places to search for the myriad opportunities awaiting your inquiry. As a longtime subscriber to both *Variety* and *The Hollywood Reporter*, I have never noticed a shortage of ripe opportunities in either of these very important trade publications. If an actual internship position isn't outwardly posted, you can deduce from the comprehensive published lists of television shows starting production where opportunities might be available.

Best of all, you don't have to call your friends at the FBI to track down phone numbers for the appropriate production offices. *Variety* and *The Hollywood Reporter* typically include direct phone numbers to the production offices of new or returning TV programs. You can immediately get on the horn to personally inquire about available openings. If there are none, there's a great possibility that the person you get on the phone will know someplace or someone who might need you.

A Daily Goldmine

A veritable treasure trove of resources and information, *Daily Variety* is now available through online subscription for $165 per year.

THE IMDB FACTOR

As an up-and-coming film director—or "wannabe," in his own words—Quentin Tarantino, like others in his aspiring position, understood the value of a knock-out résumé. Having worked as a video store attendant as a younger man, Tarantino, now one of the most successful and respected directors in Hollywood, was intimately familiar with all genres of film, particularly those on the independent circuit. Many of the films available at his local video store were films few, if any, had ever seen. So to compensate for his lack of show business experience at the start of his career, Tarantino boldly and erroneously listed films on his résumé that he had never actually performed in or directed. In most cases, they were "obscure films by great directors," according to Tarantino, who incorrectly believed that casting agents would "never have the time to confirm those résumé credits."

Unfortunately for Tarantino, he was busted on more than one occasion, even though a number of these erroneous credits remain attributed to him today in *Leonard Maltin's Movie and Video Guide.*

Over the years I have encountered an astonishing number of aspiring actors, producers, writers, and directors who have either been caught in similar shenanigans or who blatantly risk their professional reputations every day by touting fake film and television credits.

In recent years, however, it has been increasingly difficult, not to mention outright stupid, to lay claim to any professional credit that isn't legitimate to the core. Why? Since the advent of the Internet Movie Database (IMDB), an expansive, easily searchable web-based collection of verified film and television production credits, it has never been easier for networks, production companies, film studios, and others to check the facts and find out if you're fibbing. And they *do* check!

BUILD A DIGITAL RÉSUMÉ

To get a break in reality television production (or any other facet of film or television production for that matter), it is just as important—some would say *more* important—to have an outstanding digital résumé to supplement your paper one. And unless you reach the big cities and bright lights any time soon, nobody is going to tend to your digital résumé for you. This is why it is infinitely important to post on IMDB any and every verifiable film or TV credit you possess.

If you currently have no credits to list, don't make any up. Instead, create a user profile and post your photo, education, any relevant experience, and aspirations. Having an attractive digital résumé posted on a major site like IMDB is among the quickest ways to network and promote yourself, your talents, your experience, or even just your professional pipedreams.

In the spring of 2007, I was informed that a former low-level production staffer at E! had been contacted by a major television production company in response to his IMDB profile, not because of his production experience (which was limited) but because of his expressed passion for skateboarding. After a brief interview, he was hired on as an assistant producer for an MTV piloted project about extreme sports and their upcoming superstars. This example is just one of many little-known instances of IMDB doing an awful lot of networking on your behalf while you concentrate on other matters in your career.

Launched in 1990 and acquired by Amazon.com in 1998, IMDB is an online collection of information about films, actors, TV shows, production crew personnel, and even video games. According to IMDB, its website contains the biggest collection of data about film, television, and video games dating back to each medium's earliest beginnings. IMDB, however, often includes comprehensive cast and crew credits, uncredited personnel, production and distribution companies, box-office receipts, promotional info, shooting locations, famous quotes, character and plot summaries, and, perhaps most popular, message boards for public reviews and commentary. IMDB is not only a popular site for fans of entertainment content; it is also a site frequently visited by anyone who is anyone in the film and television industries.

CRACKING THE EMAIL CODE

As a young man trying to secure a foothold in broadcasting, one of the most arduous obstacles I routinely faced was attempting to get in contact with all the "right people." The process of booking celebrity guests on my series, for example, never failed to erect obfuscating hurdles. Most of the time, however, such impediments came not from a lack of celebrities wanting to appear on my show but instead from my recurrent inability to gain access to their immediate representatives: agents, publicists, managers, and the like.

As I began aiming higher in my professional aspirations and sought to take *The Michael Essany Show* to a national audience, I experienced a strikingly similar difficulty in getting my show concept and, subsequently, my program pitch in front of the right network executives and production company heads.

That was, of course, until I cracked the email code.

Over the years I've met a good number of other individuals who apply this method. Astonishingly, though, many people remain oblivious to this helpful trick for gaining an audience with those whose attention may be difficult, if not impossible, to obtain.

Let's say, hypothetically, that someone named Charlie Bell is president and CEO of XYZ Production Company in Los Angeles. For days on end, you call the front desk and bombard the only P.O. box number you have with desperate pleas for an opportunity to meet and discuss the show idea that you know in your heart is a perfect project for XYZ. You're beyond confident that if only Charlie

Bell would personally read your correspondence and brief project description, you'd promptly be invited to pitch your show.

Now, let's also say that the highest up in the company you can reach is the VP of creative development, Sarah Smith. And by some chance, you've got Sarah's email address, which is S.Smith@XYZ.com. Naturally, Sarah promises to work your information up to the top, but you still get the nagging feeling that you and your emails are being willfully ignored.

You want Charlie Bell. You *need* Charlie Bell.

The solution? Email Charlie Bell. Although you might not realize it, chances are that you already can glean Mr. Bell's direct work email address by virtue of having Ms. Smith's email address. To be sure, this approach might not work if you're trying to reach Mark Burnett or Steven Spielberg, for example, but you would be amazed at just how many higher-ups I have gained unexpected access to by cracking the email code this way.

Put simply, once you've found an email address for someone—anyone—who works at XYZ Production Company, you have the basic formula for email addresses at this particular business. In the case of Sarah Smith, the formula is *first initial + period + full last name + @XYZ.com*. Most of the time, by following this basic formula with other names (e.g., *Charlie Bell = C.Bell@XYZ.com*), you have an excellent opportunity to get your message right where you need it to go.

In the late 1990s, when I first began using this trick, I discovered that it worked approximately 60 percent of the time. And even though that means that 40 percent of my emails were returned as undeliverable, the added advantage of possessing this knowledge, which could also result in similar success for you, is worth its weight in gold. Over the years, I booked countless celebrity guests and arranged numerous high-level meetings as a result of getting my message to the right people through this occasionally clever methodology.

One warning: If you succeed in cracking the code and do manage to reach the big boys and girls upstairs, make it count. If you've prepared a wordy, unfocused, banal, and unprofessional email, there's an outstanding possibility that your first email that is opened by the head honcho will also be the last. *Make it count.*

WATCH CRITICALLY

Despite what some people believe, being a fan of reality TV doesn't necessarily give a hopeful reality TV producer much of an advantage in the competitive landscape of wannabe Mark Burnetts. What aids producers even more than simply liking to watch reality television is learning to replace a fan's eye with a critical eye.

Needless to say, watching reality television requires remarkably little effort. On the other hand, watching it critically—that is, studying the patent story arcs, noting the dramatic scene juxtapositions, contemplating the ancillary themes and musical components of the segments—could easily transform a one-hour reality TV episode into a weeklong study guide to reality television production.

Many producers who excel in reality television do more than merely watch the work of their contemporaries. Instead, they tear said works apart. They dissect the tiniest cutaways and scrutinize the surprisingly complex thematic layers that comprise what might otherwise appear as the most unsophisticated, crude bundle of video clips ever assembled.

Never forget that reality television production is an art. However, as with other tangible artistic expressions, not every "masterpiece" is destined for a museum. As we've already exhaustively explored, there is certainly no shortage of good *and* bad reality television. But once your critical eye learns to separate the two, analyze, explore, and learn as much as you possibly can about the dynamics of reality television production. Some of the most important lessons you will ever learn about production will come from this self-starting endeavor that could prove among the most beneficial experiences of your young career.

Chapter thirteen

Avoiding the Reality Drive-Through

Reality television is often credited—or criticized—for introducing the universal phenomenon that today is logged in the American pop culture lexicon as *instant celebrity.*

In the bygone era of old-school Hollywood, there was not only an established celebrity standard, there was also an established process by which one could attain that elusive and still largely respected status. The stars of yesterday earned their celebrity in large part by patiently but diligently working their way to the top of the industry through incremental steps that nurtured talent and cultivated appreciation for their chosen craft. Today, however, that long and painful road to success is frequently becoming the road less traveled.

As the leading provider of expedient celebrity, reality television has quickly deteriorated into the contemporary drive-through equivalent of "making it" in the entertainment business. With shows like *The Apprentice, America's Next Top Model, The Hills, Rock of Love,* and *The Real World* cranking out new "celebrities" on a relatively frequent basis, is it any wonder that scores of talented and professionally trained actors and musicians are growing increasingly frustrated by repeatedly losing work to flash-in-the pan instant celebrities?

Where Are They Now?

The Curious Whereabouts of Former Reality TV Darlings

William Hung

Arguably the most famous noncontestant from *American Idol*, William Hung was initially presented as a joke. Hung himself did not even know that his *American Idol* audition would be broadcast until it finally aired. Within three years, however, Hung would go on to release four albums and, according to Hung's own admission on *Larry King Live*, earn more than $1 million as an internationally recognized entertainer.

Justin Guarini

The mop-topped first-season *Idol* runner-up went on to appear in *From Justin to Kelly* and release his first album. After being dropped by his record label, a resilient Guarini independently released his second album, and a follow-up is now being planned.

Colleen Haskell

After appearing on the first season of *Survivor*, Colleen Haskell starred in the comedic film *The Animal*, also starring Rob Schneider. She has gone on to work behind the scenes in television production and as a spokesperson for various products.

Toni Ferrari

After rising to fame on *Love Cruise: The Maiden Voyage* and *Paradise Hotel*, Toni Ferrari is now working behind the scenes pitching to various networks and production companies a new reality show based on her life, entitled *I'm Really an Actress.*

Dat Phan

From *Last Comic Standing* to a small role in *Cellular* with Kim Basinger, the aspiring young stand-up comic is still touring the country and working on his career.

To be fair, some of the performers who attain national glory are tremendously talented individuals worthy of considerable praise and industry respect. But for most, 15 minutes of fame is all that will, or can, be attained in a business that hastily decides who is useful or useless. As a result of most being rendered "useless," the reality TV industry is always ready and willing to give someone else their 15 minutes.

By 2005 it was apparent that the reality television frenzy had spilled over into what is now referred to as "reality media." YouTube, for example, allows anyone with a digital camera the opportunity to become an instant celebrity. Correspondingly, the explosion of cell phones with video-enabled technology has turned ordinary folks into prolific members of the news and entertainment media.

A YouTube "Star" is Born

On September 18, 2007, *Variety* revealed that Chris Crocker, a 20-year-old who hosts a budgetless but enormously popular video series on YouTube, had signed a development deal with 44 Blue Productions to star in a documentary-style reality television show.

Incredibly, the desire for overnight fame and fortune is so strong among the masses that professional job coaches and career counselors have recorded an unprecedented spike in numerous professions now dubbed "reality TV reflecting pools." For many, the increased popularity and prevalence of these career choices have resulted directly from an accelerated viewership of reality programming. Although the bulk of reality TV fans are called to these professions as a consequence of watching others excel in a similar field, many select these particular occupations for the sole purpose of increasing their chances of getting a big break on reality television.

Top Five Job Surges Attributed to Reality TV

Interior Decorator
We can all thank Home and Garden Television (HGTV), Do It Yourself (DIY) Network, and The Learning Channel (TLC) for the surge in popularity of this career choice. Reality programs like *While You Were Out* and *Trading Spaces* have inspired a new generation of interior decorators to refurbish and redecorate all the way to the bank.

Party Planner
Life events often require talented people to properly plan and celebrate them. As a result, a great deal of reality programming on Women's Entertainment (WE tv), Style Network, and TLC is concentrated on wedding preparation and life event planning, often from the perspective of the designated party planner.

Continued...

Top Five Job Surges Attributed to Reality TV—continued

Business Consultant

Thanks to *The Apprentice*, everyone thinks they can run a business—particularly *yours*. Naturally, the booming industry that is business consultation is attributed to the popularity of reality programming.

Style Consultant

Compensated for assessing and advising others on how to look (or not to look), style consultants are quickly multiplying, largely as a result of *Queer Eye for the Straight Guy*.

Culinary Artist

From *Emeril Live* to *Iron Chef*, the reality TV market is hungry for new chefs with the talent and personality to cook up interest among viewers who are endlessly fascinated by cooking shows.

Although phrases like "overnight celebrity," "15 minutes of fame," and "flash-in-the-pan artists" are most commonly attributed to those in front of the reality TV cameras, producers are just as vulnerable to the instant make-or-break nature of reality television.

"The business used to recycle producers," says legendary TV host, producer, and media mogul Dick Clark. "Once you were in, you were in. It's different now."

Indeed, reality show producers are often relegated to the ash heap of television history just as quickly as the fleeting celebrities they helped to engender.

"The value of not putting all your eggs in one basket is particularly true for television producers today," warns Clark. "Unless you want a career that spans six weeks, I urge the younger guys coming up to be as prolific as their sanity allows."

THE JUGGLING ACT

Successful producers like Dick Clark and Mark Burnett have been widely recognized for juggling a multitude of projects at any given time. As Clark has noted, savvy producers focus on the big picture—namely, their careers—fully aware that it's harder to be professionally dismissed after a failed project if other projects are in development.

Unfortunately, most reality series last only one short season. Yet the majority of first-time reality producers don't realize that producing a ratings juggernaut like *Survivor* is considerably more difficult to do than the unscripted genre deceptively leads them to believe. As a result, many producers abandon their long-held aspirations after a single project fails to prove successful.

On the other hand, producers who bring to the table a vast array of projects and programming concepts stand a much better chance of emerging as premier reality show producers than those who invest all their time, money, and energy in one project that might or might not ever see the light of day.

"The most important thing for a new producer to do is get an active start," advises Dick Clark. "When I was a kid, I ended up on camera for the first time by an odd mistake. Somebody just put me there. And I began to realize as the years went by that I wouldn't be able to do this forever. So I started doing the production end. I still do some on-camera work, but 90 percent of what I do is *behind* the lens. And if you're going to do that, you have to do a mess of things all at once. It's the only way to keep up and make a steady living. There are so many uncertainties in television production that you really can't afford to approach another way."

Though there are numerous "gimmicks" routinely employed by former reality TV stars working to extend the viability and longevity of their careers, there are considerably fewer options for reality TV producers hoping to be known for more than one failed series.

Without a doubt, this is the reason that the principle of hitting the ground running at the start of your career is ultimately just as vital to the length and quality of your career as anything else you will ever do. When Mark Burnett started his own production company, ·Mark Burnett Productions, he unveiled a slew of projects, many of which never reached the mainstream. Yet his portfolio kept Burnett a leading and prolific producer whose name quickly became synonymous with the reality medium itself.

Although upstart producers typically don't have vast reserves of financing power or industry connections, a viable strategy for newcomers looking to pitch and produce a reality project involves taking your work directly to the troika of reality television's most open markets: Comedy Central, Discovery, and MTV. As of early 2008, these three growing and undeniably successful major cable networks still accept unsolicited programming pitches from new and untested producers and writers.

THE $60 BATTLE PLAN

By now, of course, you probably have at least one reality TV brainchild that you are wholly optimistic about. If you have only one, quickly develop two more into similar, properly formatted pitches. Tailor one unique project to each network, trying in some way to home in on the niche viewing audiences held by the individual networks.

Next, for the purposes of protecting your work, register each individual show idea ($20 each) with the WGA. Fortunately, the registration process is remarkably straightforward and will only require you to enter the basic information that's likely already included in your pitch. The registration is instant and should consume only a few minutes of your time. The site will require your Social Security or driver's license number for identification purposes. Finally, you'll be given a registration number to include in your written pitch.

Although few networks will review unsolicited proposals, none to my knowledge will review unregistered ones. Not only does a WGA registration moderately protect your work, it also protects the network from any accusations of intellectual property theft down the line.

Once you're all set, review your respective presentations and mail them (by snail mail) to your first three prospective networks:

MTV Networks
Series Development
2600 Colorado Avenue
Santa Monica, CA 90404

Comedy Central
Coordinator of Development
1775 Broadway
New York, NY 10019

Discovery Communications
Development Liaison
7700 Wisconsin Avenue
Bethesda, MD 20814

Most of the time, the typical unsolicited pitch will not garner a response (if any at all) for up to eight weeks.

Although this strategy obviously applies most suitably to producers trying to break into the business, the process of continually generating program concepts and pitching to new and former contacts is the best, and some would argue the *only*, way to overcome the perpetual threat of lasting only as long as the first project you manage to sell.

The *Hollywood Creative Directory*

For $64.95 you can purchase the *Hollywood Creative Directory*, a comprehensive reference guide with current contact information for production companies, television shows, and network executives. The book, which is revised three times yearly, is available at www.hcdonline.com. A new online edition of the directory was launched recently and is updated daily. A subscription to the online version runs $249.95 per year.

In 2001 I sat down with Jim Lehrer, longtime host of the *News Hour* on PBS. During the course of our interview, Jim shared one of the most interesting and lasting insights ever gleaned during a conversation on my program: "Some of the dumbest people I know," said Lehrer, "are those who, on paper, have the most experience and education in their field. I say this because after they attained their master's or reached their desirable level of success, they never cracked another book or entertained a fresh idea. They simply stagnated."

In the television industry—particularly within the genre of unscripted programming—any producer who stagnates or similarly fails to continuously expand his or her knowledge of market trends, viewership patterns, and programming developments cannot possibly expect a lasting career that grows with the industry.

It is indeed a simple assertion, but cultivating a lasting, profitable, and gratifying career in reality television has more to do with basic communication skills than it does production skills. For many producers who've arranged their first pitch meeting or sold their first reality show, a palpable demeanor of cocksureness becomes apparent. Countless producers believe after even a minimal amount of success that they "get it." But as discussed earlier, there is no wise old sage of reality television who truly knows all. The reality genre is a consistently evolving field that demands a consistently studious approach by producers at all levels, from those just out of college to Mark Burnett himself.

TALKING THE TALK

The basic communication skills I just alluded to are twofold. First and foremost, a good producer possesses the willingness and ability to listen—to criticism, feedback, industry moods, and more. Just as important, conversely, is the ability to speak or present what others need to hear, specifically during a project pitch. For those who grow conceited and believe that their apparent confidence is enough to sell a soft pitch, they will find themselves sorely mistaken almost all the time. Though presenting self-confidence and faith in one's project is absolutely fundamental, failing to deliver a presentation just as thoughtful and charming as the one a first-time producer would deliver is a veritable death sentence for a project, even if it's an outstanding idea with real potential.

AN EMERGENT TREND

In some circles within the television industry, although to a reduced extent after the 2007–2008 writers' strike, many producers in the reality television genre have begun flirting with scripted programming largely to diversify their résumés and build production credibility for the future.

Ideally, successful producers will eventually incorporate and launch their own production companies, as discussed, for more leveraged creative and financial reasons. At the moment, however, the growing trend is to develop production companies that specialize in scripted *and* unscripted programming, thus doubling the base of potential production opportunities.

Although producers looking to break into the television industry as reality show producers should focus exclusively at first on only the reality genre, an emergent theory for extending one's reach and longevity in the business is to diversify production experience and credits to the fullest extent possible.

Although reality television doesn't appear to be going away, it's virtually impossible to predict what audiences will demand 10 or 15 years down the road. If the reality craze subsides, even just temporarily, producers solely invested in the reality business could find themselves at a tremendous financial and creative disadvantage—or an outright loss.

Just as Dick Clark warned against putting all your eggs in one basket when trying to break into reality television, indeed, maintaining a rewarding career as a producer—of any format of programming—primarily still depends on talent, experience, tenacity, and foresight. Having the foresight early in your career to amass the sundry credentials necessary to be an indispensable part of any type of television production is precisely the most valuable advice any new producer can receive on the journey to becoming a Hollywood mogul.

Chapter | fourteen

Making Sense of Reality

Some have argued that every reality television program should be immediately preceded by the obligatory disclaimer, "Don't try this at home." However, it wouldn't be altogether clear if such a warning would apply to the particular content of the program or to the general idea of producing reality television. As we've seen, either could prove remarkably perilous.

Having been wholly seduced by the wiles of television's hottest industry, I have appreciated my past and present experiences in reality television. And although I have always sought to encourage up-and-coming reality show producers and performers to embrace the medium, it's equally important to concede that the business is *not* for everyone.

Reality television ruins lives beyond the occasional naïve soul who intrepidly signs up for a tour of duty in front of the lens. The ugly underside of reality TV is the vast array of immensely talented producers and secondary production staffers abruptly eaten alive by a medium that uses people in ways inconceivable to outsiders. In this regard, *Survivor* is more than just reality TV's hottest show. It's also an accurate metaphor for the industry itself.

Surviving the reality television experience begins by making sense of the genre. Together we have begun the survival process by exploring the basic steps to becoming an experienced warrior of reality TV production. And with this book, unlike the majority of textbooks and reference guides available on the subject, I hoped to introduce some of the less discussed, more abstract components of the production process.

In reality TV, success *and* survival are exclusive products of knowing what to expect from the business and reacting accordingly every step of the way. Although reality television is an art, it certainly isn't a science. As you might have learned in college or in film school or through sundry production guides or even hands-on experience, virtually *anyone* can learn to produce reality television, albeit to varying degrees of quality. For that reason, in this volume I tried to refrain from tackling the more technical aspects of production that have been readily available on bookshelves for decades. Instead, I aimed to take you through the motions of creating a programming concept, seeing it to fruition, and extending professional momentum beyond a fleeting tenure.

Of course, as with other products and services that are widely available, individual results may vary. But as plenty of moguls have exhibited through their unique success stories, if you take your work seriously, aggressively create opportunities for yourself, and learn the essential nature of the business in which you toil, you'll begin your journey 10 steps ahead of the average guy who ineptly embarks on a career in reality TV simply because it looks "easy, fun, and lucrative."

WHERE WE'VE BEEN. WHERE YOU'RE GOING

The first thing to grasp about unscripted programming is that all reality television is not of the same variety. As we've explored, reality television is the melting pot of diverse programming categories frequently lumped into one broad genre.

CATEGORIES OF REALITY PROGRAMMING

Documentary reality	Competition reality	Celebrity reality
Self-improvement reality	Makeover reality	Renovation and design reality
Professional reality	Forced environment reality	Romance reality
Aspiration reality	Fear-based reality	Sports reality
Undercover reality		

Ultimately, whether you're producing a new game show or introducing audiences to innovative home-renovation techniques, the bottom line for all programs placed in the reality rubric is the human element. If your game show is inventive, that's certainly a vital and positive start. But unless it also conveys real human emotion and the personal stories behind the contestants, audiences will likely never bond with your product. Conversely, the eventual success or failure of a home improvement program equally depends on skilled storytelling. Incredibly enough, the families who reside in the renovated houses are just as important as the houses. No matter how you cut it, audiences grow enamored with programs that regularly feature individuals by whom they are charmed and to whom they can relate. Across the expansive board of reality television categories, this is the only imperative variable common to each.

SOMETHING BORROWED, SOMETHING NEW

The advent of reality TV accompanied the advent of television itself. Those who would do well as producers should first study the long, fascinating history of reality television. Internet resources alone are insufficient for gauging programming trends and audience preferences for programs that might very well date back to the Golden Era of television.

Borrowing lessons from the history of reality television is only the first step. The next involves creating programming concepts that are dramatically different from anything familiar to reality TV viewing audiences. The era of recycled reality programming is over. Today more than ever, network executives and production companies are exhibiting a penchant for risk. In the past, it was common for the shows purchased to only emulate other successful programming concepts. Now that reality television is established among modern audiences, networks realize the value of revolutionizing the contents of a formerly revolutionary programming genre. In the past, creativity was secondary to viability. In 2008 and beyond, the reality TV industry stands poised and ready for a complete makeover. Producers who can cook up programming ideas to help reinvent the reality wheel will likely prove an indispensable commodity to networks in the foreseeable future.

LOTS OF EGGS IN LOTS OF BASKETS

Mark Burnett and Dick Clark are "active producers." That is, they consistently invent and pitch programming ideas. Some sell. Many do not, even for these established titans of television production.

For the fledgling producer who is new to the industry, selling a show is exponentially more cumbersome. But reality television, according to Dick Clark's example, responds well to the law of averages. In other words, producers who concentrate on 12 program concepts or pitches instead of one have an accelerated opportunity to gain a foothold in the business and begin producing television.

Though this pearl of wisdom might actually seem like mere common sense, the record shows that most newcomers to television typically focus on a single program idea and devote months to circulating that lone concept to every network and production company with a physical mailing address—even those that traditionally don't toil in the reality genre. In most cases, regrettably, these aspiring producers rarely achieve the professional heights they might very well have been capable of reaching.

If you think it's difficult to predict which reality shows will sink or swim during a new season, trying to imagine which of your ideas will sell is even more challenging. But by diversifying their pitch portfolios and disseminating a wide variety of targeted proposals to well-researched production companies, aspiring producers will fare much better than their counterparts who fail to apply strategy behind their lofty ambitions.

LIFE'S A PITCH

Anyone willing to hear a pitch from you should be allowed to hear it. Whether it's the CEO of Disney or the receptionist at your dentist's office, never miss an opportunity to pitch. If it doesn't amount to a sold project, it at least results in pitching experience. And, as we've seen, *how* you pitch can ultimately mean just as much as *what* you pitch.

Overall, the reality television industry demands that a producer be two things: a work horse and show horse. And because persistence is vital in getting executives to hear your pitch, sometimes it is necessary to be a horse's ass if it eventually helps to facilitate a meeting.

Ten Steps to Successful Project Pitching

1. Research current reality programming to familiarize yourself with current trends, opportunities, and network and audience preferences.

2. Prepare a brief, descriptive outline of your show idea(s), typically three to five pages for reality-based concepts (two to five pages are standard for scripted projects).

3. Go online and register your written show concept with the Writers Guild of America.

4. Target your submissions to networks and production companies that are well suited to the nature of your project.

5. Persistently follow up to schedule pitch meetings at any rank or level available.

6. Prepare to the hilt. For once, the producer is the performer. Present yourself and your project confidently, passionately, and briefly.

7. If possible, attach a credible production company, recognizable talent, or experienced counselor to the project and bring him or her to the pitch meeting.

8. Present as many relevant and compelling examples and resources possible (video clips, handouts, testimonies, etc.).

9. Leave enough creative wiggle room in your presentation to let executives imagine what they want to see on the small screen. Endear others to your vision, but let them also incorporate their own.

10. Repeat as necessary.

HOMEMADE REALITY TV

As we've seen, there are no guarantees in reality television. In many instances, for any number of reasons, the pitch meeting never happens. But even in the wake of such a disappointing reality, all hope is not lost for garnering the attention of network executives and production companies looking for exactly what it is that you have to offer.

The do-it-yourself approach to selling and producing projects often begins with a wannabe producer becoming a formidable presence on YouTube, Mania TV, MySpace, and Facebook. From filming your reality show pitch or segments of the actual program to networking with new people and making connections in new places, exposure remains the most critical of variables to an aspiring producer.

Pitch meeting or not, how well you network is entirely up to you. And those who devote the time and attention to exposing their projects and connecting with the "in crowd" are going to eventually find Hollywood knocking on *their* door.

POWER OF ATTORNEY

Confidence is the mother's milk of reality television. Without it, you can't sell a project. Without it, you can't produce a project. But there is one aspect of the reality TV experience that should remove any and all traces of confidence from your mind. It's the confidence that you're smart enough and savvy enough *not* to get screwed. The nature of reality television is so highly exploitative—for producers and performers alike—that it is imperative to seek and obtain proper legal counsel after your first show sells and the contract is delivered to your door.

Eventually, if you hang in through the ups and downs of the business, there's an excellent possibility that you will end up producing *something*. But there's no chance for you to produce *anything* without first *signing something*. From protecting your rights to preserving your dignity, an adequate attorney is always better than an excellent agent in defending your interests and safeguarding your good name.

Although we have examined numerous ways of protecting your work (registering program concepts with the WGA, for example), an attorney who is well versed in entertainment law can quickly—and sometimes inexpensively—take you through the motions of securing your intellectual property to an extent that online registrations simply cannot.

Also valuable to an aspiring producer, particularly one independently producing a pilot, is that an attorney can help draft and organize the vast array of legal forms requisite for video production. From preparing specialized documents for obtaining permission for location shoots to drafting personal release forms to indemnify producers from any right to privacy lawsuits by individuals captured on tape, an attorney more than protects a producer's work; he or she also protects the producer's career.

Ways to Protect Intellectual Property and Avoid Production-Related Lawsuits

1. Use nondisclosure forms when pitching your projects.

2. Obtain legal protection for your ideas to the fullest extent your time or budget allows.

3. Don't sign *anything* without first consulting an attorney versed in copyright, patent, or entertainment law.

4. Just as you seek to protect your intellectual property, respect others seeking to protect theirs.

5. When producing a project, secure permission in writing for everything—even that which might not technically require permission.

THE DIRTY WORK

Many established producers will tell you that physically producing a project is, surprisingly, the easiest aspect of the entire production process. In most instances, it's the frustration that transpires before and after the shooting that generates the greatest stress for people attached to the project.

Nonetheless, the process is only simple for those who have already learned the fundamentals of the reality TV game. At all times, across the immense spectrum of unscripted programming categories, you must follow an established structure of production basics. If you don't, the only things you will be recognized for producing are ulcers.

Reality TV Production Basics

- Projects live and die according to the calendar. Set a production schedule that everyone is aware of and agrees to. Meet, if not beat, all corresponding deadlines.

- Before the cameras capture a vision for the finished project, come up with your own.

- Maintain open lines of communication at all levels of production to avoid the myriad problems that can result from not doing so.

Continued...

- Get comfortable with Murphy's Law. Setbacks and unexpected problems are synonymous with reality TV production. Set backup plans and contingencies for every conceivable situation.

- Operate within budget at all times. Don't anticipate "cutting corners later."

- Give your production crew and cast the same respect and understanding you afford to your superiors.

- Allow twice as much time for location shoots as you currently anticipate.

- Trust your team. Let others do their work so that you may concentrate wholly on doing your own.

- If it's not detrimental to the project, invite your crew to share your vision. If they're only shooting tape without a clear understanding of what is to become of it, they can't perform as well as you need and expect them to.

CULTIVATING A CAREER

Although reality television is not internationally renowned for giving rise to enduring careers, there are numerous ways to extend the fleeting momentum awarded by reality television success into a lasting, gratifying career.

For starters, even if your passion burns exclusively for reality television, don't naïvely limit yourself to producing strictly within the unscripted genre. Be prolific and creative in as many facets of television production as possible. The experience and credibility you'll gain by doing so can be parlayed into a host of opportunities behind the scenes if and when your reality show tanks or fails to even launch.

Just as important is having consistent awareness so that you avoid growing stagnant or complacent. Network and audience preferences evolve constantly. If you, too, can uninterruptedly mold your work to the programming whims that surround you, your product will always be fresh, your ideas will remain cutting-edge, and your odds of staying employed will be excellent.

Although these qualities are rarely spoken of as linking to the prospect of cultivating a lasting career, those who work with character and integrity at all times do more to cement their professional footing than most realize. Those who earn respect by respecting others are a surprisingly rare but much appreciated commodity in television production. By maintaining high ethical standards of conduct, you not only perform a great service to yourself and those on your team, you also elevate the integrity and class of a medium hardly known for either.

Last, as we've touched on more times than Donald Trump has echoed, "You're fired," don't become known for doing only *one* thing. Promote yourself to a level where you are known as a multifaceted, dynamic, and versatile producer who regularly juggles an enormous workload, even if the responsibilities are largely self-imposed.

Reality TV is a cash run only for those willing to play games, eat bugs, and frequently debase themselves on national television. For producers, reality television can also be highly lucrative, but only for those who are serious about their work, dedicate themselves wholly to their craft, and maintain their sanity through setback after setback while chasing an elusive dream. Ultimately, nothing is more conducive to a long-lasting career than the desire and determination to have one.

YOUNIVERSAL REALITY

When *Time* magazine announced that the much coveted Person of the Year for 2006 was "You," the "you" they were primarily referring to was *you:* the contemporary breed of ambitious upstart looking to capitalize on revolutionary media capable of launching new careers, impacting diverse cultures, and, to no small degree, powerfully influencing the modern world as we know it. Even though it is unlikely that the greatest heroes and legends of our century will ultimately prove to have been the reality TV producers, this unprecedented epoch of "you" presents equally unprecedented opportunities for those courageous enough to assume the front lines of this exciting movement.

Never at any other time in global history has the world at large been more accommodating to and accepting of individual influence. With the dawn of Internet media, the emergence of reality entertainment, and the dwindling influence of more established, traditional forms of news and broadcast media, the 21st century is undoubtedly poised to be an era dominated by average Joes and Janes.

That said, it is absolutely essential to completely disregard everything you have previously read in dated works about the improbability or virtual impossibility of breaking into the entertainment business as a producer with no contacts, wealth, or influence. Ironically enough, those who currently possess those ideal "attributes" are not by default nearly as far ahead of their lesser-equipped contemporaries as they once were. If anything, the business today is rejecting almost by rote those who have the established pedigrees for performing and producing. The world as a whole is hungry for change. And nowhere is this universal truth more transparent than in the world of network and cable broadcast television.

Indeed, the formidable barricades once in place are now minimal hurdles than can readily be jumped. For those who treat their work and their peers with reverence, react to obstacles with irreverence, and always strive to evolve with the art and business behind the industry, the unknown producer of today could very well become an iconic producer of tomorrow.

It's a process that begins with a reality check and results in the experience of a lifetime.

Glossary of TV Production Terms

A

A-roll Video that is used for both visual *and* audio presentation purposes.

above the line The creative elements of a television production project, including but not limited to writers, producers, directors, talent, and the like. These are the names/titles that often appear above the bold line on a standard production budget or worksheet.

A/B-roll splicing Cutting between two video sources playing simultaneously.

accent light A light such as a key light, a kicker, or a backlight that calls attention to one particular subject.

action axis ("180-degree rule") An imaginary line between two subjects; used to secure the continuity of camera movements and direction.

ad-lib Impromptu comment or action otherwise unrehearsed and delivered for the first time on camera.

aerial shot High- and wide-angle view of a subject, often captured from a lift or crane, if not from a low-flying helicopter.

AFM (audio frequency modulation) 8mm and Hi8 video format analog soundtrack.

AFTRA (American Federation of Television and Radio Artists) AFTRA is a performers' union that represents a variety of talent: actors in radio and television, radio and television announcers, news anchors, recording artists, commercial promo and voice-over announcers, stunt persons, a vast array of "specialty acts." AFTRA currently has more than 80,000 members in local divisions throughout the United States. The two areas with the greatest concentration of AFTRA members are Los Angeles and New York City. Essentially, AFTRA negotiates wages and working conditions for its members. AFTRA is affiliated with the AFL-CIO and the International Federation of Journalists.

AGC (automatic gain control) Inbuilt feature of many camcorders that automatically balances a microphone's volume with unavoidable surrounding environmental audio or "noise."

ambient sound The natural environmental audio, or "background soundtrack," present at the location of filming. Unlike the primary audio—designated characters speaking, for example— ambient sound can consist of elements like the air conditioning humming in the room during, before, and after the dialogue between characters.

amplification The process of magnifying an audio signal.

anamorphic The aspect ratio of most films made with anamorphic lenses today is 1:2.35. The conventional television image's aspect ratio is 1:1.33. Anamorphic is a widescreen film process (e.g., CinemaScope and Panavision) used to create an image wider than the conventional television image.

artificial light Human-made illumination that originates from any source that is not natural light: lamps, candles, fluorescent bulbs, studio lights, and so on.

ASCAP (American Society of Composers, Authors, and Publishers) ASCAP is a nonprofit organization that safeguards its members' copyrights (for musical works) by monitoring public performances of their music through broadcast or live performance. ASCAP collects licensing fees from those who perform proprietary works of ASCAP members and then returns that money collected in the form of royalties to the member whose music was performed or "used" in some capacity. In the U.S., ASCAP competes with two other performing rights organizations: BMI (Broadcast Music Incorporated) and SESAC (Society of European Stage Authors and Composers). Like BMI and SESAC, ASCAP is an important organization with which to familiarize yourself, particularly if the need for clearing music for broadcast ever becomes a necessity on your projects (which it almost certainly will).

aspect ratio The width-to-height ratio of a television image. (The industry standard for a conventional monitor is 4:3; 16:9 for HDTV.)

assemble (or edit) The process of organizing video clips in the sequence in which they will appear in the final product.

assemble edit Shooting video segments in desired sequence in order to form a complete body of work or program.

associate producer Individual who primarily serves as the communication link between a production company and the myriad staff associated with the physical production process.

atmosphere Manufactured "human traffic" provided by extras to facilitate the desired atmosphere for a particular shoot.

audio dub The process of imposing or recording over an existing videotape soundtrack while leaving the prerecorded images unaltered

audio engineer Production crew member chiefly responsible for the functionality of audio capturing and recording devices on set or location.

audio mixer Integral production equipment used to compile multiple microphone sources and direct the collective signal to one designated location or recording source.

authoring The final phase of editing in most digital editing software packages is the "authoring" process, or compiling video, audio, and graphical components of a project into a finished product.

available light The lighting available at a particular shooting location—either natural light or artificial light, or a combination of both.

B

B-roll Video imposed over the primary video/audio track (A-roll) only for visual purposes.

baby legs A short video camera tripod used for low-level or special shots.

backlight Directional illumination (natural or manmade) placed behind the subject being filmed. Back lighting separates the foreground subject from its background by creating a heightened sense of depth.

barn doors Accessories tantamount to blinders used for video lights that aid in controlling light distribution.

basic storyboard The act of drawing or sketching pictures of scenes as you would like them to unfold on camera. Although reality TV production is supposed to be "natural" and not premeditated, storyboards are just as common to reality TV production as they are scripted film and television projects.

batch capture The process by which some digital editing systems capture entire batches of video clips or raw footage from videotape.

bed Background music played in conjunction with narration or foreground dialogue.

Betacam Broadcast-quality video camera utilized in production for most television series.

bidirectional microphone Microphone that absorbs sound equally from two sides.

bleeding Video image defect recognized by the blurring of colors, which "bleed" into other images.

BMI (Broadcast Music Incorporated) A music licensing company and a performing rights organization. BMI, which tracks public performances of 6.5 million works, collects license fees on behalf of its songwriters and other music publishers. BMI then disperses those moneys as "royalties" to the BMI members whose works have been performed. Originally established as competition for ASCAP, BMI is a nonprofit organization that in recent years has reached new heights in collections and distributions. According to industry estimates, in 2007 BMI distributed more than $700 million in royalties to the songwriters, composers, and copyright owners it represents. BMI issues licenses to users of music, including television networks and radio stations; so-called new media, including the Internet and mobile technologies; satellite audio services (e.g., XM and Sirius); nightclubs, hotels, bars, and restaurants; symphony orchestras, concert bands, and classical chamber music ensembles; digital jukeboxes; live musical performances and concerts.

boom Vertical camera move most commonly made possible by a *boom arm*.

boom arm A bar that extends parallel from the top of a tripod on which a video camera can be positioned. It allows for a fluid combination of camera movements, including panning and tilting.

boom microphone A microphone suspended by a retractable pole above and in front of a subject or performer.

bump Additional compensation paid to a performer or extra in return for performing a feat that goes above and beyond the call of duty; specifically any difficult stunt or activity that isn't typically performed by an extra or minimal on-camera participant.

C

C-47 Clothespins used to secure gels to barn doors.

cable (or public) access television Channel designated by local cable television provider for community-related programming. Cable access centers provide free use of video production equipment and studio facilities to members of a community.

call sheet A printed list of assignments for designated performers and production members, including when and where to arrive for a subsequent day of work.

call time A scheduled time to report to the production location or set for work, usually printed on a call sheet.

cameo lighting The process of illuminating foreground subjects against a black background through directional light.

camera log Detailed list of scenes recorded on a corresponding video tape.

camera operator Production crew member primarily responsible for capturing subjects on video within frame.

casting The process by which participants (amateur or professional) are auditioned and hired for a particular television series.

casting company An organization that provides performers and extras to networks and television production companies.

casting director Principle individual providing, auditioning, or recommending talent to a TV production company.

CATV (Community Antenna Television) A system of broadband distribution using coaxial cable rather than over-the-air broadcast.

character generator Equipment that can superimpose text over video during a live broadcast or in post-production.

chroma key (blue/green screen effect) Once complicated but now commonplace special effect method of inserting an image from one video source behind the image of another. A key color is designated as the transparent canvas for absorbing the super-imposed image, e.g., a weatherman stands in front of a green screen on which weather-related graphics are superimposed on the evening newscast.

close-up (tight shot) A compactly framed camera shot in which the main subject is viewed closely and prominently on the screen.

color commentator A television sports announcer, often a former athlete and/or coach, with hands-on expertise in the sport being broadcast. Increasingly in the world of reality television, color commentators are becoming a mainstay, particularly on programs like *American Gladiators*.

contingency An amount added to a production budget in anticipation of potential over-budget expenses.

continuity A sensible ordering of video clips to convey a story. Also refers to shots matching within a scene, as when someone is eating ice cream and the ice cream is gone in the second shot and back again in the third shot.

cookie Lighting accessory characterized by intricate patterns of cutouts that create shadows for effects purposes.

copyright The exclusive legal right to reproduce or perform any proprietary material (a book, song, photo). The use of copyrighted material on television, for example, warrants both permission from and a royalty fee payable to the holder of the copyrighted material. If there is no copyright, the material is said to be in the "public domain" and may be freely used by all.

cost per mil (CPM) The advertising rate charged to television advertising sponsors, which is quantified per 1000 viewers. *Mil* equals 1000. The CPM is the cost per 1000 viewers.

craft services The show business equivalent of "catering," craft services refer to the various food and refreshments provided to cast and crew on set during production.

craning A fluid or swinging camera movement deriving its name from the mechanical crane on which the video camera may be suspended. In a crane shot, the entire camera, mounted on a crane, is swept upward or downward.

crawl Text or graphics that horizontally "crawl" across the screen, usually from right to left along the bottom of the screen.

credits Comprehensive listing of crew and cast involved in the production of a television program or series, usually scrolling at the conclusion of a broadcast.

cross-fade (or dissolve) The fading out of one audio or video source as another fades in so that they briefly overlap.

cue Instruction to begin, end, or influence on-camera activity during a shoot.

cume Short for *cumulative*; refers to the total audience or number of viewers for a program after multiple broadcasts, excluding repeat viewers.

cut A shot change from one scene or image to another.

cutaway An important shot or series of shots taken by a camera operator to cover up potential edits. The cutaway shot is typically related to the immediate vicinity of the shooting location and can be used to cut away from the person speaking so that the editor can remove any unwanted audio during post-production. In reality television, cutaways are among the greatest causes of "ethical dilemmas," particularly on account of changing the context of one's comments, not just cleaning up the audio for continuity purposes.

D

deal memo An offer memorandum between a production company and crew member that details the specifics of a production or performance contract (salary, length of production, guaranteed conditions, etc).

demographics The characteristics of a viewing or listening audience, usually classified in terms of age, gender, income, race, or the like. Demographics are particularly useful to television networks in setting advertising rates for companies with products or services to sell to a particular or targeted demographic group.

designated market area (DMA) A geographic area where the resident population receives the same local television and radio station content offerings. One who resides in Northwest Indiana, for example, will primarily receive the local television and radio broadcasts (primarily news-related) originating from Chicago, the nearest major city and metropolitan area. Since these market regions occasionally overlap, the people residing on the edge of one media market can also receive content from other nearby markets. DMAs are widely used in assessing ratings, which are compiled in the United States by Nielsen Media Research (TV) and Arbitron (radio).

dialogue Written or improvised speech among characters on television or radio.

development deal Typically the first contract signed between a performer or producer and a major network, production company, or record label. A development deal usually provides an opportunity for emerging talent to have their skills directed to appropriate work and exploited for profit and an increased public profile.

director Individual who directs (often with the assistance of a First AD) the in-studio scenes of a television program; responsibilities often delegated to producers for on-site or remote location shoots.

dollying The process by which a camera is moved toward or away from a subject (typically on a *dolly,* or small wheeled vehicle), removing the need for zooming.

dub To duplicate a video and/or audio track by playing the original recording on one deck and copying it on another.

DV Digital Video, a specific video format; both a tape format and a data format specification.

DVCAM Digital Betacam tape format.

DVE (digital video effect) Any digital special effect that modifies a video image.

E

edit To condense, rearrange, or otherwise alter the events captured on video for the purposes of producing a quality and efficient product for broadcast.

edit bay Location of editing equipment and stored footage for use during the editing or compilation process.

edit decision list (EDL) The comprehensive and ordered list of time codes, edit-in and edit-out points, and special effect instructions for an editor's use in preparing the final cut of a production.

edit master A tape containing the finished, polished product of a video production.

edit points *Edit-in* and *edit-out* points are designated during the review of raw video footage in preparation for shot assembly.

electronic field production (EFP) The use of a single video camera and portable editing equipment to produce a segment or entire program on location.

essential area Also known as the *safe action area*, the essential area is a production term referring to the inner 80 percent of the screen containing the landscape where action is to be filmed.

establishing shot The opening shot used to educate the audience about scene location.

executive producer A producer not charged with technical aspects of the production process but who is responsible for the overall series or program production.

extra On-screen talent not vital to a scene or overall production but contributing to the atmosphere of the filming environment, e.g., the need for a small crowd in a cafeteria while the main characters exchange dialogue.

F

fade to black Expression used to mean *fade to the end of a scene* or, more literally, to diminish the image on screen by fading to a background.

feed A video/audio signal transmitted from one source to another.

field of view Width of a shot that is visible with a lens set at a particular focal length.

film look (a.k.a. *filmizing*) An informal term referring to any process that makes video footage look like it was shot on film.

film-style production Shooting scenes out of sequence for purposes of convenience, with scenes to be assembled in correct order later.

first AD (first assistant director) A veritable assistant to the principle director, the first AD helps to coordinate the cast and crew in the physical production of a television program or series. The first AD helps execute the director's vision by sometimes doing the actual direction, placing performers in their places, and even yelling the obligatory "Action!"

fishpole Long, often retractable pole used to suspend a microphone above a subject being filmed.

floor director Production crew member who reports directly to the supervising producer or director regarding the set and other locations for filming.

fluid head Type of tripod utilizing various lubricants to provide for the smoothest possible camera adjustments and movements.

flying erase head Editing feature incorporated in many cameras and VCRs to reduce or eliminate video or audio glitches between edits. All 8mm and digital equipment has flying erase heads.

FPS (frames per second) Number of frames captured on film per second.

frame The individual picture image on a tape or one complete screen on a video monitor.

framing Securing a shot in the camera's viewfinder for desired angle, content, and exposure.

freeze frame A single frame placed on pause and used as a still or vidcap (video capture).

F/X Special effects.

G

gaffer Production member charged with the placement, relocation, maintenance, and operation of lighting instruments.

gain The amplification of signal strength.

gel Colored cellophane-like material situated in front of a light source (natural or artificial) to project its hue onto the subject or scenery being filmed.

generation Production reference to a master copy and its duplicate recordings, e.g., a copy of the master would be known as a *second-generation copy.*

generation loss Prior to the advent of digital video editing, which does not produce generation loss, it was common for a reduction of quality to be observable between the master and its duplicate copies, particularly of myriad video tape formats.

genre A variety of programming (e.g., scripted, reality, sports-related, etc.). A *genre* alludes to an established grouping of television programs recognized for their particular narrative structure or thematic content.

glitch Brief picture distortion or disturbance.

grip Production crew member assigned to handle set-related responsibilities, including props and scenery.

H

head The top portion of a tripod that enables panning and tilting of the camera.

headroom The space between the top of the primary on-camera subject's head and the top of the camera frame.

head writer Individual overseeing the collective work of other writers (while also producing material) during the production of a television series.

Hi8 (high-band 8mm) Newer version of 8mm format characterized by greater luminance resolution.

I

insert editing Recording video or audio over a small or large portion of existing footage without disturbing the footage that precedes and follows.

in-camera editing Amateur video-editing technique performed by shooting scenes in appropriate sequence and then stopping the record function after each scene is filmed.

iris A component of a video cameras lens that regulates the amount of light entering the camera and influencing the picture being captured.

J

jog shuttle VCR-mounted manual control for viewing and editing video footage.

jump cut Sudden, noticeable, unattractive cut between shots identical in their setting but slightly different on account of a subject's changed position or action.

K

key grip The primary grip who coordinates with the gaffer in executing light effects and other illumination needs as they arise during production.

key light The primary source of lighting for a particular scene, either natural or artificial.

L

Lavalier microphone (lapel mic) A small microphone that can be situated on an article of clothing easily concealed from the camera's view.

letterbox Also known as *widescreen effect,* a letterbox presentation is the process by which a widescreen film is presented on video. It is also the way in which a high-definition television (HDTV) broadcast appears on a conventional television set. The letterbox presentation is noted by the top and bottom of the video frame appearing blackened, with the video appearing inside the stretched or elongated center frame.

linear editing Old-school post-production technique of editing scenes in chronological (linear) order by VCR-to-VCR tape deck editing.

live to tape Unedited program recorded and aired identical to its original presentation.

LTC (longitudinal time code) The process of identifying frames through numbers imprinted lengthwise along the perimeter of a tape.

M

master The edited, polished copy of a program ready for broadcast or duplication.

medium shot (MS) Camera angle or view showing an individual subject from the waist to the head.

model release Release form, to be signed by subjects appearing on screen, which informs a participant of production-related matters and protects production staff from a right-to-privacy lawsuit.

monitor TV set or screen receiving a video feed for playback or review.

monopod One-legged version of a tripod used to level or steady a video camera.

montage A series of video clips assembled to convey a story, foreshadow an event, or establish a mood.

N

natural light Any nonartificial illumination (primarily the sun) resulting from natural sources.

Nielsen ratings A widely recognized system of audience measurement pioneered by Nielsen Media Research to discover audience size, demographics, viewing patterns, and so on.

noise Undesirable audible static or interference on a recorded soundtrack or live feed.

nonlinear editing Process of digital editing that utilizes a hard drive instead of tape to store, assemble, and manipulate video clips.

NTSC National Television Standards Committee.

O

OTF "On-the-fly" method of interviewing, most common in the reality TV production genre.

overkill Emphasizing a worn character, subject, or storyline to an excessive or unwarranted extent during live or post-production.

P

PA (production assistant) A low-level position responsible for many of the mundane but critical production-related tasks on a set or filming location. Many successful executive producers began their careers as production assistants by "cutting their teeth" and paying their dues in this truly underappreciated and underpaid position.

pan To horizontally pivot a camera from a stationary position.

pay or play A standard contract provision obligating a network or production company to compensate a producer or performer for his or her work on a project, even if the series is never developed.

PCM (pulse code modulation) A method of encoding digital audio.

post-production The process of editing footage to produce a finished product for broadcast or distribution.

POV (point of view) A camera perspective equivalent to the subject's view.

producer Integral production crew member or executive largely responsible for supervisory and financial responsibilities in the overall production of a television, cinematic, or similar commercial broadcast or performance enterprise.

public domain Any recorded material that is not copyrighted which may be used or rebroadcast on television or radio programs without paying a licensing fee or royalty.

R

ratings See *Nielsen ratings.*

raw footage Unedited, uncut footage directly removed from the video camera.

reel Brief segment of clips showcasing a producer's or performer's sample work or an example of what a proposed project currently looks like or will look like.

remote A production location (or temporary makeshift set) other than the sound stage used for primary filming.

reveal The moment (particularly on reality TV) when the series-revolving "surprise" or "secret" is revealed to either viewers or show participants, e.g., the revelation that "Joe Millionaire" isn't really a millionaire.

riser A dais or stage on which talent perform at a height best suited to the perspective of television cameras.

rough cut A working edit of a video production characterized by a rough approximation of shot juxtaposition and storyline presentation.

S

SAG (Screen Actors Guild) The Screen Actors Guild is a U.S.-based labor union representing more than 100,000 film and television "principal performers" and "background performers" around the world. Founded in 1933, SAG was created to help eliminate the flagrant exploitation of actors who were routinely forced into unfavorable multiyear film contracts that didn't, for example, provide for the contract's expiration or even include restrictions on work hours or minimum rest periods. According to SAG's Mission Statement, the Guild strives to "negotiate and enforce collective bargaining agreements that establish equitable levels of compensation, benefits, and working conditions for its performers; collect compensation for exploitation of recorded performances by its members, and provide protection against unauthorized use of those performances; and preserve and expand work opportunities for its members." In addition to its main office in Hollywood, SAG also maintains local branches in Phoenix, Boston, New York, Philadelphia, Washington, D.C., Nashville, Atlanta, Miami, Dallas, Houston, Chicago, Detroit, Denver, Salt Lake City, San Diego, Seattle, Portland, Las Vegas, Honolulu, and San Francisco.

SESAC (Society of European Stage Authors & Composers) As the smallest of the three major performance rights organizations in the United States (the others are BMI and ASCAP), SESAC "deals with all aspects of the music business, from creation to licensing and administration." Unlike ASCAP and BMI, which operate on a nonprofit basis and distribute all royalties collected back to their composer and publisher affiliates, SESAC retains some income as profit. SESAC is also different from its two competitors in that it does not offer "open membership." One must be approved to join.

script Copy to be performed or spoken by an on-camera participant. A script may also provide direction or guidelines to production staff and crew regarding camera positioning, scenery, lighting, or numerous additional production-related directives.

set The designated location (often a sound stage) where a television show or movie is filmed.

share Within the established framework of television ratings, a *share* is the percentage of homes with turned-on television sets that are tuned to a particular show.

sitcom (TV sitcom) A *situation comedy* written, produced, and performed by professionals, usually before a live studio audience within a customized set or soundstage.

sizzle reel Brief segment of clips used to sell or promote a performer's hyped talents. A sizzle reel commonly presents the best example of the featured performer's work. In a bygone era, this would have been called a *demo tape*.

shotgun microphone A unidirectional microphone designed to focus on a sole subject.

sound stage A manufactured set within a soundproofed building tailored to a unique project.

stock footage Canned video footage of ordinary occurrences—an airplane landing, a school bus departing, people crossing the street, etc.—readily available to editors as B-roll.

sweeps A very important time period in which Nielsen Media Research determines the ratings of network television programs. In the United States, sweeps are currently held in February, May, July, and November. Traditionally, during sweeps periods, networks broadcast more original or "first-run" programming as well as a greater verity of miniseries, TV movies, and other hyped specials. During a sweeps period, many television networks employ massive schemes for ratings in the content of their programming.

sweetening A sound effects process that commonly takes place during post-production where, for example, more applause and laughter are added to the original recording of the live studio audience that witnessed the show taping.

syndication The distribution of television programs to local, national, or international stations and networks by their production companies. The term *syndication* refers to both the second broadcast run of a program after a network's initial license period (e.g., *The Cosby Show*, 1984–92) and any show that was created expressly for syndication.

T

talent General title for performers or participants on a program on screen.

tally light Small, usually red light atop a studio camera to indicate that recording has begun.

TelePrompTer (or *prompter*) A device acting as an electronic cue card that projects copy (lines or direction) on mirrors placed directly in front of a camera's lens. A prompter enables talent to follow a script or receive instruction without diverting eye contact away from the camera.

three-shot Camera perspective trained on three subjects.

tripod Three-legged video camera base.

two-shot Camera perspective commonly used in interview situations which includes two primary subjects.

time code (longitudinal time code) Running clock recorded on a batch of raw video (appearing lengthwise at the bottom of the screen) providing hours, minutes, seconds, and frame numbers for each particular scene. A time code simplifies the editing process, allowing for precise access by editors and keeping audio and video in sync.

U

underscore Music that blends into the background of the primary action and lends to the emotional "feel" of the scene.

unscripted programming (reality TV) Television programming that ostensibly operates without a functioning script.

V

voiceover (VO) Any narration accompanying a video, usually presented in conjunction with a soundtrack.

W

wipe A special effect used as a transition device between scenes, typically where a line moves across the screen, apparently removing one shot as the next replaces it.

WGA (Writers Guild of America) A large labor union actively representing writers of television and film and employees of TV and radio news.

workprint Duplicate of an original or "master" video tape or reel primarily used for producing rough-cut variations.

Index